UMBRAL

BOOK ONE † OUT OF THE SHADOWS

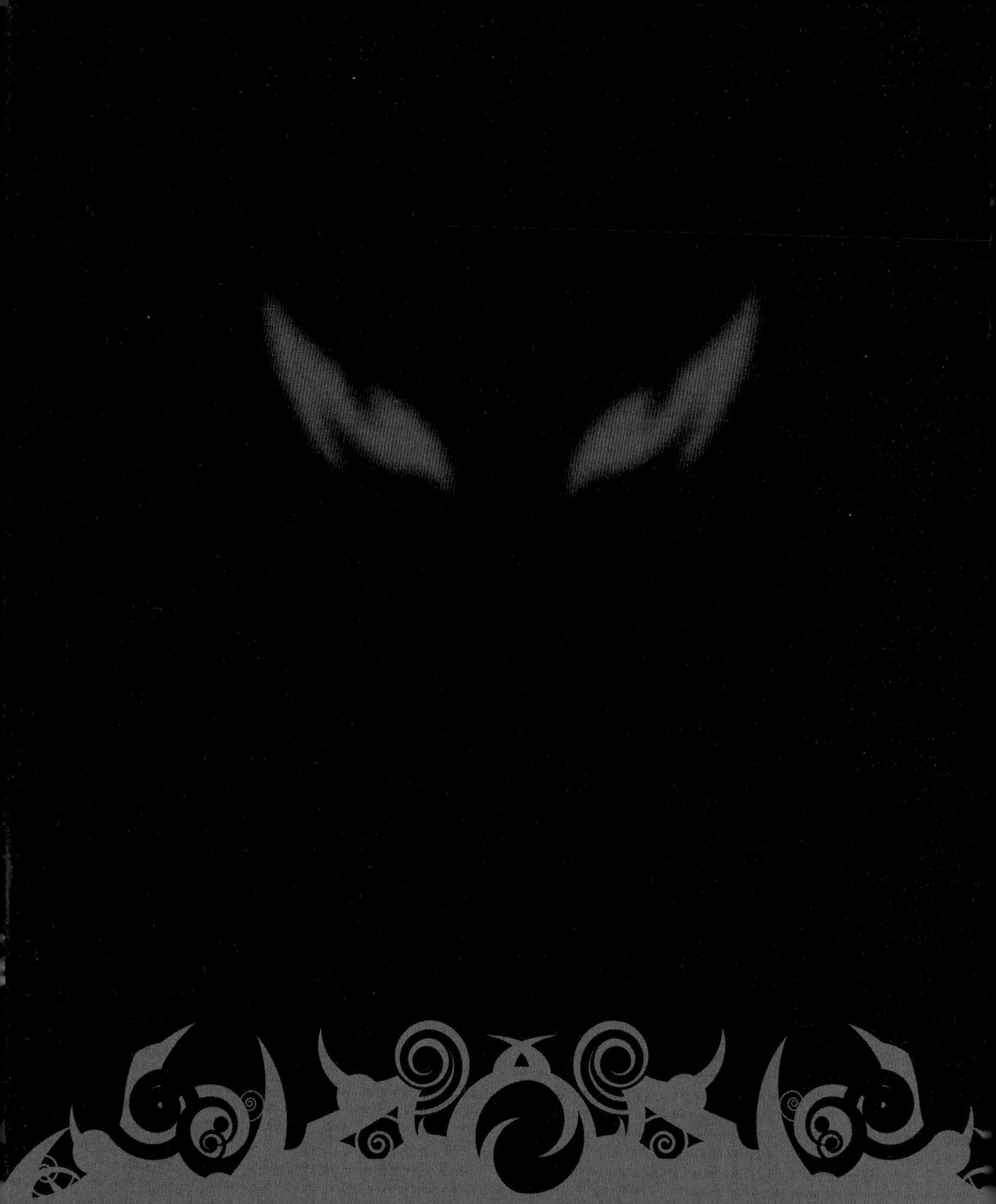

THEUMBRAL.COM

IMAGE COMICS, INC.
Robert Kirkman – Chief Operating Officer
Erik Larsen – Chief Financial Officer
Todd McFarlane – President
Marc Silvestri – Chief Executive Officer
Jim Valentino – Vice-President

Eric Stephenson – Publisher
Ron Richards – Director of Business Development
Jennifer de Guzman – Director of Trade Book Sales
Kat Salazar – Director of PR & Marketing
Jeremy Sullivan – Director of Digital Sales
Emilio Bautista – Sales Assistant
Branwyn Bigglestone – Senior Accounts Manager
Emily Miller – Accounts Manager
Jessica Ambriz – Administrative Assistant
Tyler Shainline – Events Coordinator
David Brothers – Content Manager
Jonathan Chan – Production Manager
Drew Gill – Art Director
Meredith Wallace – Print Manager
Monica Garcia – Senior Production Artist
Jenna Savage – Production Artist
Addison Duke – Production Artist
Tricia Ramos – Production Assistant
IMAGECOMICS.COM

UMBRAL BOOK ONE: OUT OF THE SHADOWS. FIRST PRINTING. MAY 2014.

ISBN: 978-1-60706-984-3. Contains material originally published in magazine form as UMBRAL #1-6.

Published by Image Comics, Inc. Office of publication: 2001 Center Street, 6th Floor, Berkeley, CA 94704.

Printed in the U.S.A. For information regarding the CPSIA on this printed material call: 203-595-3636 and provide reference # RICH- 560499. For international rights, contact: foreignlicensing@imagecomics.com

SCRIBE
ANTONY JOHNSTON

ILLUMINATOR
CHRISTOPHER MITTEN

PAINTERS
JOHN RAUCH & JORDAN BOYD

FLOURISHER
THOMAS MAUER

UMBRAL **CREATED BY JOHNSTON & MITTEN**

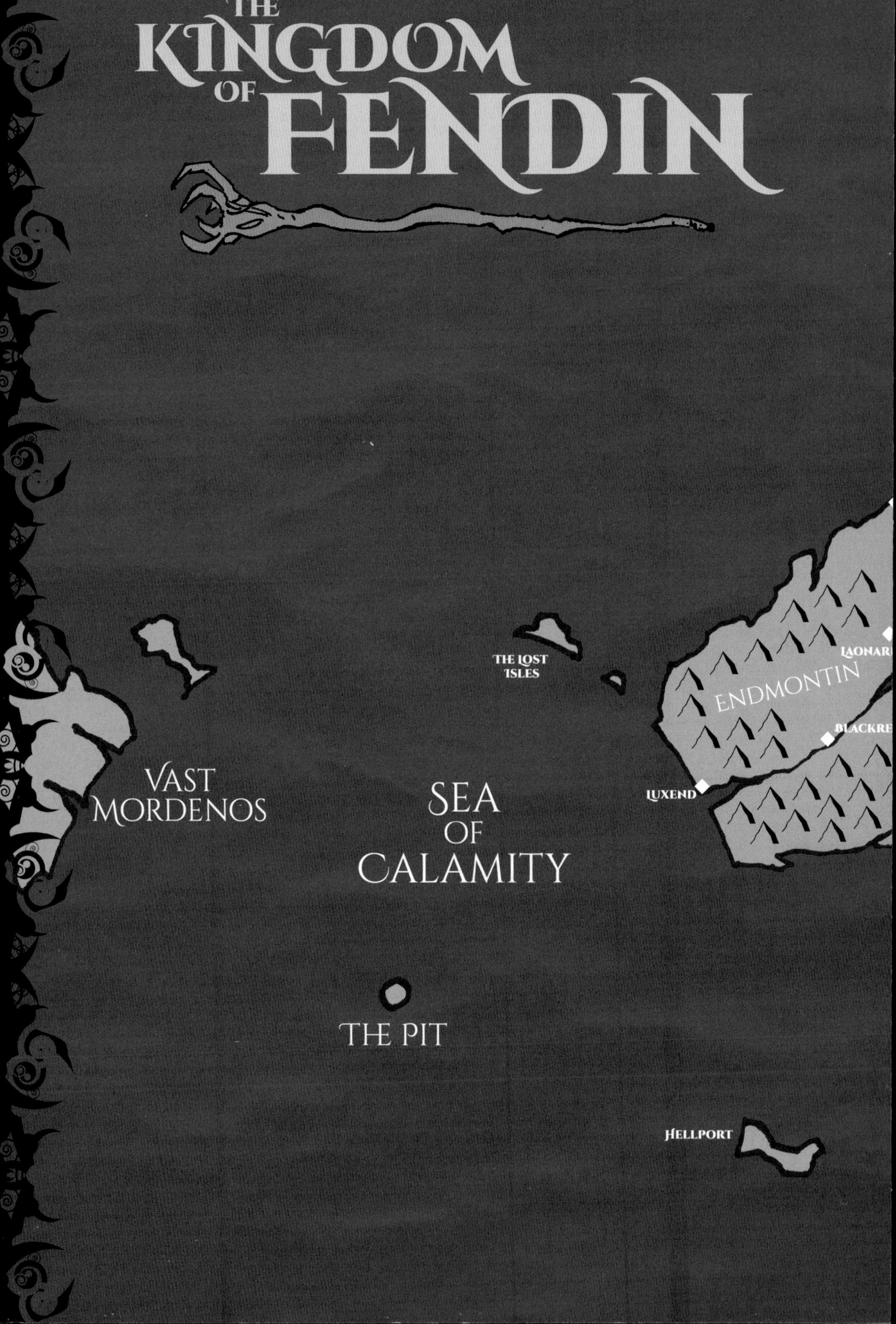
THE KINGDOM OF FENDIN
THE LOST ISLES
ENDMONTIN
LAONAR
BLACKRE
VAST MORDENOS
SEA OF CALAMITY
LUXEND
THE PIT
HELLPORT

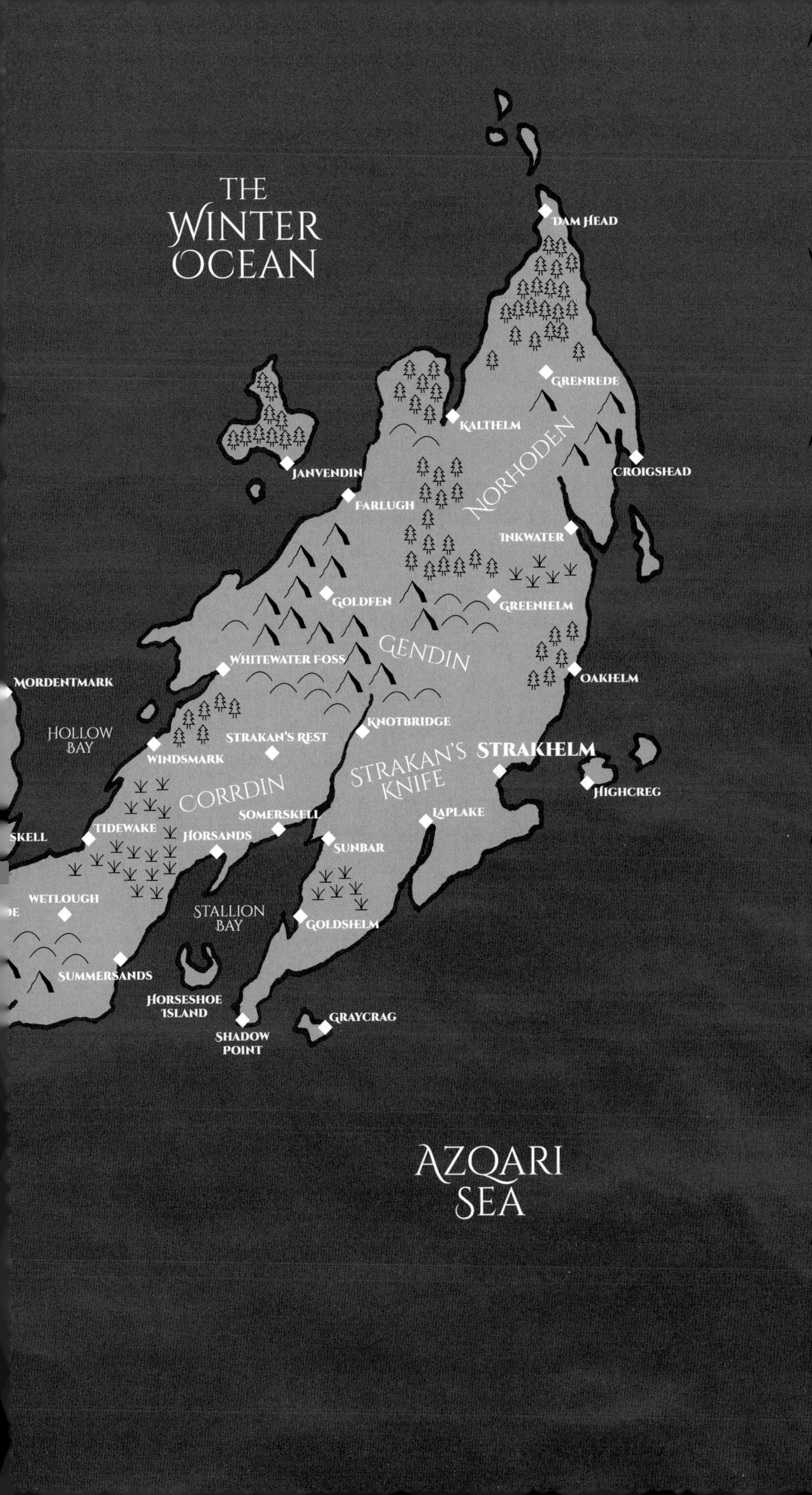

THE WINTER OCEAN
DAM HEAD
GRENREDE
KALTHELM
NORHODEN
CROIGSHEAD
JANVENDIN
FARLUGH
INKWATER
GOLDFEN
GREENHELM
GENDIN
WHITEWATER FOSS
OAKHELM
MORDENTMARK
HOLLOW BAY
KNOTBRIDGE
STRAKAN'S REST
WINDSMARK
STRAKAN'S KNIFE
STRAKHELM
HIGHCREG
CORRDIN
SOMERSKELL
LAPLAKE
TIDEWAKE
HORSANDS
SUNBAR
WETLOUGH
STALLION BAY
GOLDSHELM
SUMMERSANDS
HORSESHOE ISLAND
SHADOW POINT
GRAYCRAG
AZQARI SEA

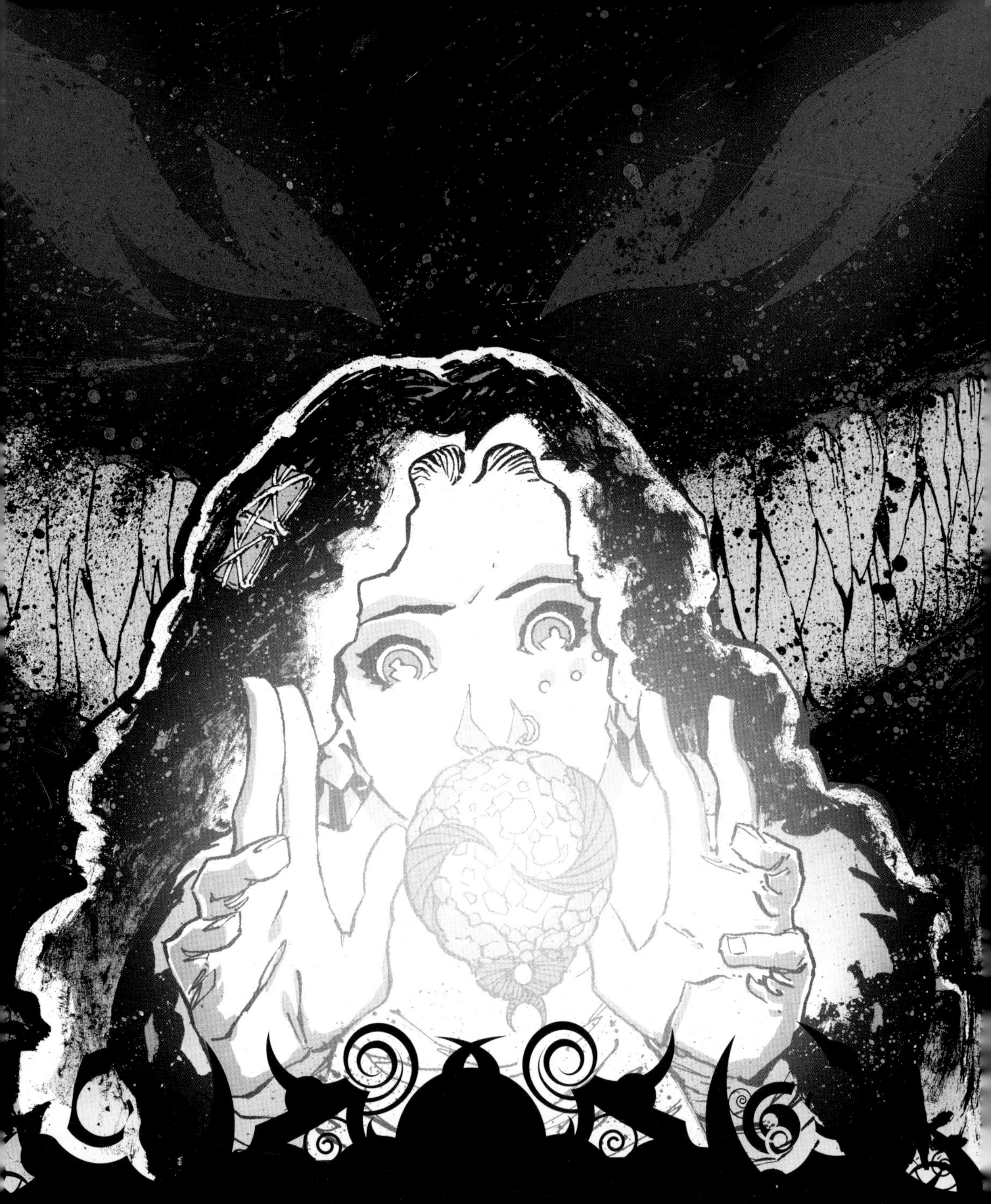

THE DAY DAWNED TWICE

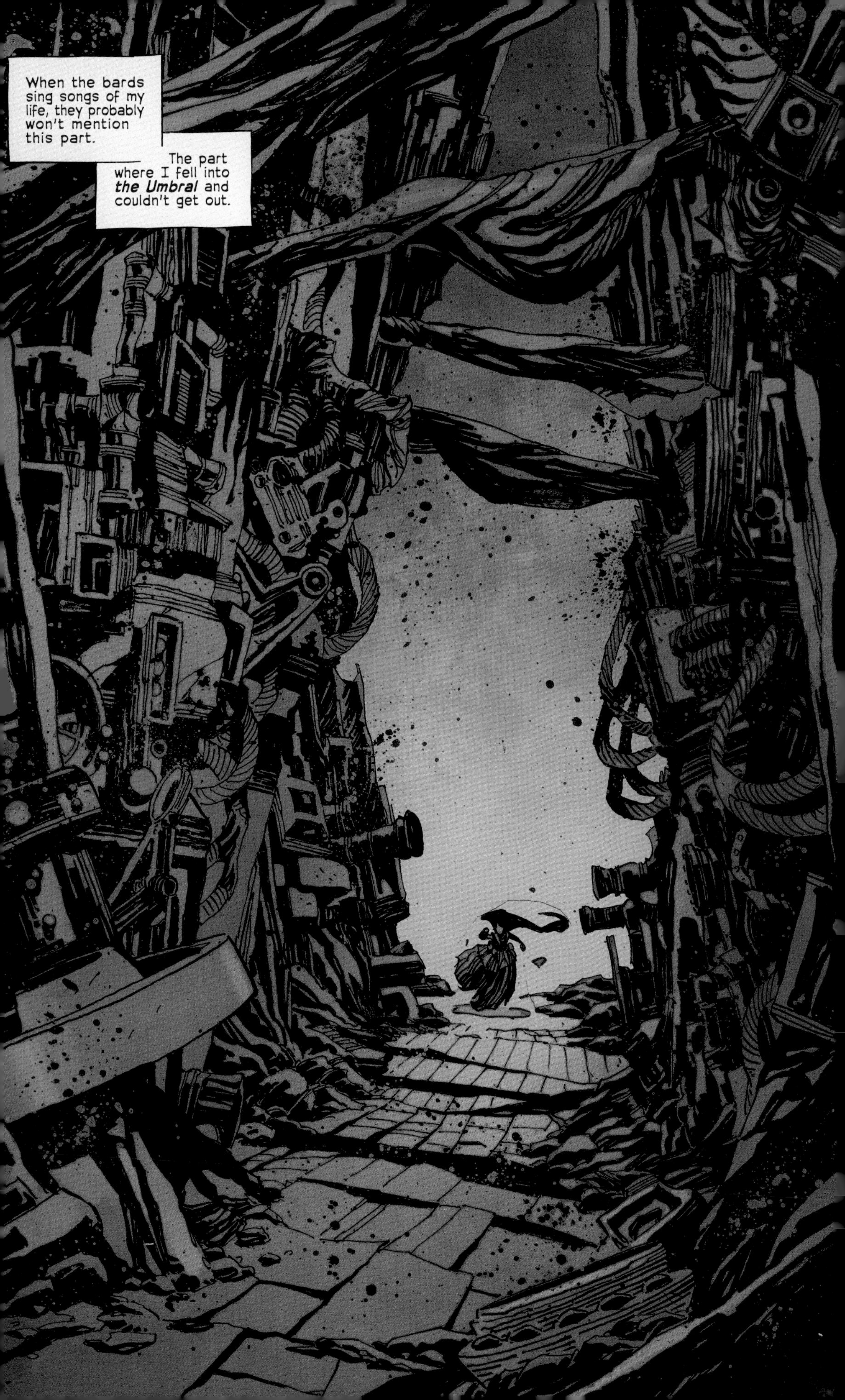
When the bards sing songs of my life, they probably won't mention this part.
The part where I fell into *the Umbral* and couldn't get out.

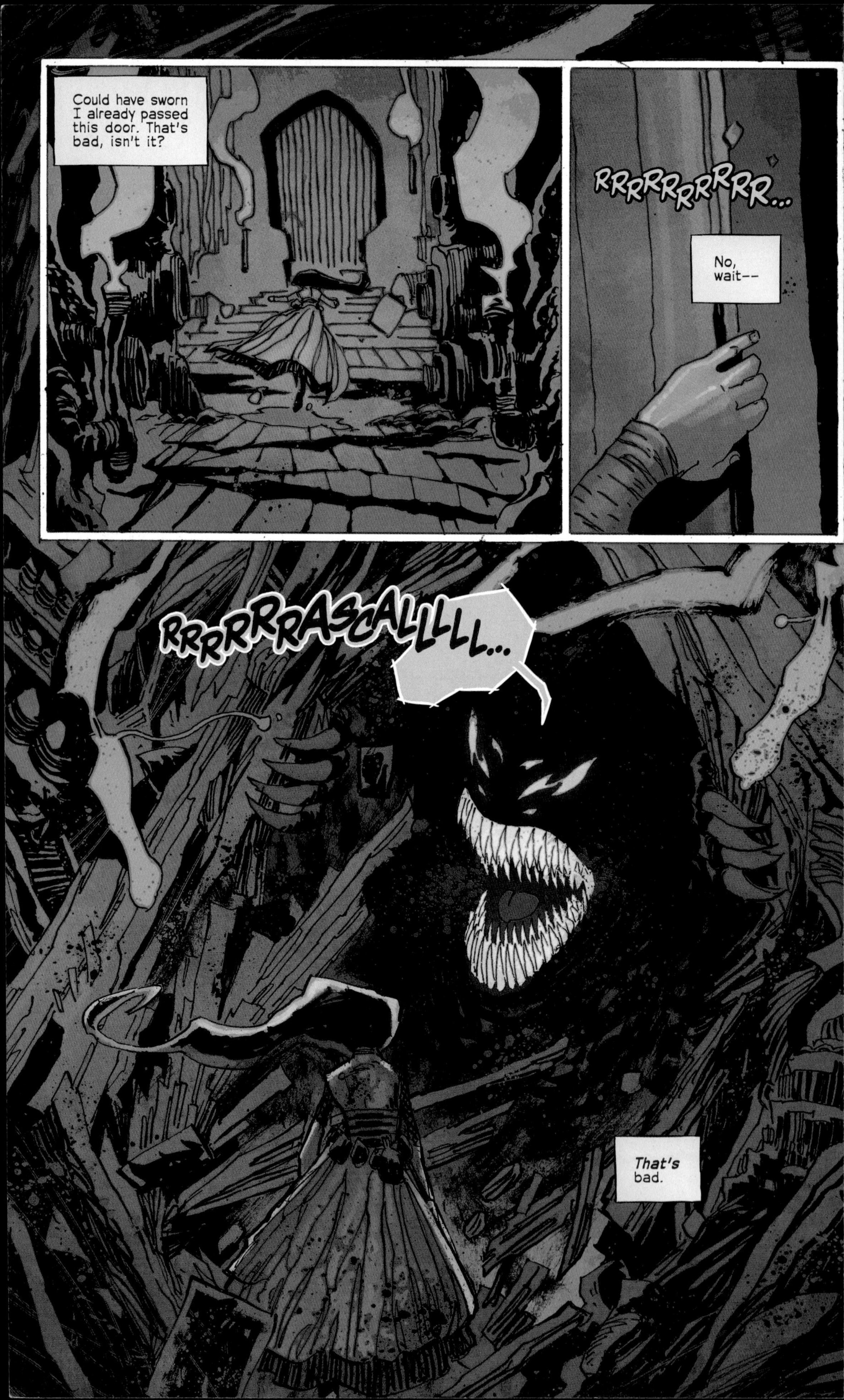

Could have sworn I already passed this door. That's bad, isn't it?
RRRRRRRRRR...
No, wait--
RRRRRRASCALLLLL...
That's bad.

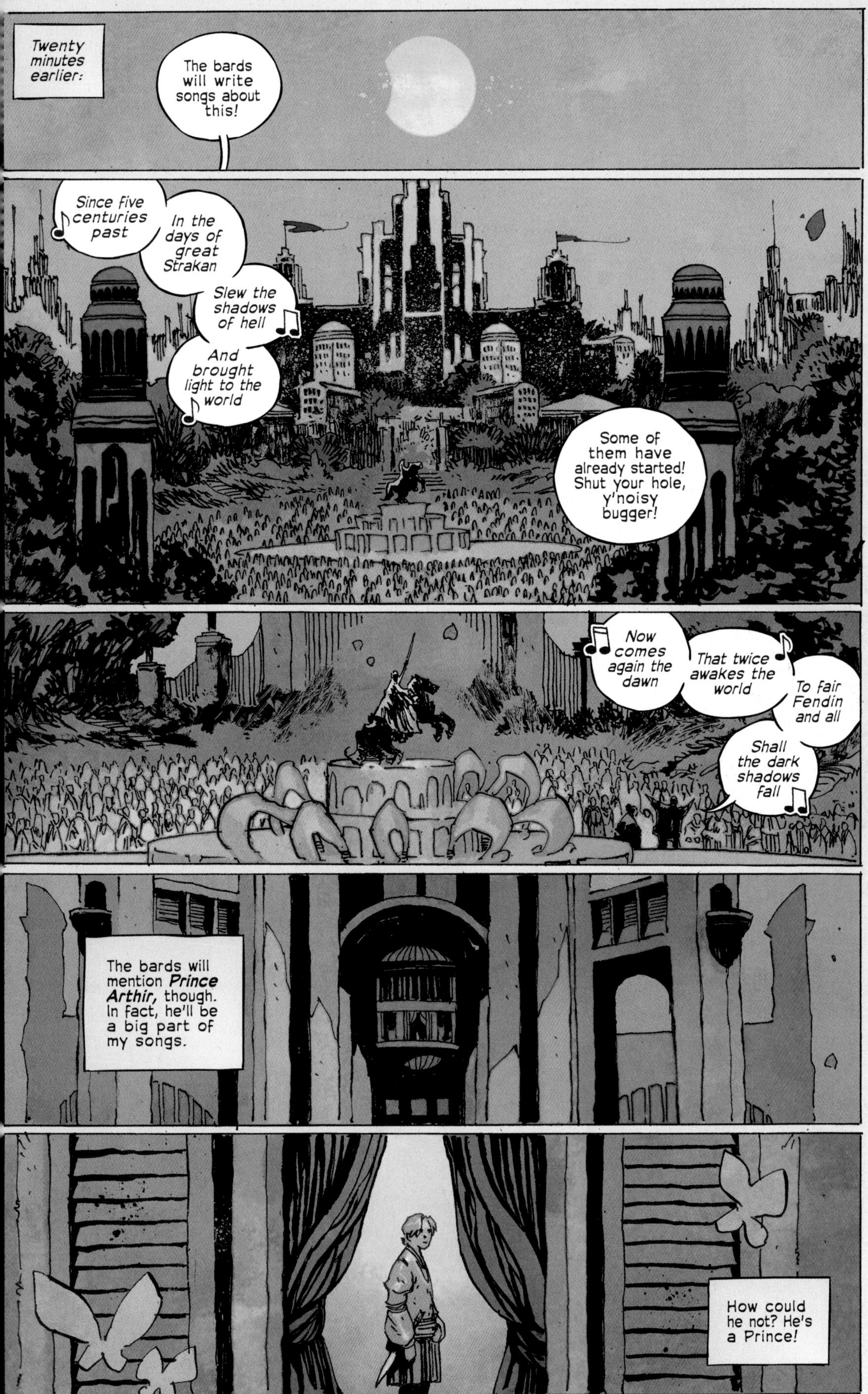

Twenty minutes earlier:
The bards will write songs about this!
Since five centuries past
In the days of great Strakan
Slew the shadows of hell
And brought light to the world
Some of them have already started! Shut your hole, y'noisy bugger!
Now comes again the dawn
That twice awakes the world
To fair Fendin and all
Shall the dark shadows fall
The bards will mention **Prince Arthir,** though. In fact, he'll be a big part of my songs.
How could he not? He's a Prince!

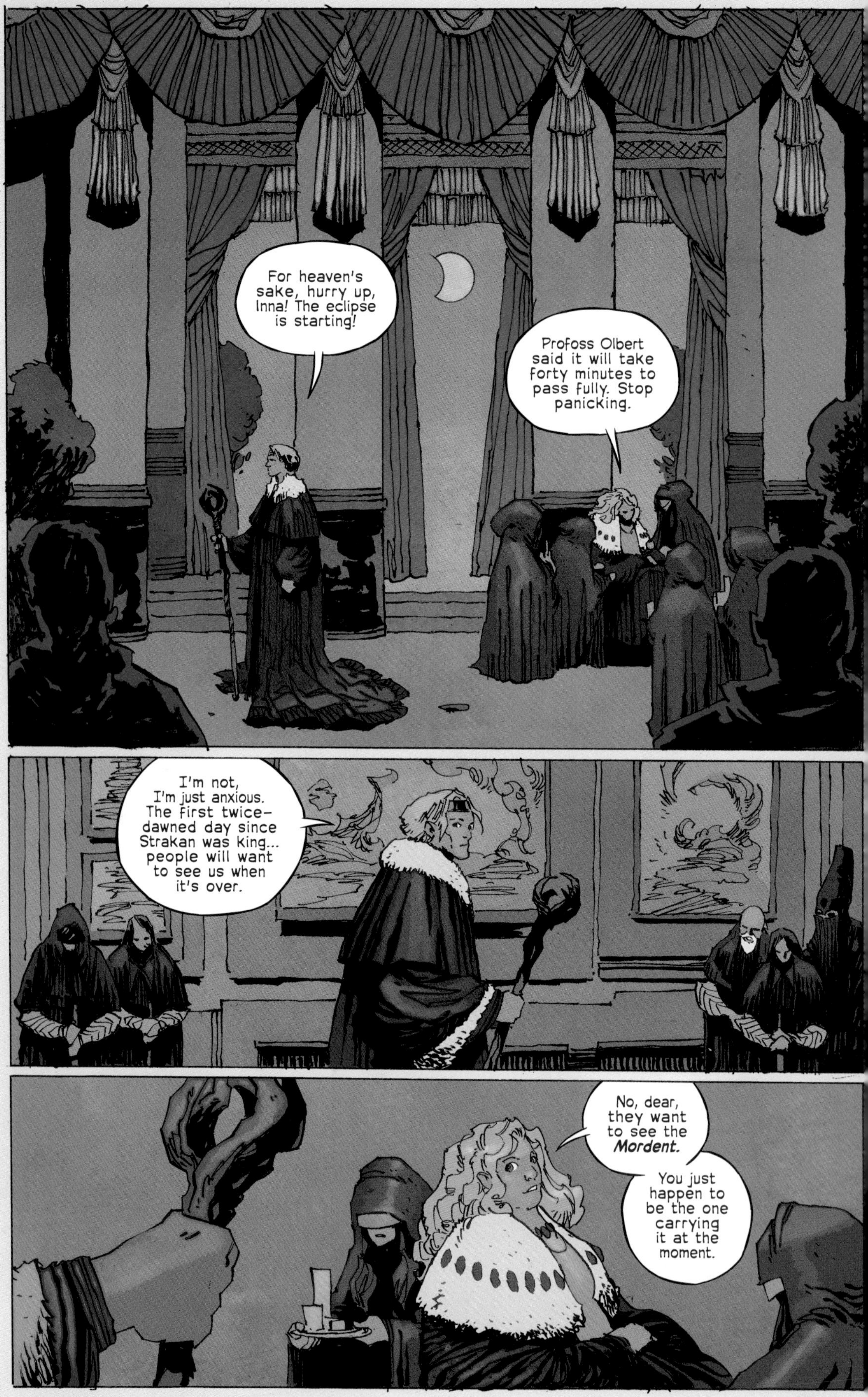
For heaven's sake, hurry up, Inna! The eclipse is starting!
Profoss Olbert said it will take forty minutes to pass fully. Stop panicking.
I'm not, I'm just anxious. The first twice-dawned day since Strakan was king... people will want to see us when it's over.
No, dear, they want to see the *Mordent.*
You just happen to be the one carrying it at the moment.

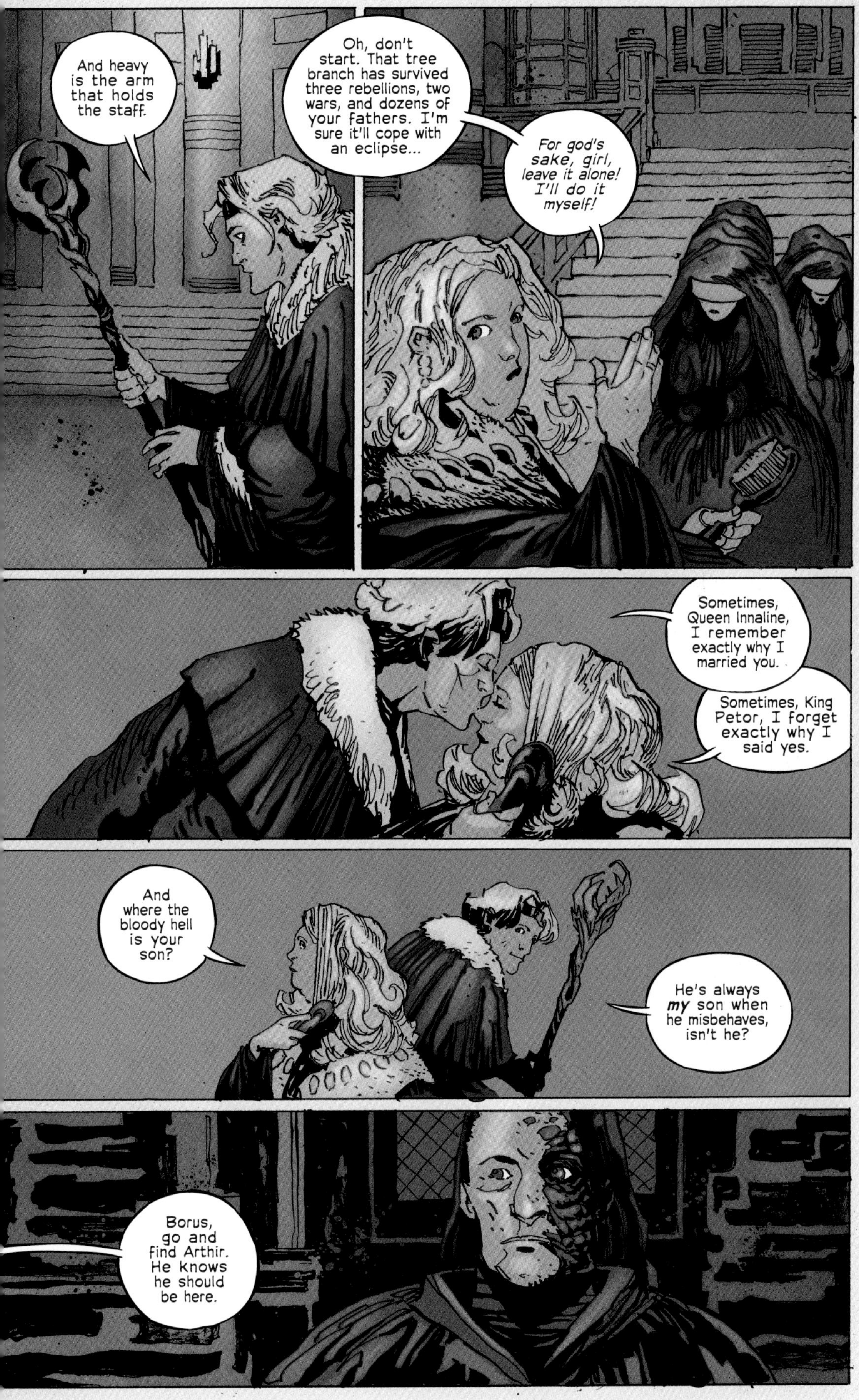
And heavy is the arm that holds the staff.
Oh, don't start. That tree branch has survived three rebellions, two wars, and dozens of your fathers. I'm sure it'll cope with an eclipse...
For god's sake, girl, leave it alone! I'll do it myself!
Sometimes, Queen Innaline, I remember exactly why I married you.
Sometimes, King Petor, I forget exactly why I said yes.
And where the bloody hell is your son?
He's always my son when he misbehaves, isn't he?
Borus, go and find Arthir. He knows he should be here.

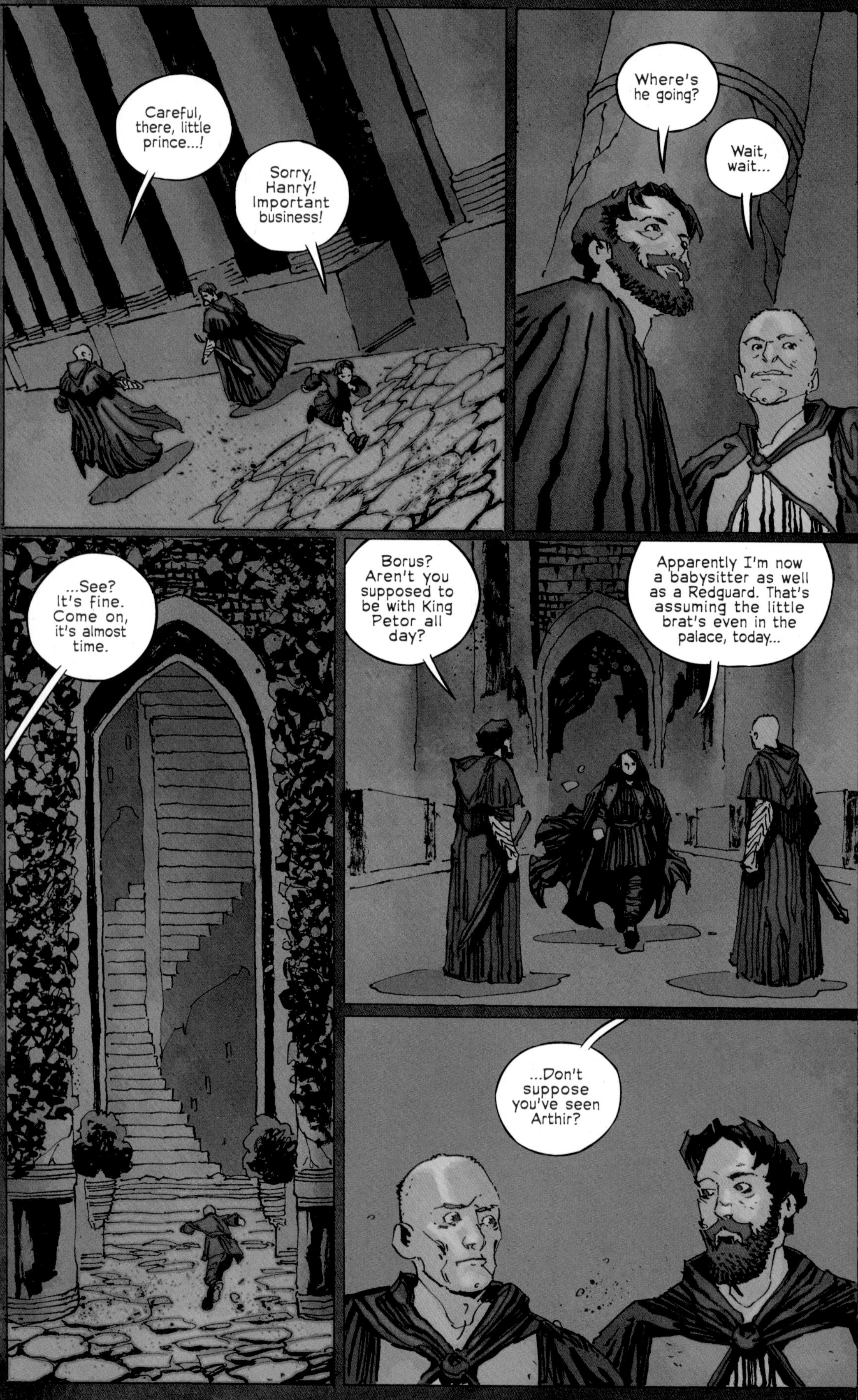
Careful, there, little prince...!
Sorry, Hanry! Important business!
Where's he going?
Wait, wait...
...See? It's fine. Come on, it's almost time.
Borus? Aren't you supposed to be with King Petor all day?
Apparently I'm now a babysitter as well as a Redguard. That's assuming the little brat's even in the palace, today...
...Don't suppose you've seen Arthir?

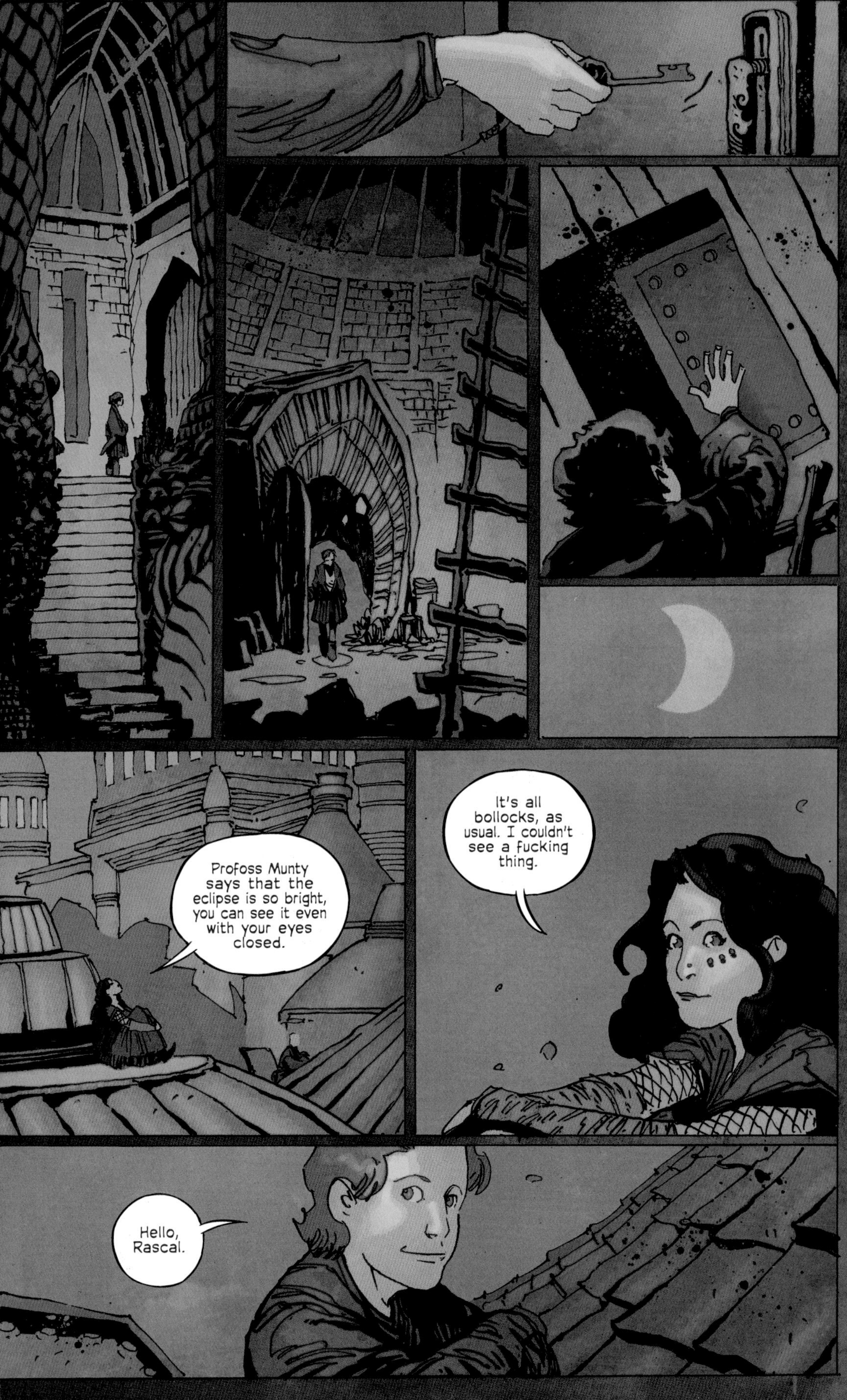

Profoss Munty says that the eclipse is so bright, you can see it even with your eyes closed.
It's all bollocks, as usual. I couldn't see a fucking thing.
Hello, Rascal.

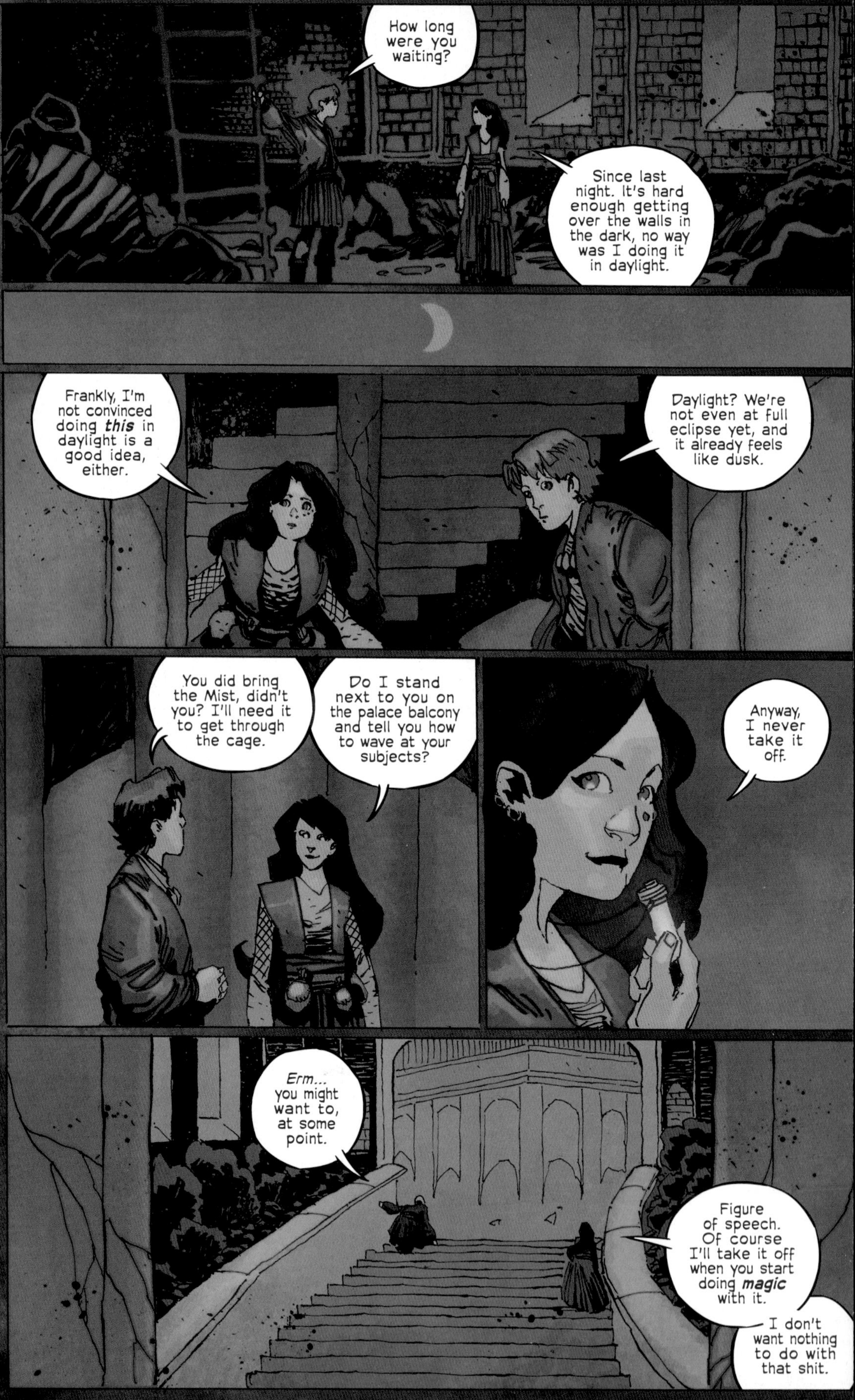
How long were you waiting?
Since last night. It's hard enough getting over the walls in the dark, no way was I doing it in daylight.
Frankly, I'm not convinced doing *this* in daylight is a good idea, either.
Daylight? We're not even at full eclipse yet, and it already feels like dusk.
You did bring the Mist, didn't you? I'll need it to get through the cage.
Do I stand next to you on the palace balcony and tell you how to wave at your subjects?
Anyway, I never take it off.
Erm... you might want to, at some point.
Figure of speech. Of course I'll take it off when you start doing *magic* with it.
I don't want nothing to do with that shit.

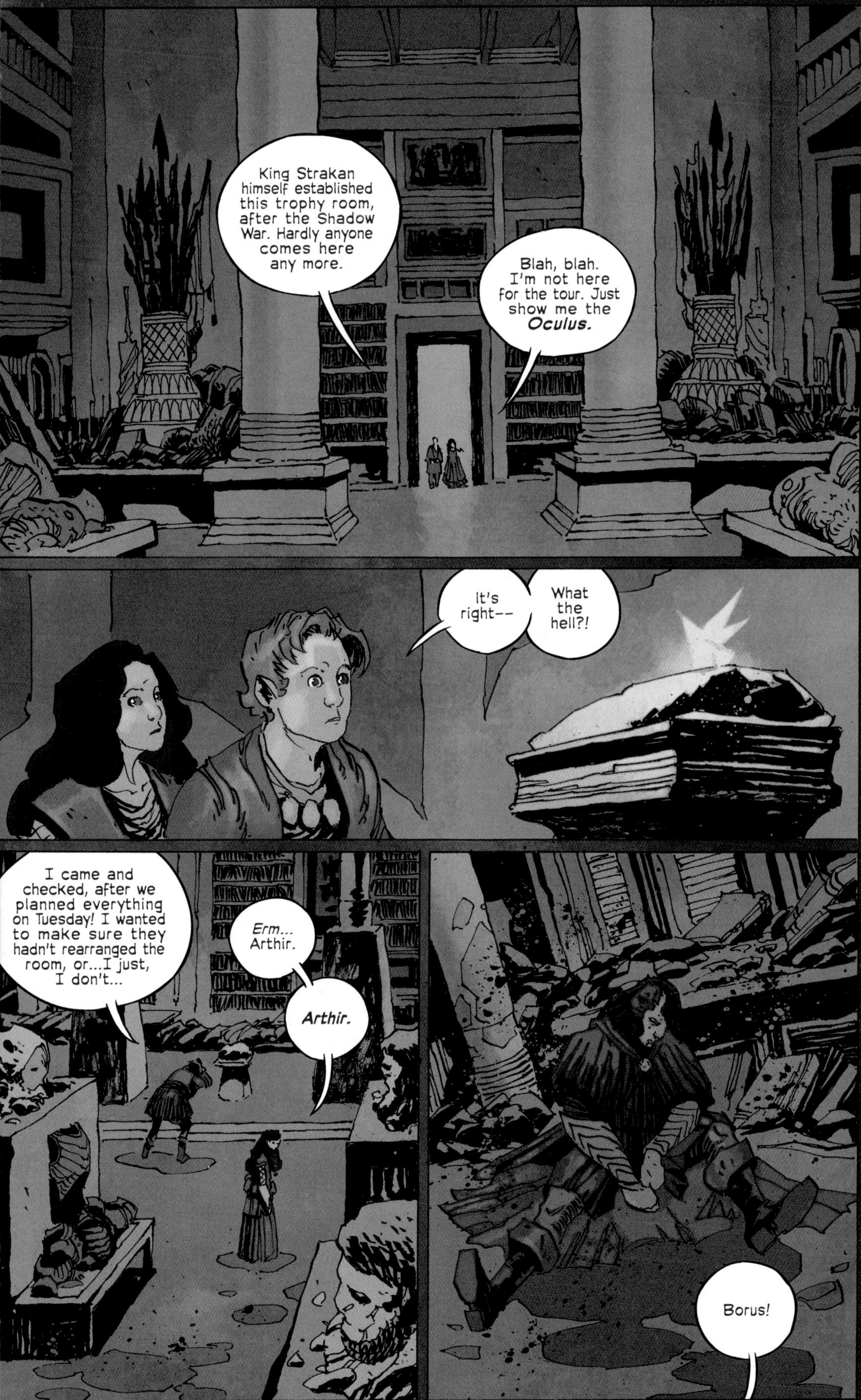
King Strakan himself established this trophy room, after the Shadow War. Hardly anyone comes here any more.
Blah, blah. I'm not here for the tour. Just show me the *Oculus.*
It's right--
What the hell?!
I came and checked, after we planned everything on Tuesday! I wanted to make sure they hadn't rearranged the room, or...I just, I don't...
Erm... Arthir.
Arthir.
Borus!

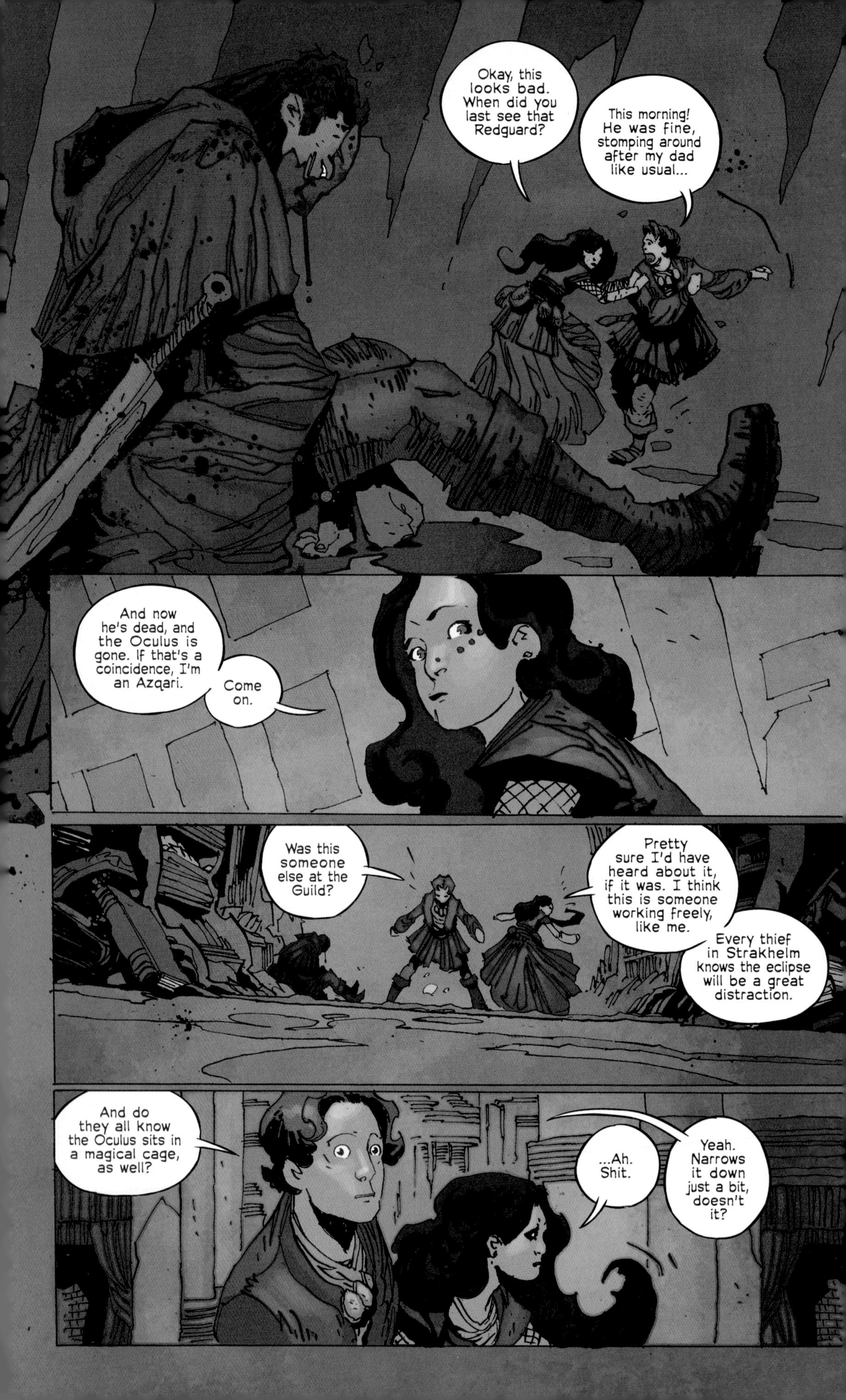
Okay, this looks bad. When did you last see that Redguard?
This morning! He was fine, stomping around after my dad like usual...
And now he's dead, and the Oculus is gone. If that's a coincidence, I'm an Azqari.
Come on.
Was this someone else at the Guild?
Pretty sure I'd have heard about it, if it was. I think this is someone working freely, like me.
Every thief in Strakhelm knows the eclipse will be a great distraction.
And do they all know the Oculus sits in a magical cage, as well?
Yeah. Narrows it down just a bit, doesn't it?
...Ah. Shit.

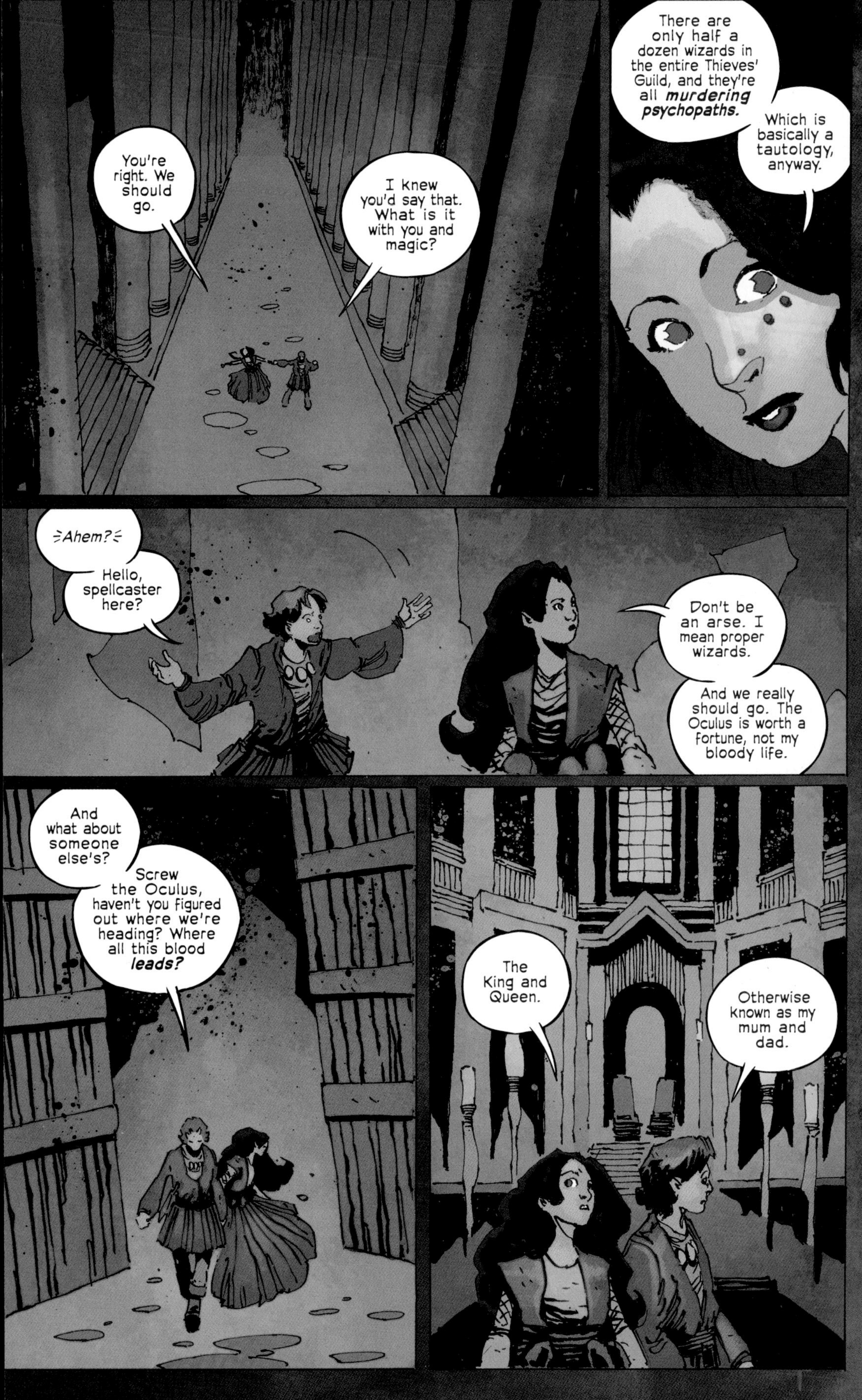

You're right. We should go.
I knew you'd say that. What is it with you and magic?
There are only half a dozen wizards in the entire Thieves' Guild, and they're all ***murdering psychopaths.***
Which is basically a tautology, anyway.
Ahem?
Hello, spellcaster here?
Don't be an arse. I mean proper wizards.
And we really should go. The Oculus is worth a fortune, not my bloody life.
And what about someone else's?
Screw the Oculus, haven't you figured out where we're heading? Where all this blood ***leads?***
The King and Queen.
Otherwise known as my mum and dad.

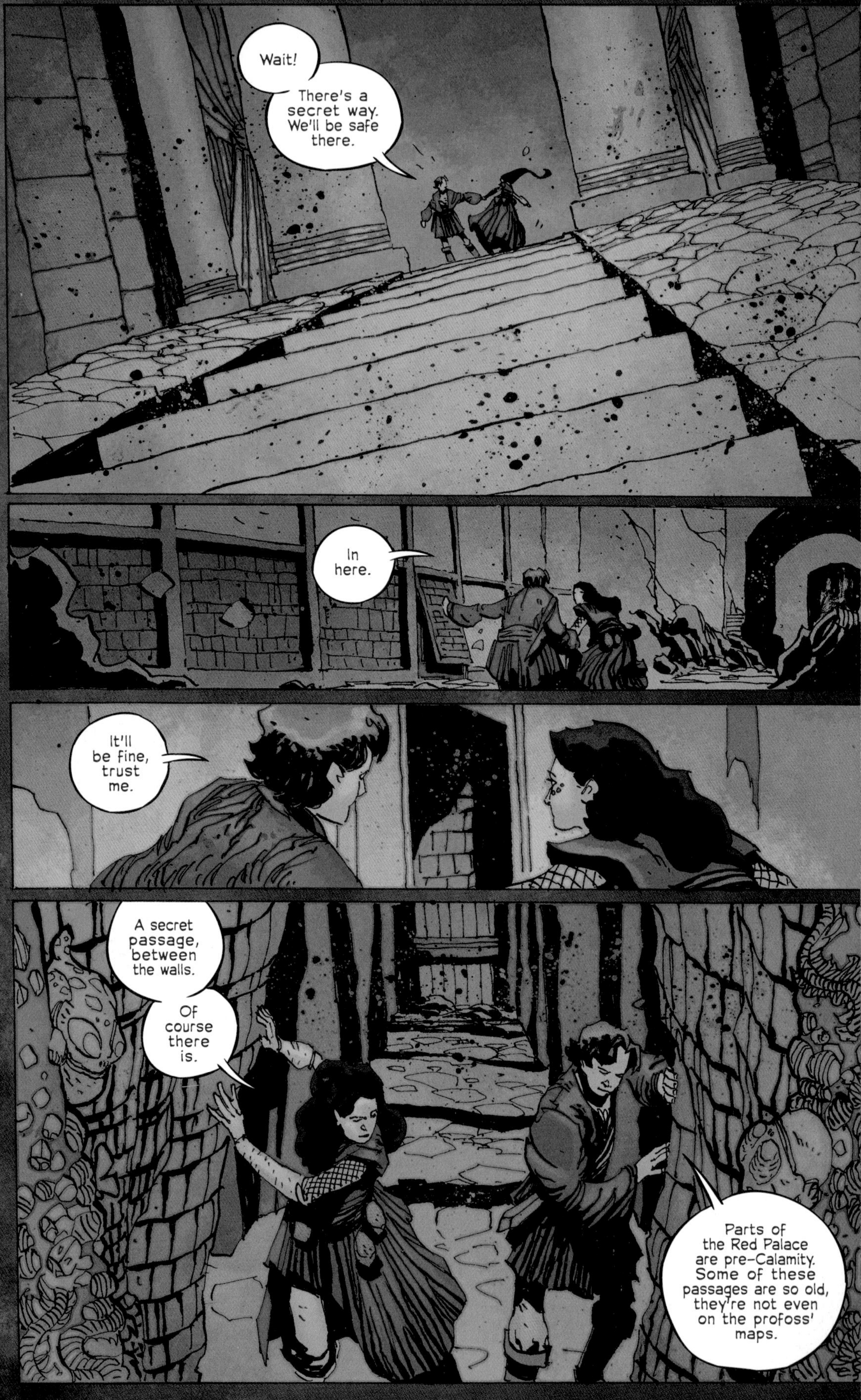
Wait!
There's a secret way. We'll be safe there.
In here.
It'll be fine, trust me.
A secret passage, between the walls.
Of course there is.
Parts of the Red Palace are pre-Calamity. Some of these passages are so old, they're not even on the profoss' maps.

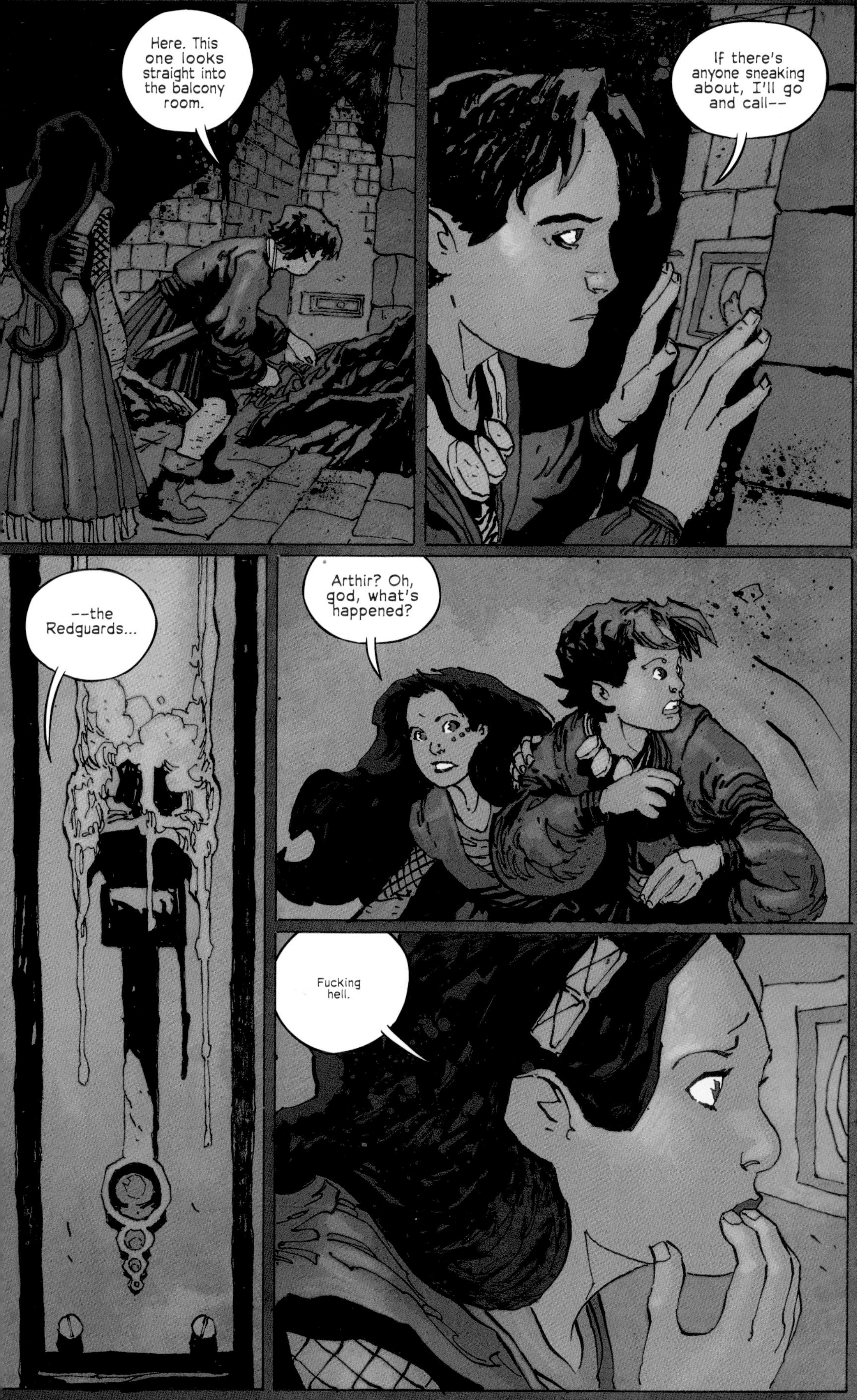
Here. This one looks straight into the balcony room.
If there's anyone sneaking about, I'll go and call--
--the Redguards...
Arthir? Oh, god, what's happened?
Fucking hell.

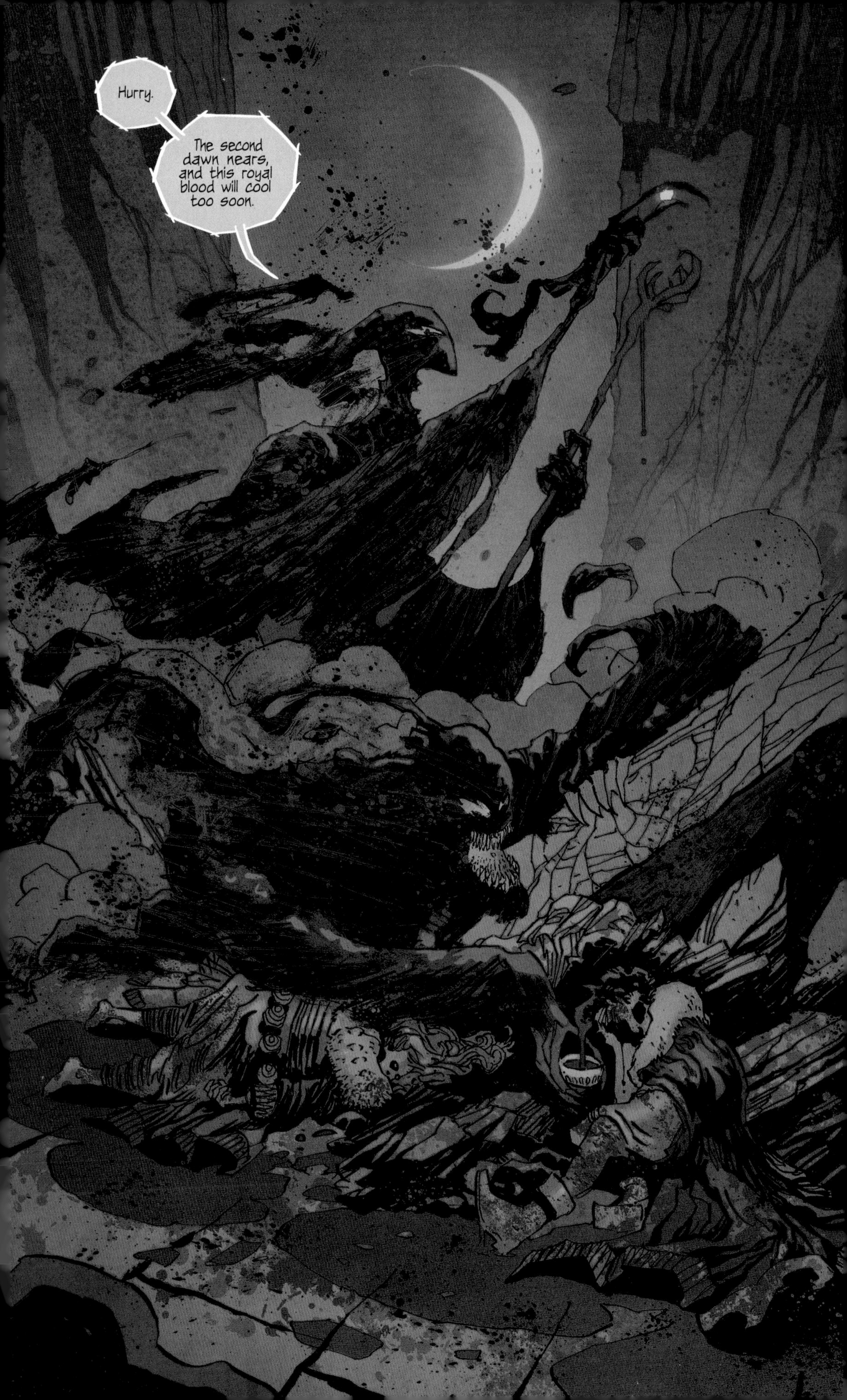
Hurry.
The second dawn nears, and this royal blood will cool too soon.

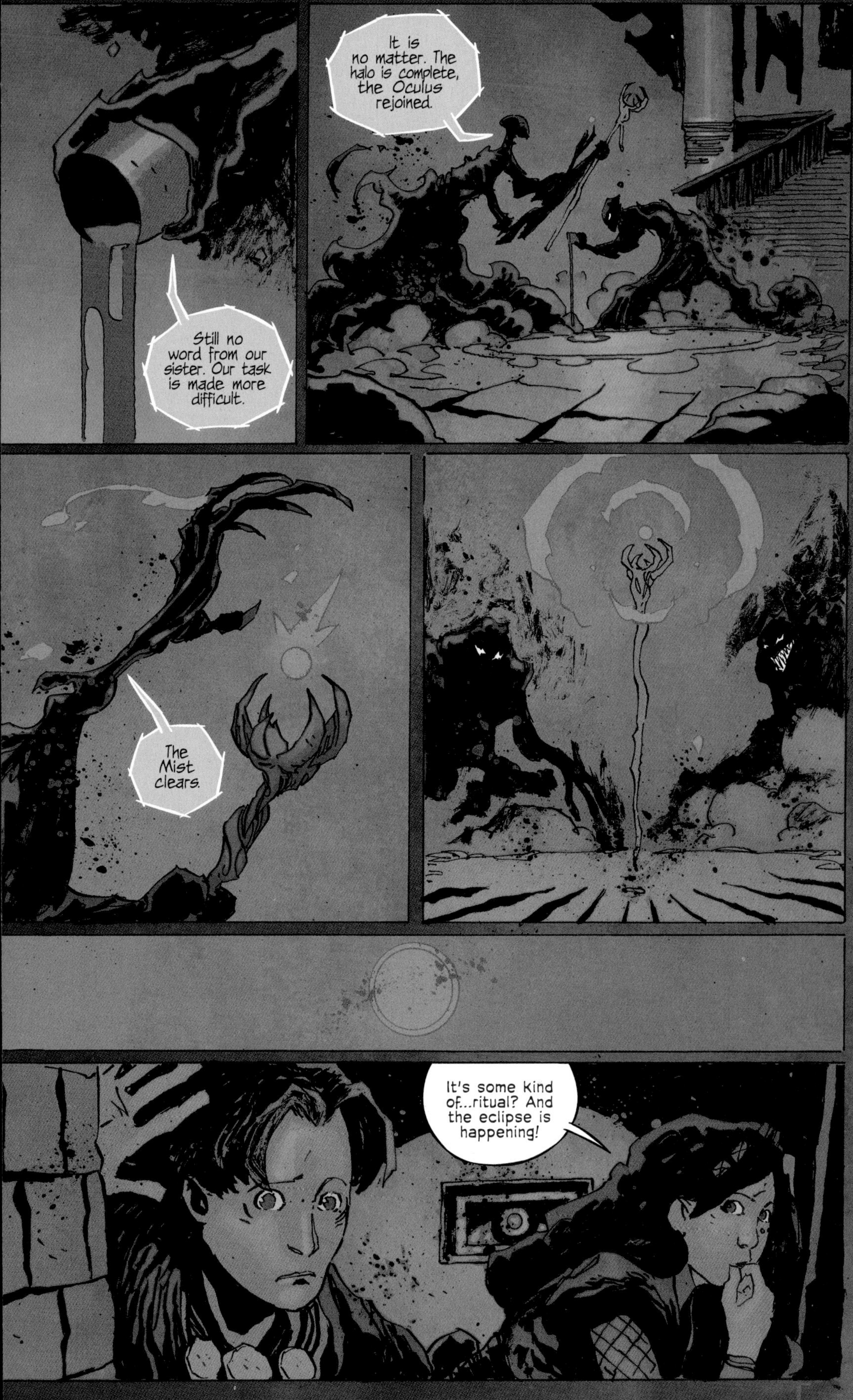
It is no matter. The halo is complete, the Oculus rejoined.
Still no word from our sister. Our task is made more difficult.
The Mist clears.
It's some kind of...ritual? And the eclipse is happening!

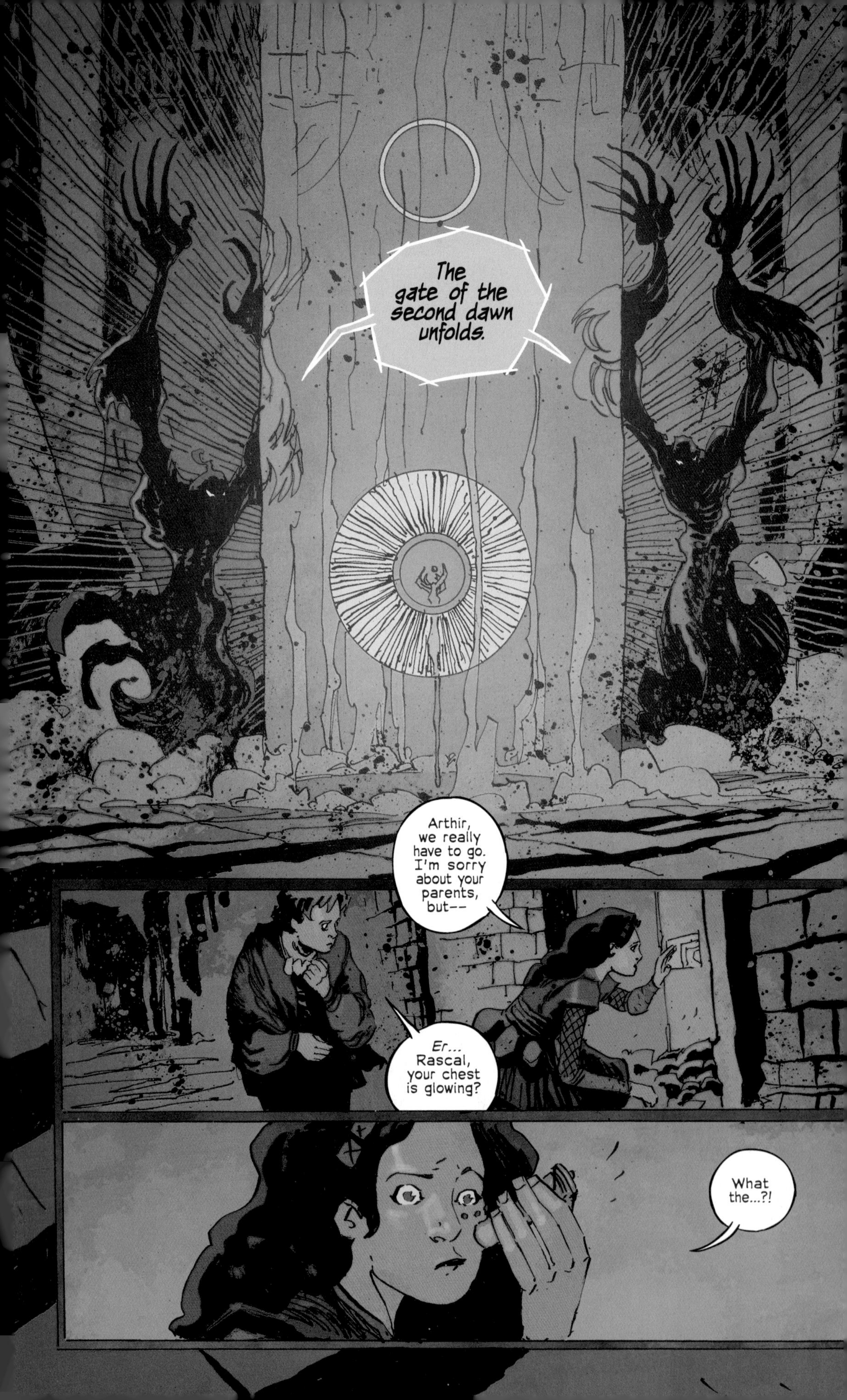

The gate of the second dawn unfolds.
Arthir, we really have to go. I'm sorry about your parents, but--
Er... Rascal, your chest is glowing?
What the...?!

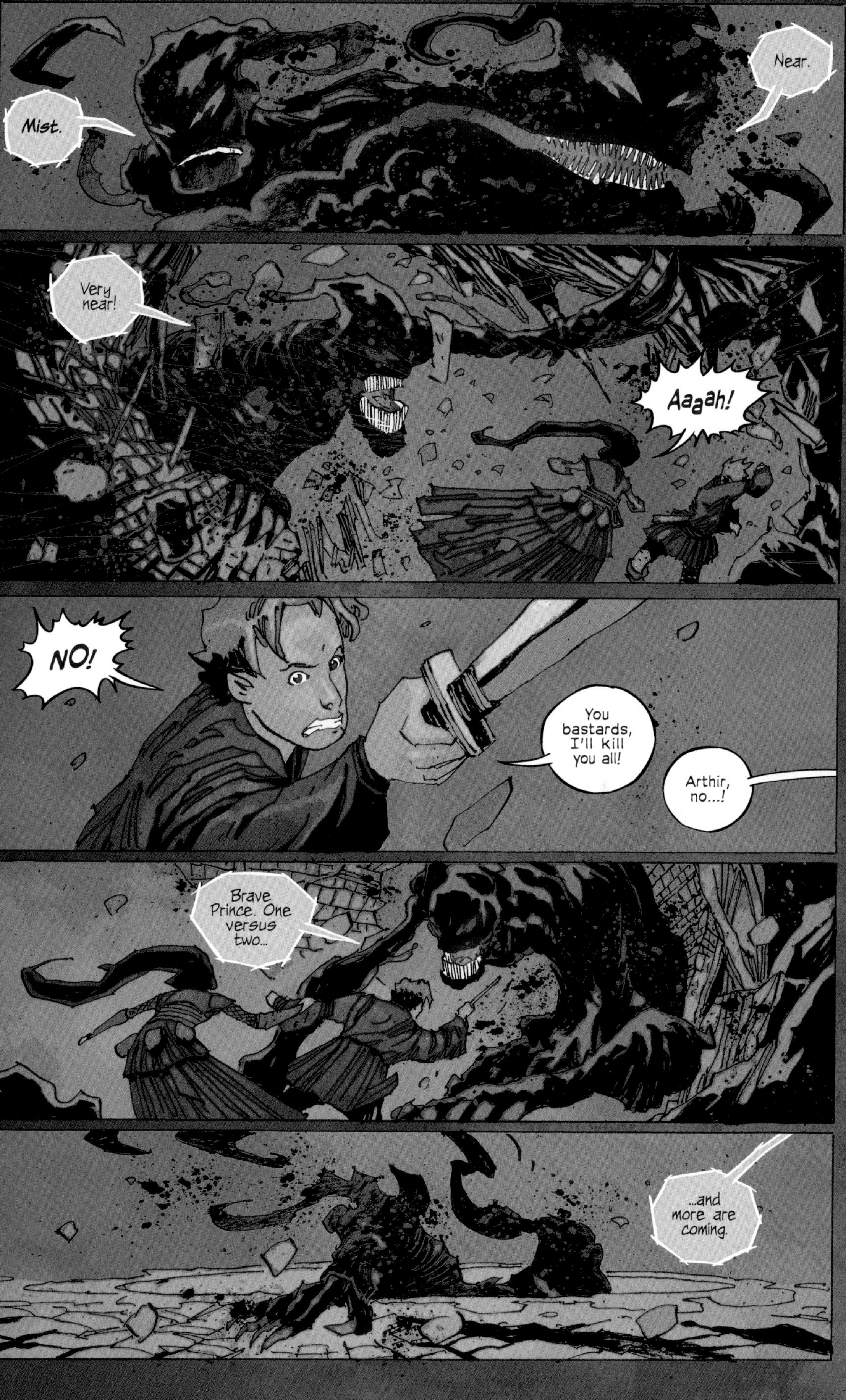
Mist.
Near.
Very near!
Aaaah!
NO!
You bastards, I'll kill you all!
Arthir, no...!
Brave Prince. One versus two...
...and more are coming.

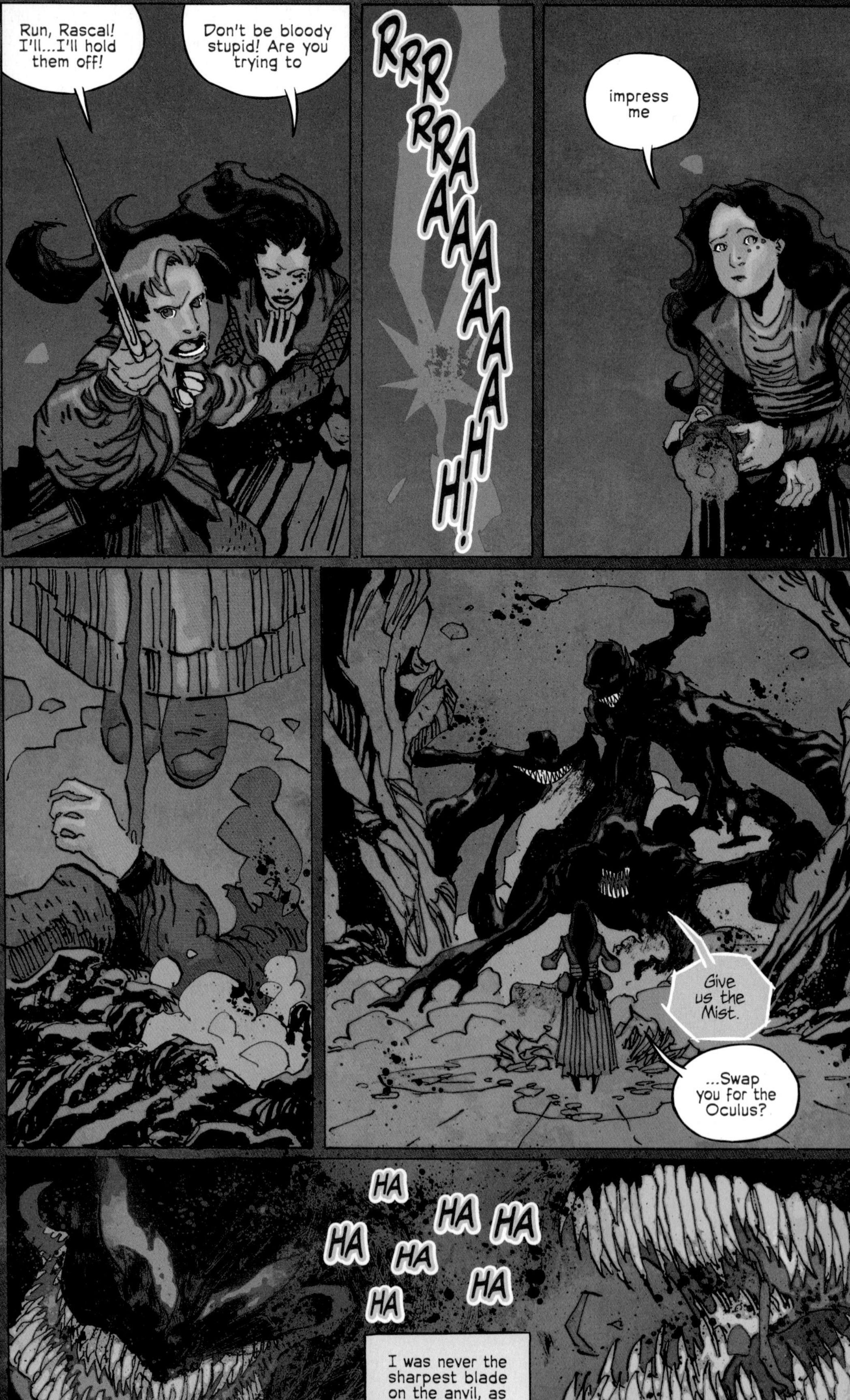
Run, Rascal! I'll...I'll hold them off!
Don't be bloody stupid! Are you trying to
RRRRRAAAAAAAAAAH!
impress me
Give us the Mist.
...Swap you for the Oculus?
HA HA HA HA HA HA HA HA
I was never the sharpest blade on the anvil, as they say.

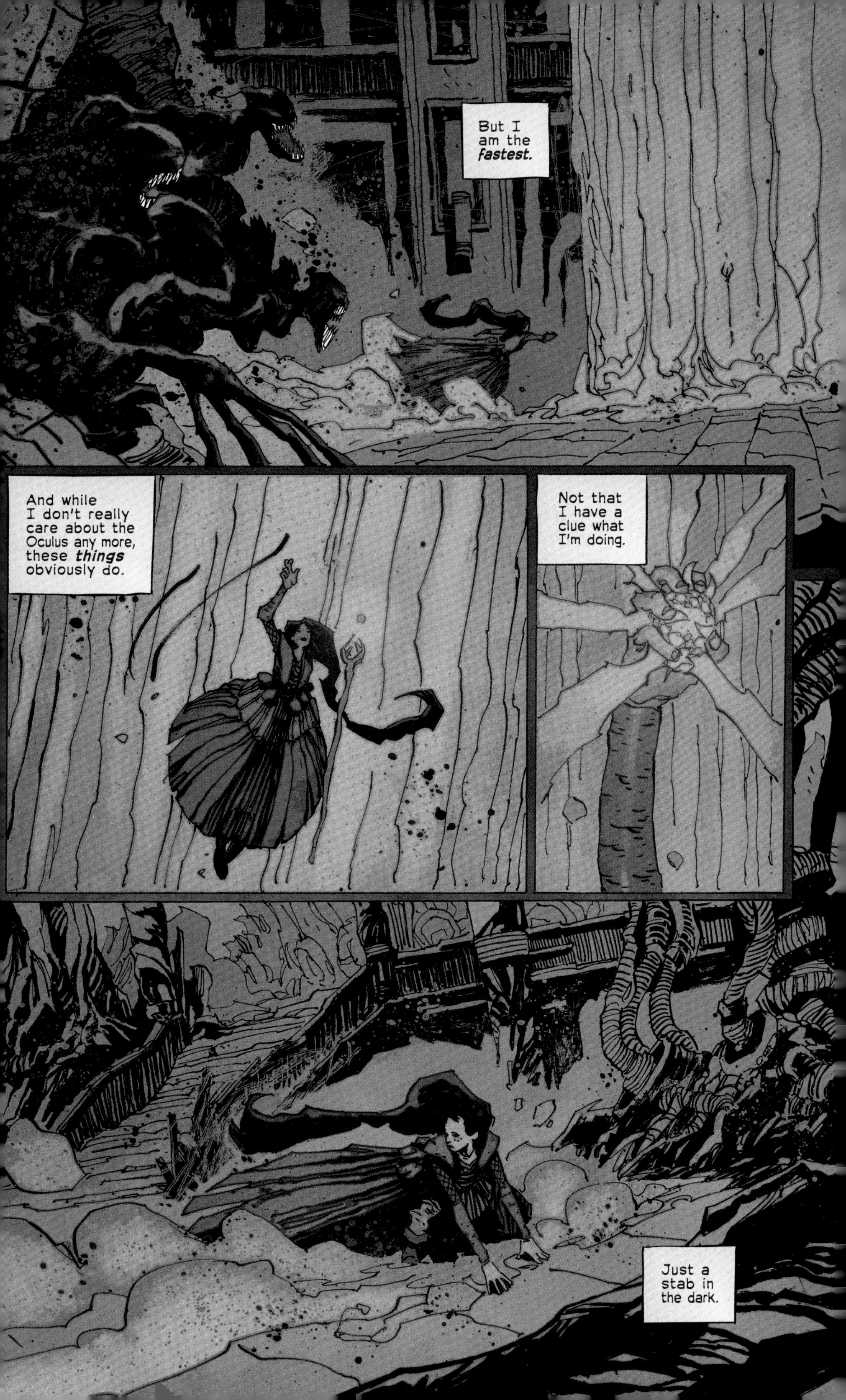

But I am the *fastest.*
And while I don't really care about the Oculus any more, these *things* obviously do.
Not that I have a clue what I'm doing.
Just a stab in the dark.

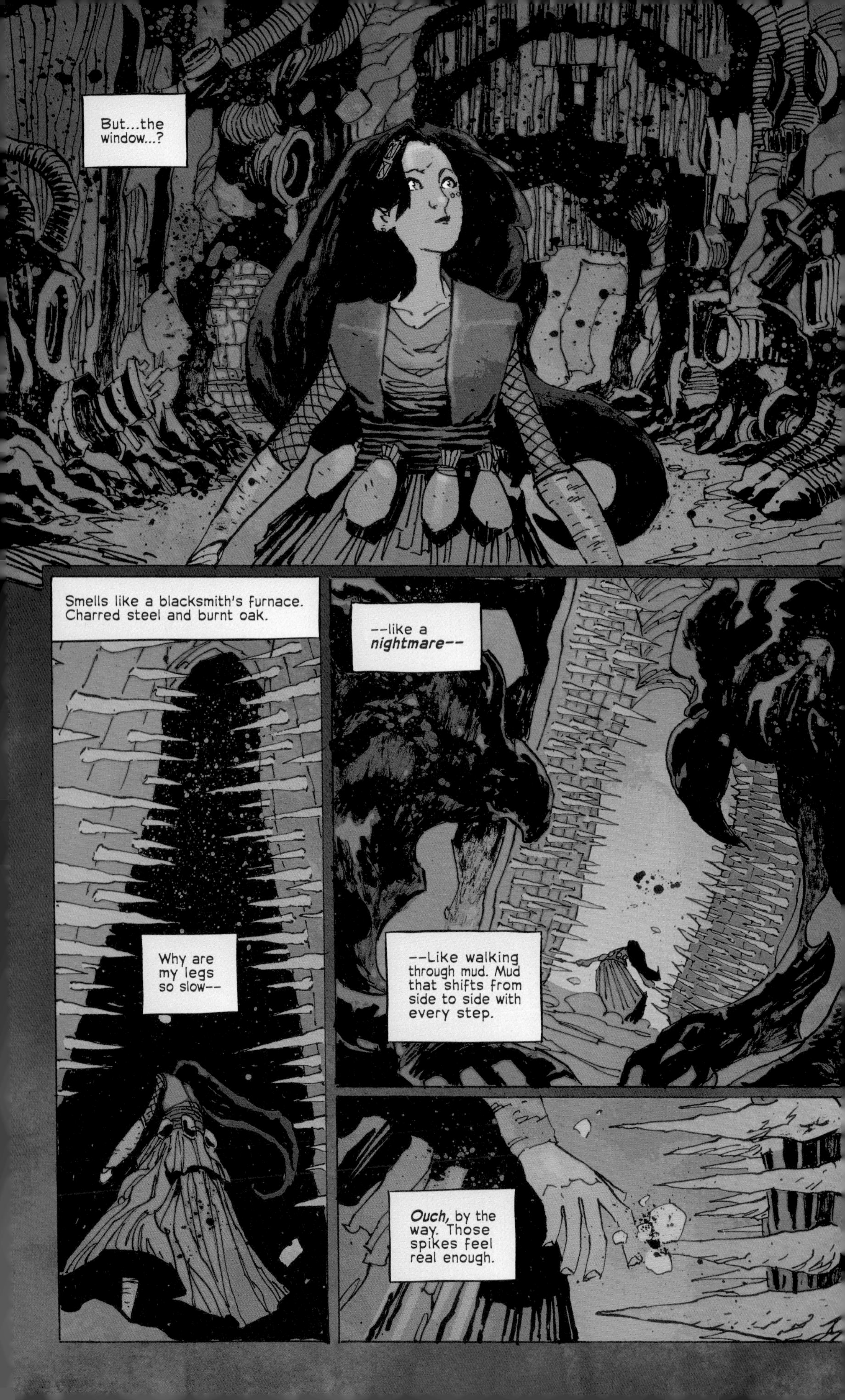
But...the window...?
Smells like a blacksmith's furnace. Charred steel and burnt oak.
--like a *nightmare*--
Why are my legs so slow--
--Like walking through mud. Mud that shifts from side to side with every step.
Ouch, by the way. Those spikes feel real enough.

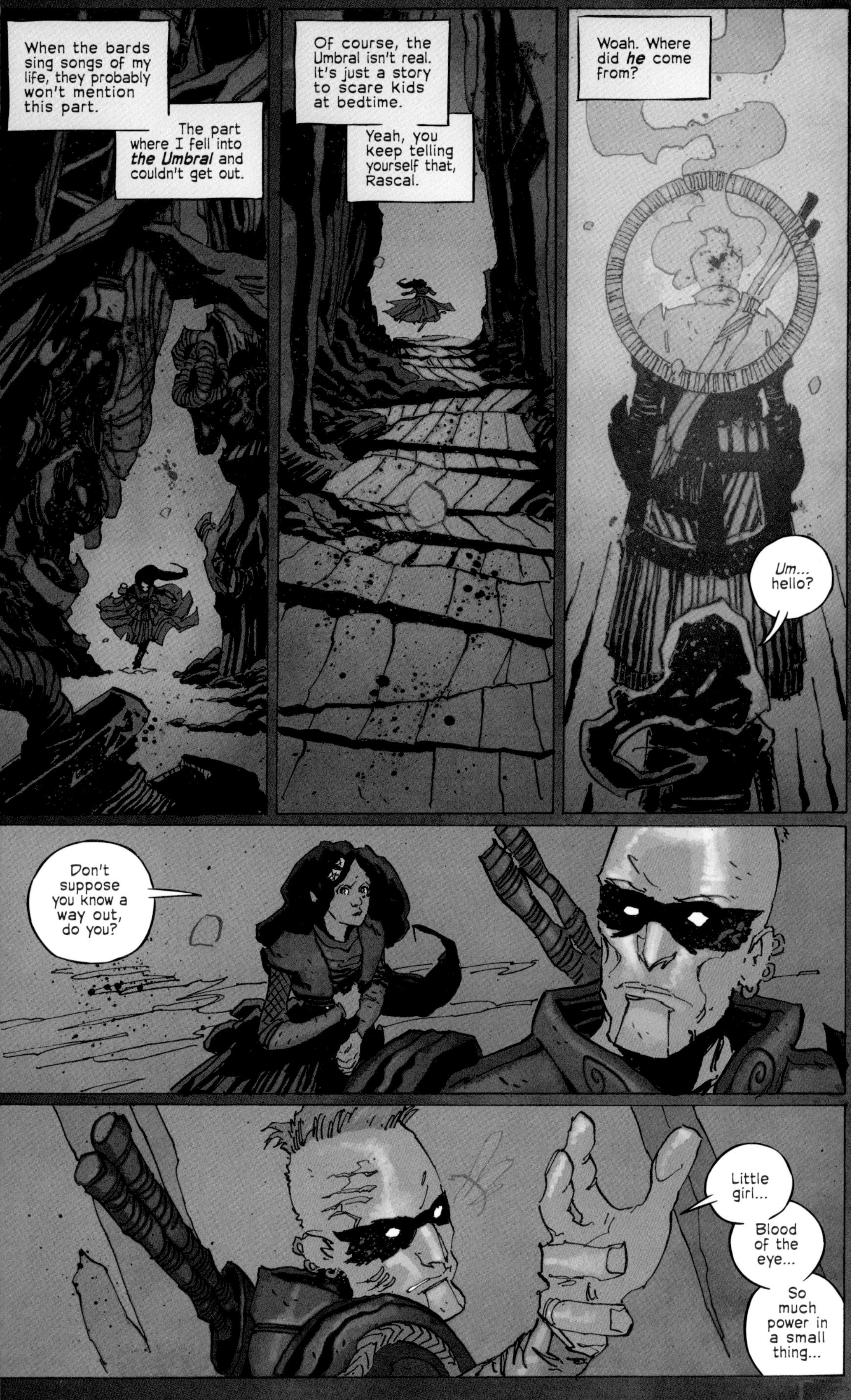
When the bards sing songs of my life, they probably won't mention this part.
The part where I fell into *the Umbral* and couldn't get out.
Of course, the Umbral isn't real. It's just a story to scare kids at bedtime.
Yeah, you keep telling yourself that, Rascal.
Woah. Where did *he* come from?
Um... hello?
Don't suppose you know a way out, do you?
Little girl...
Blood of the eye...
So much power in a small thing...

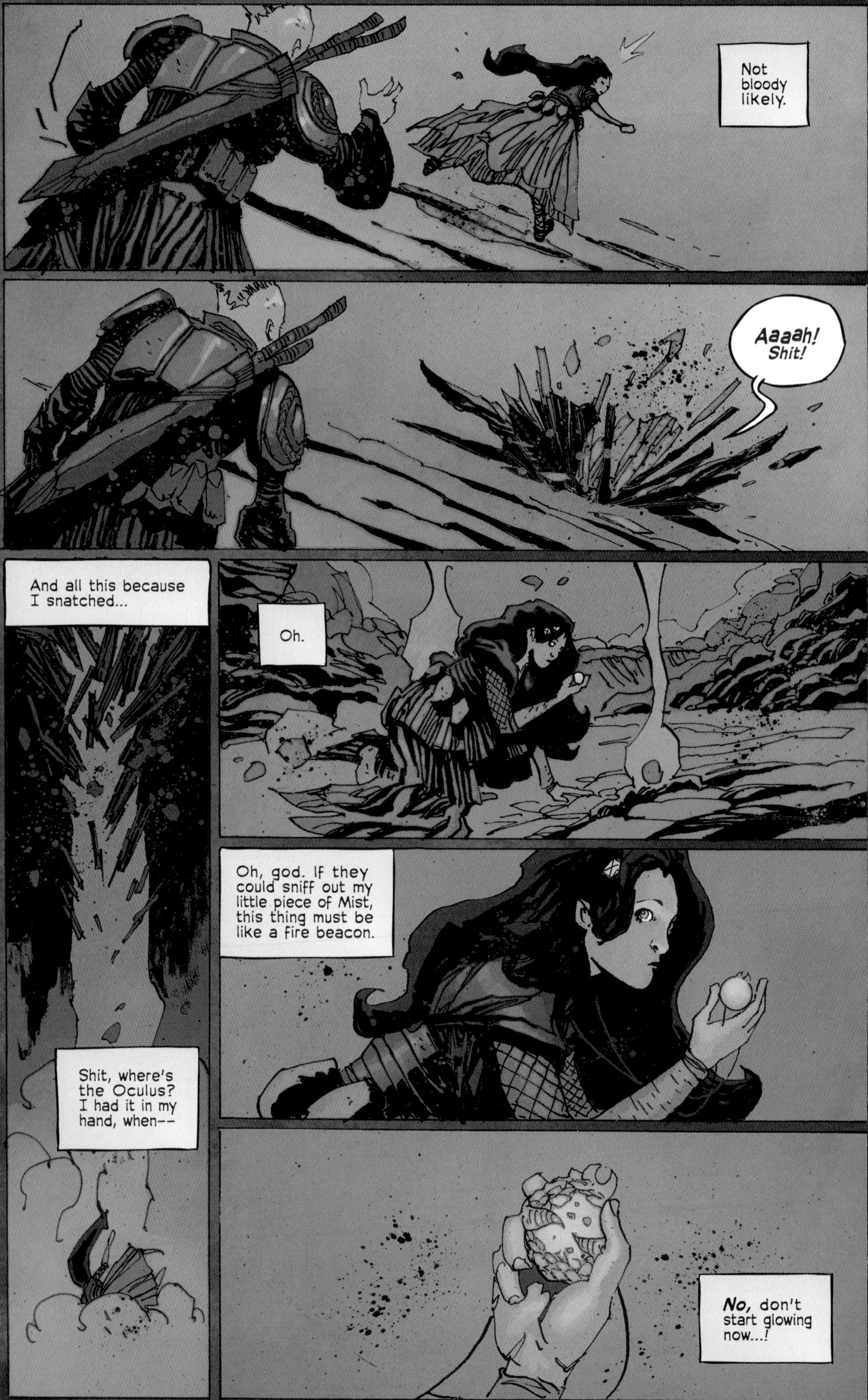
Not bloody likely.
Aaaah! Shit!
And all this because I snatched...
Oh.
Oh, god. If they could sniff out my little piece of Mist, this thing must be like a fire beacon.
Shit, where's the Oculus? I had it in my hand, when--
No, don't start glowing now...!

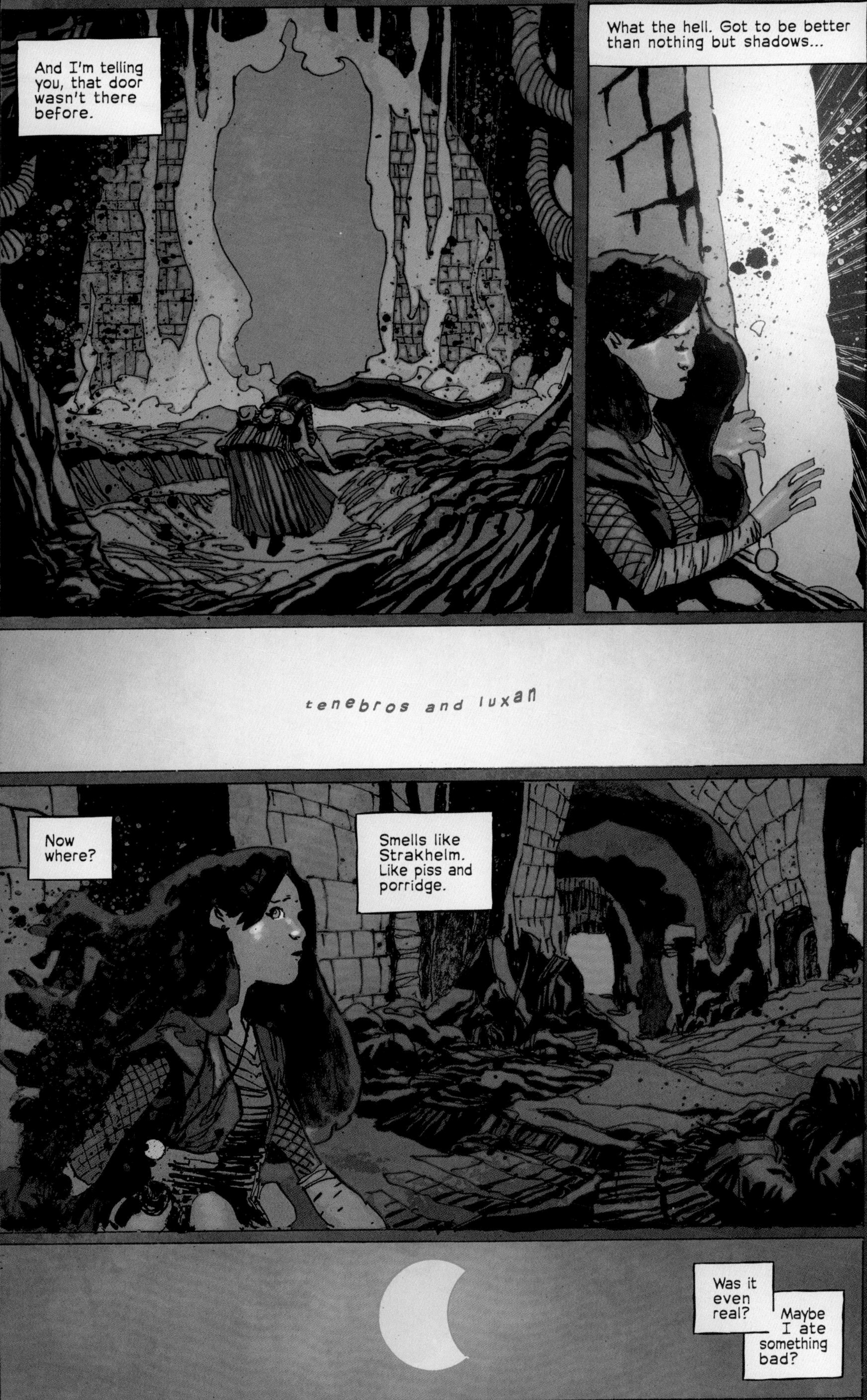
And I'm telling you, that door wasn't there before.
What the hell. Got to be better than nothing but shadows...
tenebros and luxan
Now where?
Smells like Strakhelm. Like piss and porridge.
Was it even real?
Maybe I ate something bad?

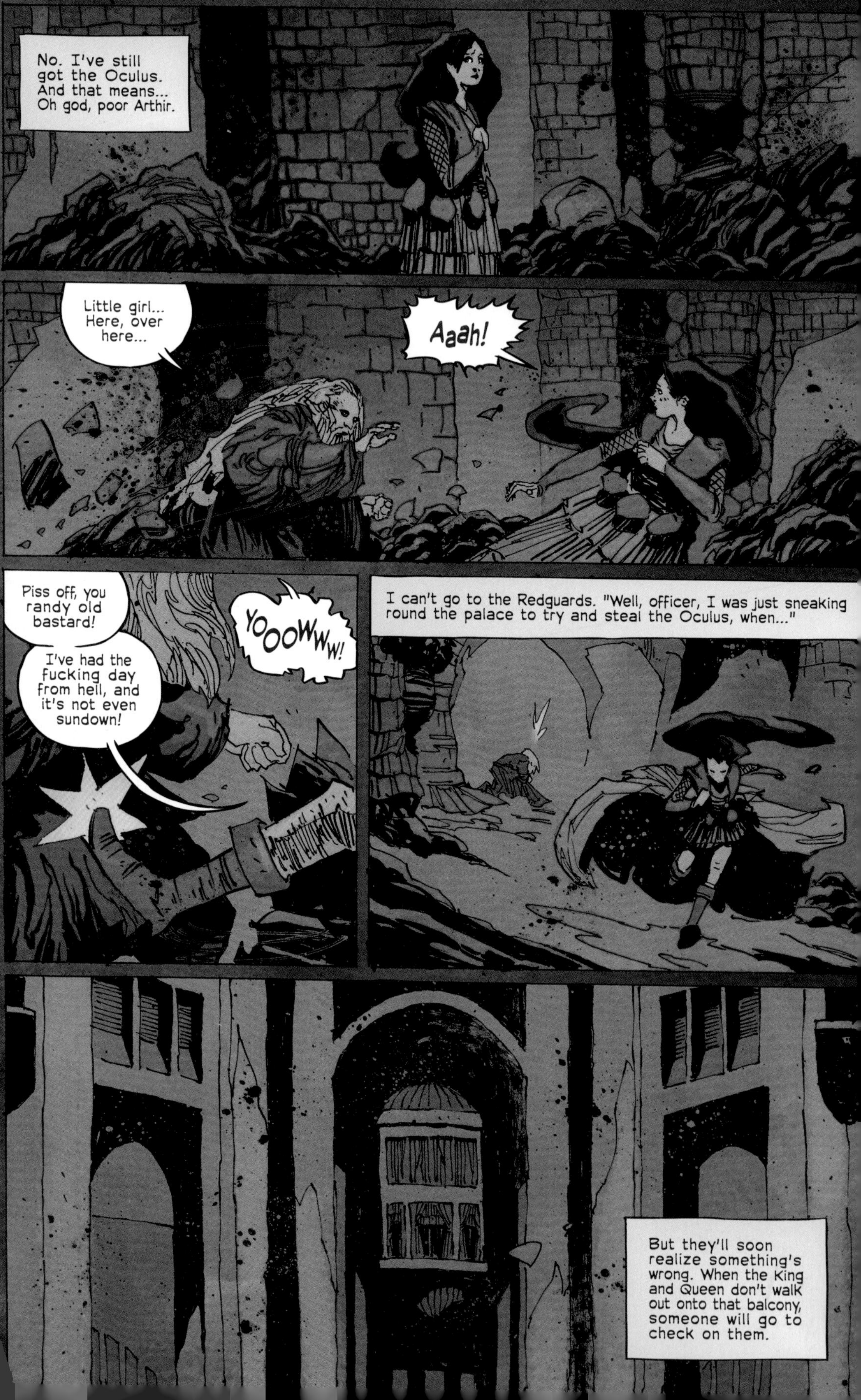

No. I've still got the Oculus. And that means... Oh god, poor Arthir.
Little girl... Here, over here...
Aaah!
Piss off, you randy old bastard!
I've had the fucking day from hell, and it's not even sundown!
YOOOWWW!
I can't go to the Redguards. "Well, officer, I was just sneaking round the palace to try and steal the Oculus, when..."
But they'll soon realize something's wrong. When the King and Queen don't walk out onto that balcony, someone will go to check on them.

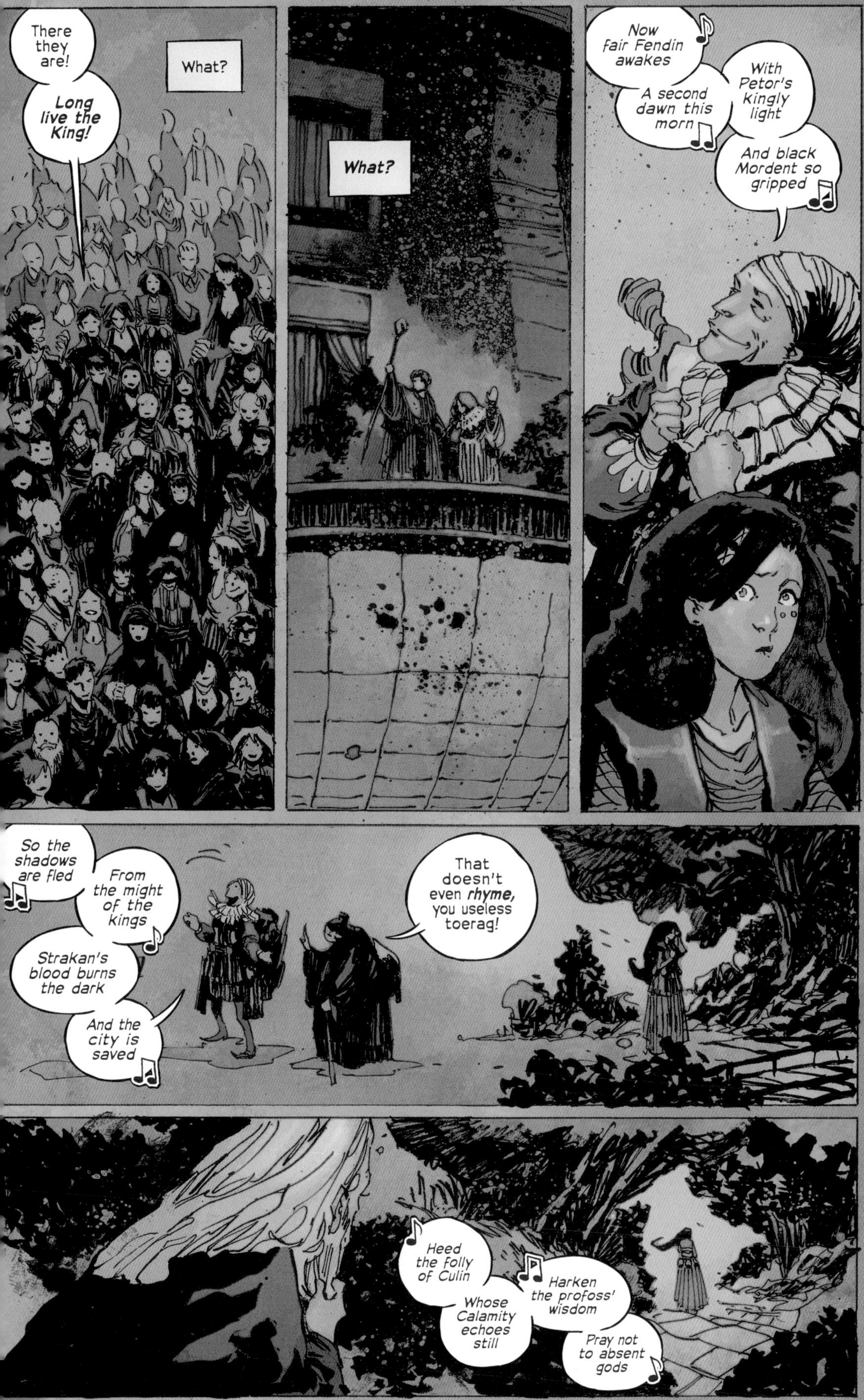
There they are!
What?
Long live the King!
What?
Now fair Fendin awakes
A second dawn this morn
With Petor's kingly light
And black Mordent so gripped
So the shadows are fled
From the might of the kings
Strakan's blood burns the dark
And the city is saved
That doesn't even rhyme, you useless toerag!
Heed the folly of Culin
Whose Calamity echoes still
Harken the profoss' wisdom
Pray not to absent gods

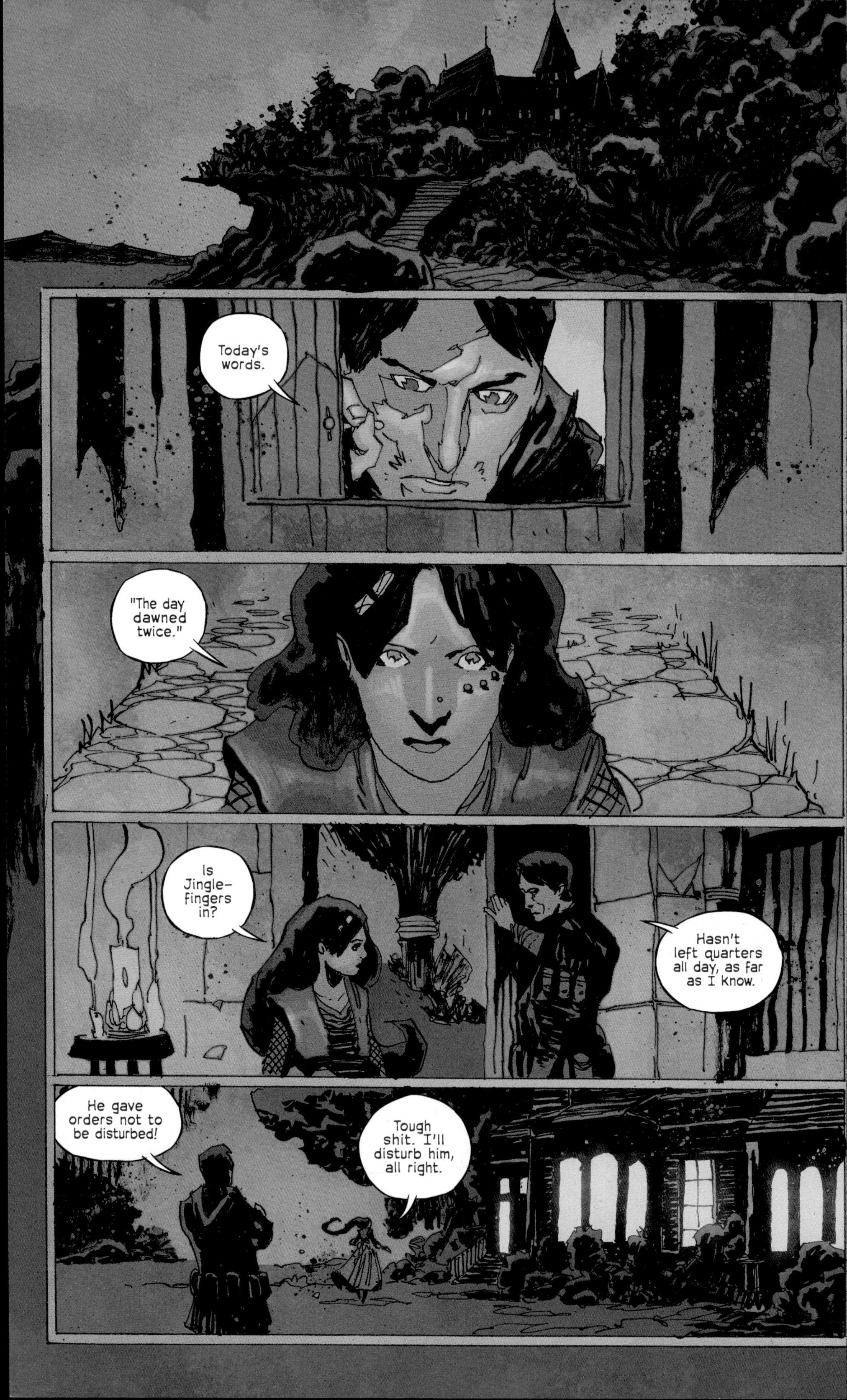
Today's words.
"The day dawned twice."
Is Jingle-fingers in?
Hasn't left quarters all day, as far as I know.
He gave orders not to be disturbed!
Tough shit. I'll disturb him, all right.

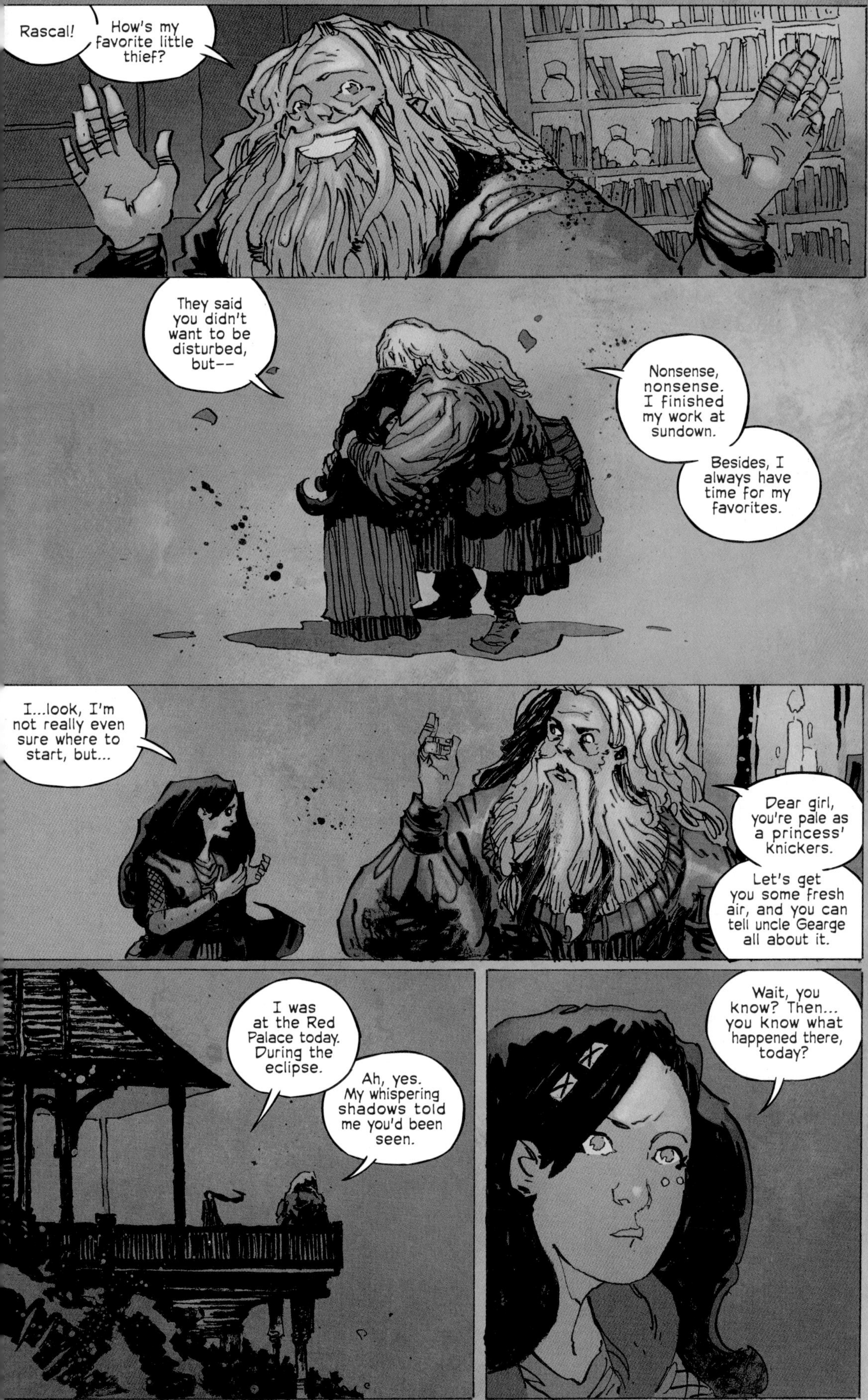
Rascal!
How's my favorite little thief?
They said you didn't want to be disturbed, but--
Nonsense, nonsense. I finished my work at sundown.
Besides, I always have time for my favorites.
I...look, I'm not really even sure where to start, but...
Dear girl, you're pale as a princess' knickers.
Let's get you some fresh air, and you can tell uncle Gearge all about it.
I was at the Red Palace today. During the eclipse.
Ah, yes. My whispering shadows told me you'd been seen.
Wait, you know? Then... you know what happened there, today?

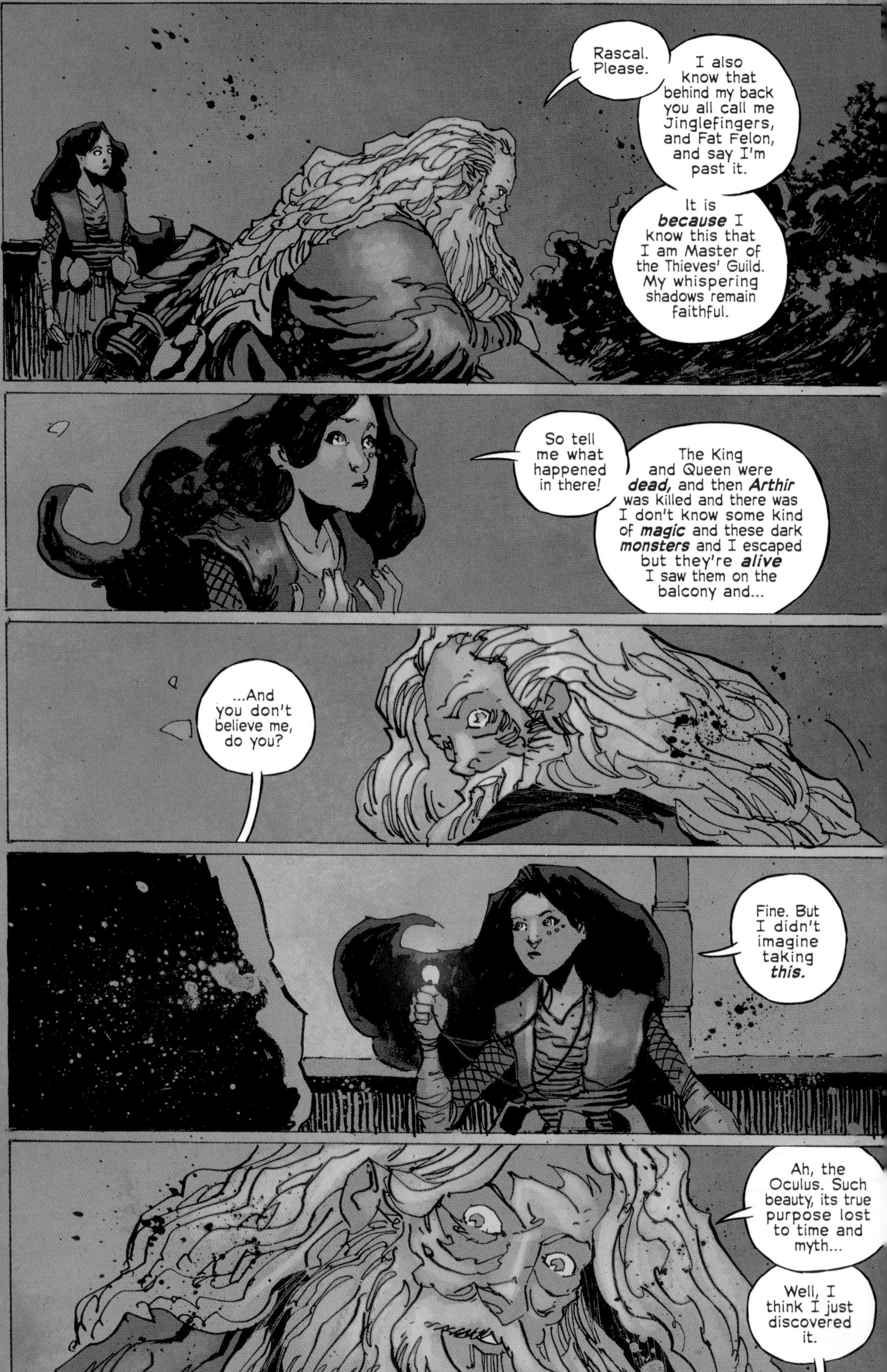
Rascal. Please.
I also know that behind my back you all call me Jinglefingers, and Fat Felon, and say I'm past it.
It is *because* I know this that I am Master of the Thieves' Guild. My whispering shadows remain faithful.
So tell me what happened in there!
The King and Queen were *dead,* and then *Arthir* was killed and there was I don't know some kind of *magic* and these dark *monsters* and I escaped but they're *alive* I saw them on the balcony and...
...And you don't believe me, do you?
Fine. But I didn't imagine taking *this.*
Ah, the Oculus. Such beauty, its true purpose lost to time and myth...
Well, I think I just discovered it.

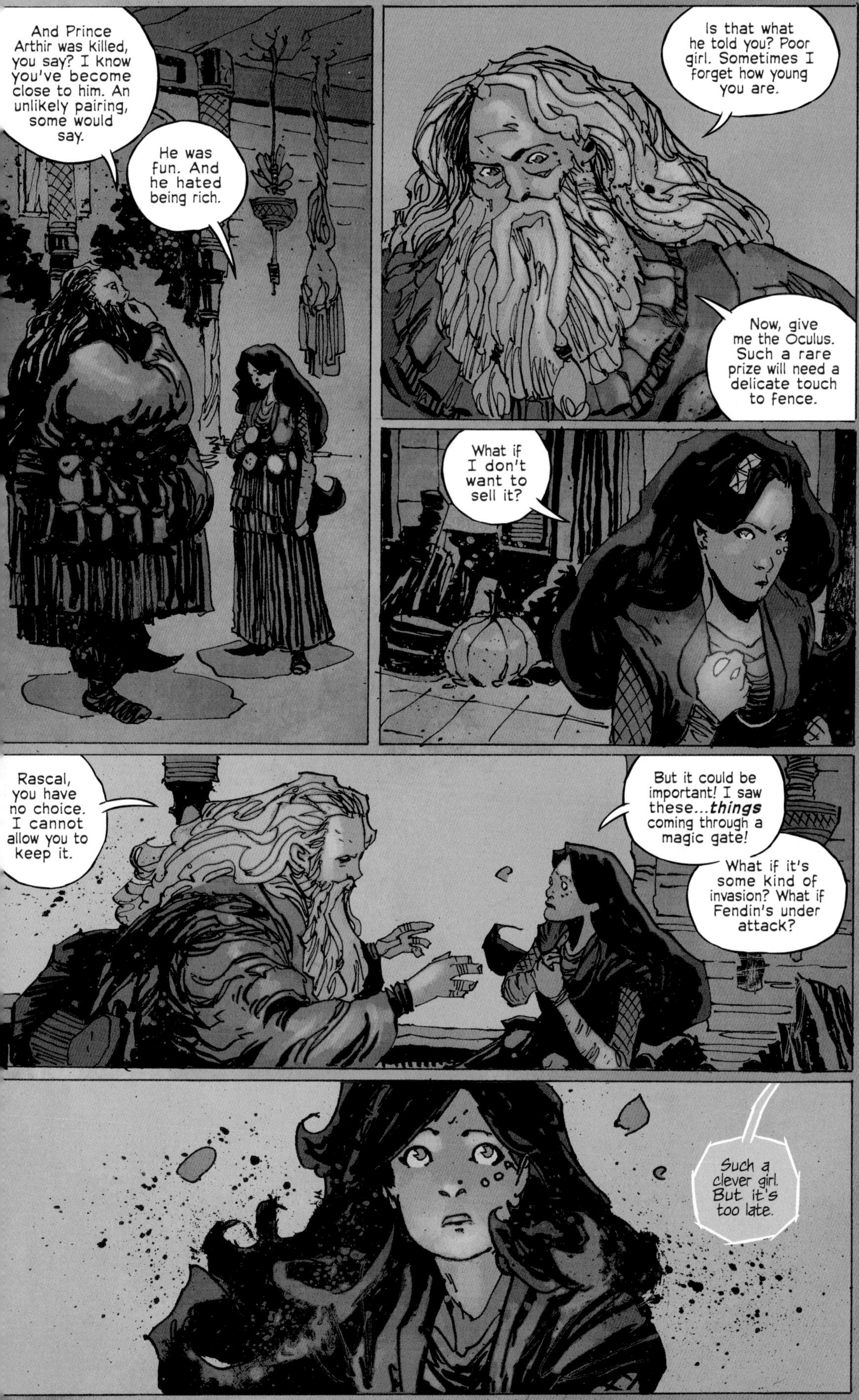
And Prince Arthir was killed, you say? I know you've become close to him. An unlikely pairing, some would say.
He was fun. And he hated being rich.
Is that what he told you? Poor girl. Sometimes I forget how young you are.
Now, give me the Oculus. Such a rare prize will need a delicate touch to fence.
What if I don't want to sell it?
Rascal, you have no choice. I cannot allow you to keep it.
But it could be important! I saw these...*things* coming through a magic gate!
What if it's some kind of invasion? What if Fendin's under attack?
Such a clever girl. But it's too late.

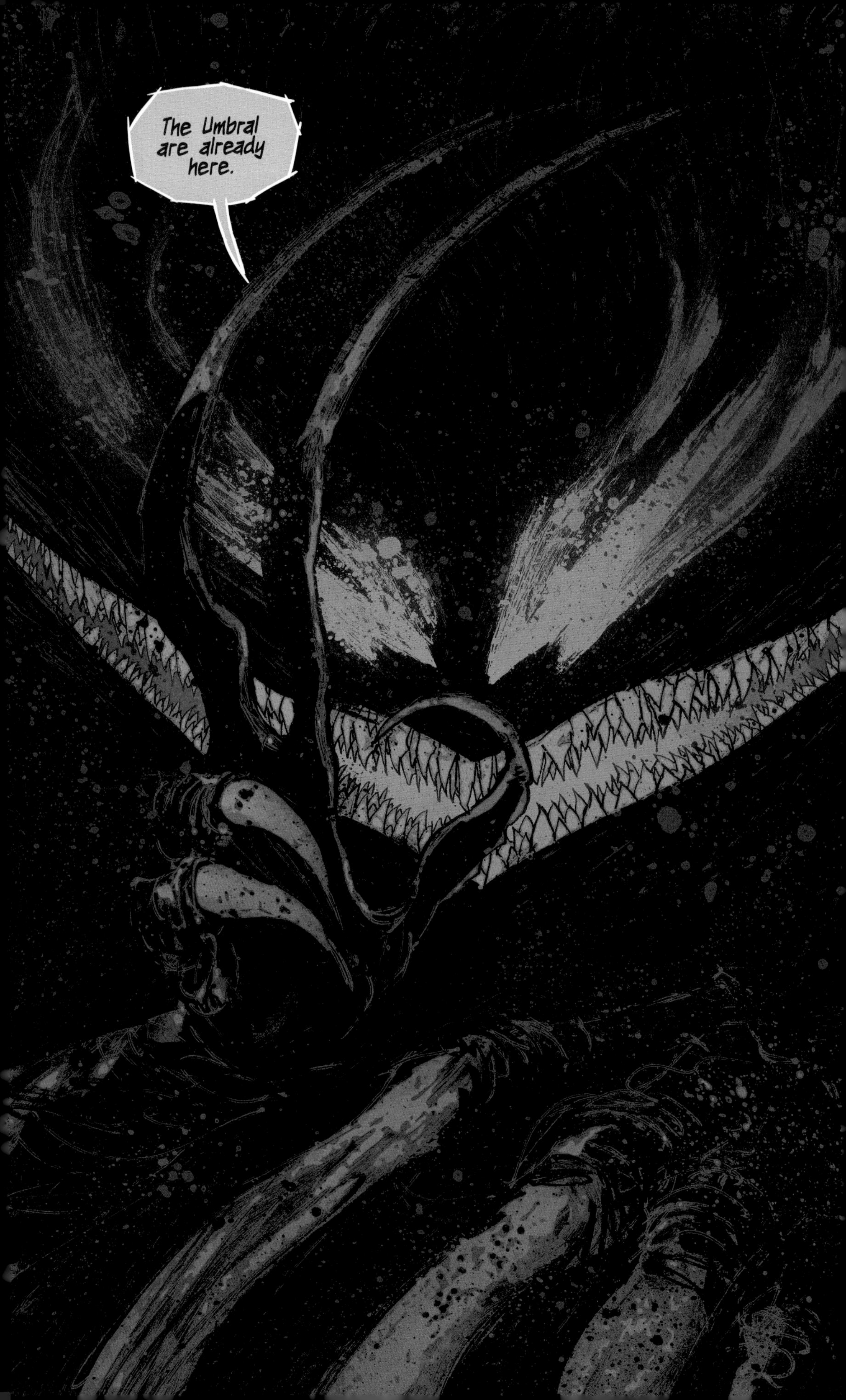
The Umbral are already here.

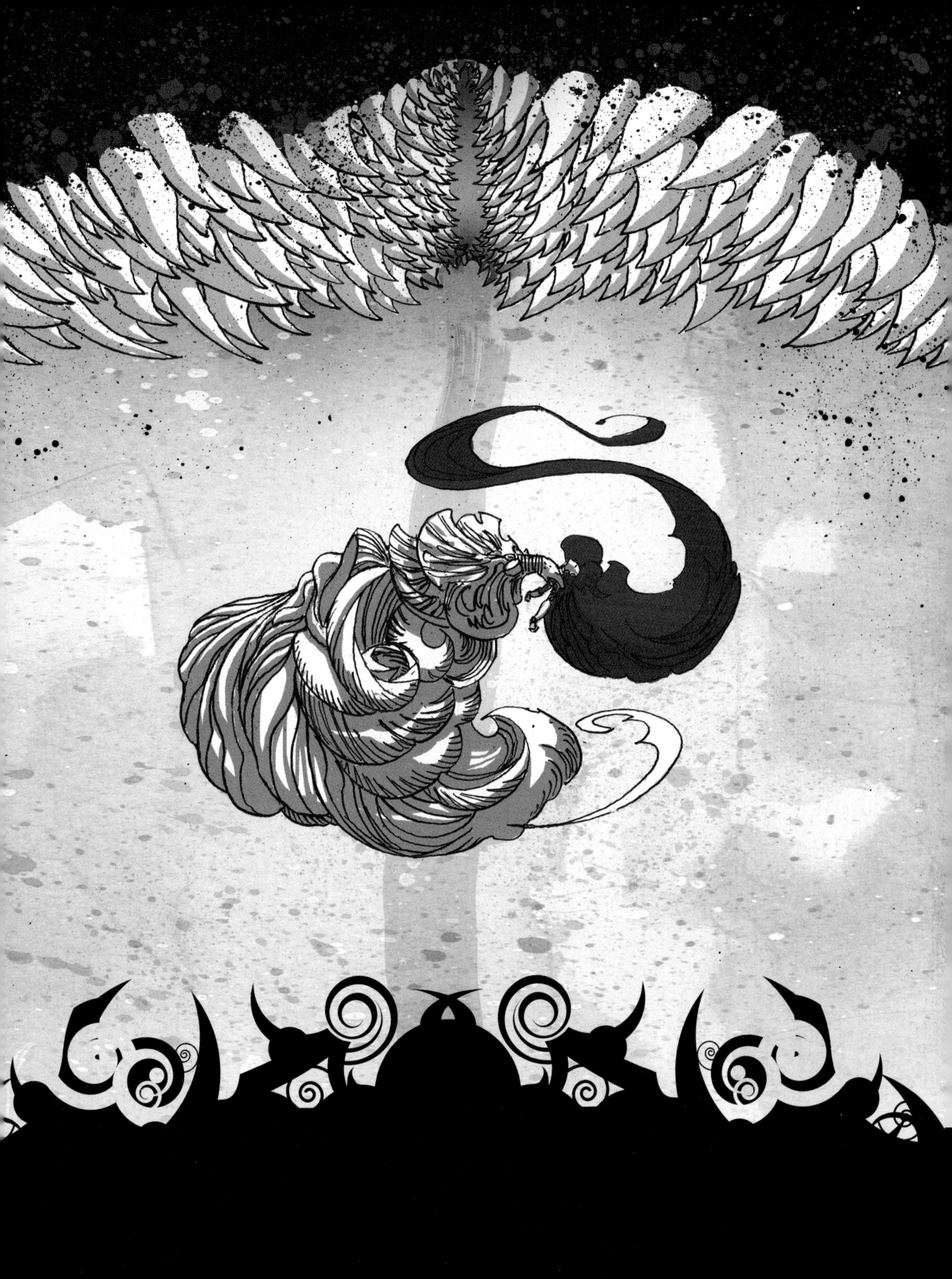

FALLING INTO DARK

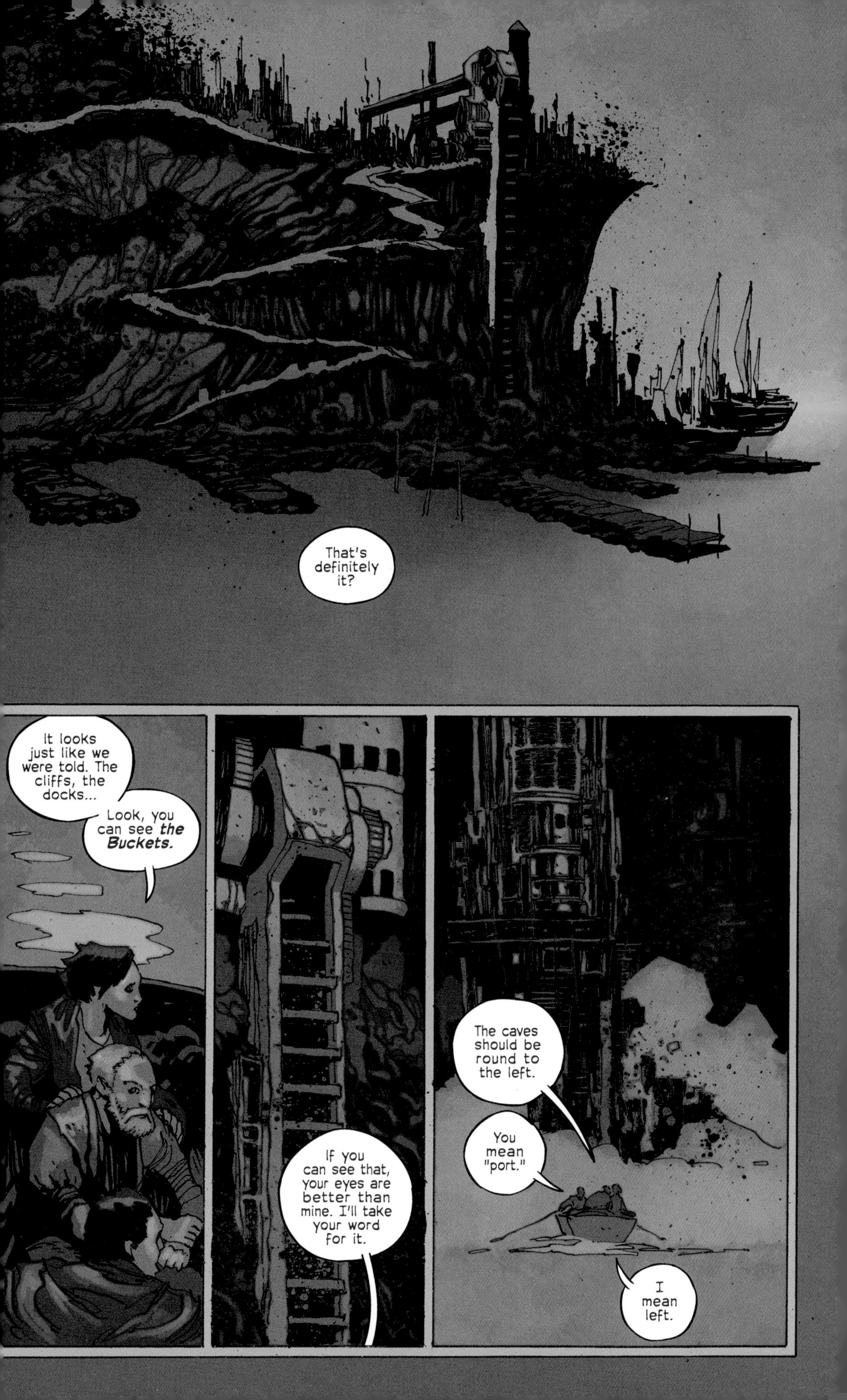
That's definitely it?
It looks just like we were told. The cliffs, the docks...
Look, you can see *the Buckets.*
If you can see that, your eyes are better than mine. I'll take your word for it.
The caves should be round to the left.
You mean "port."
I mean left.

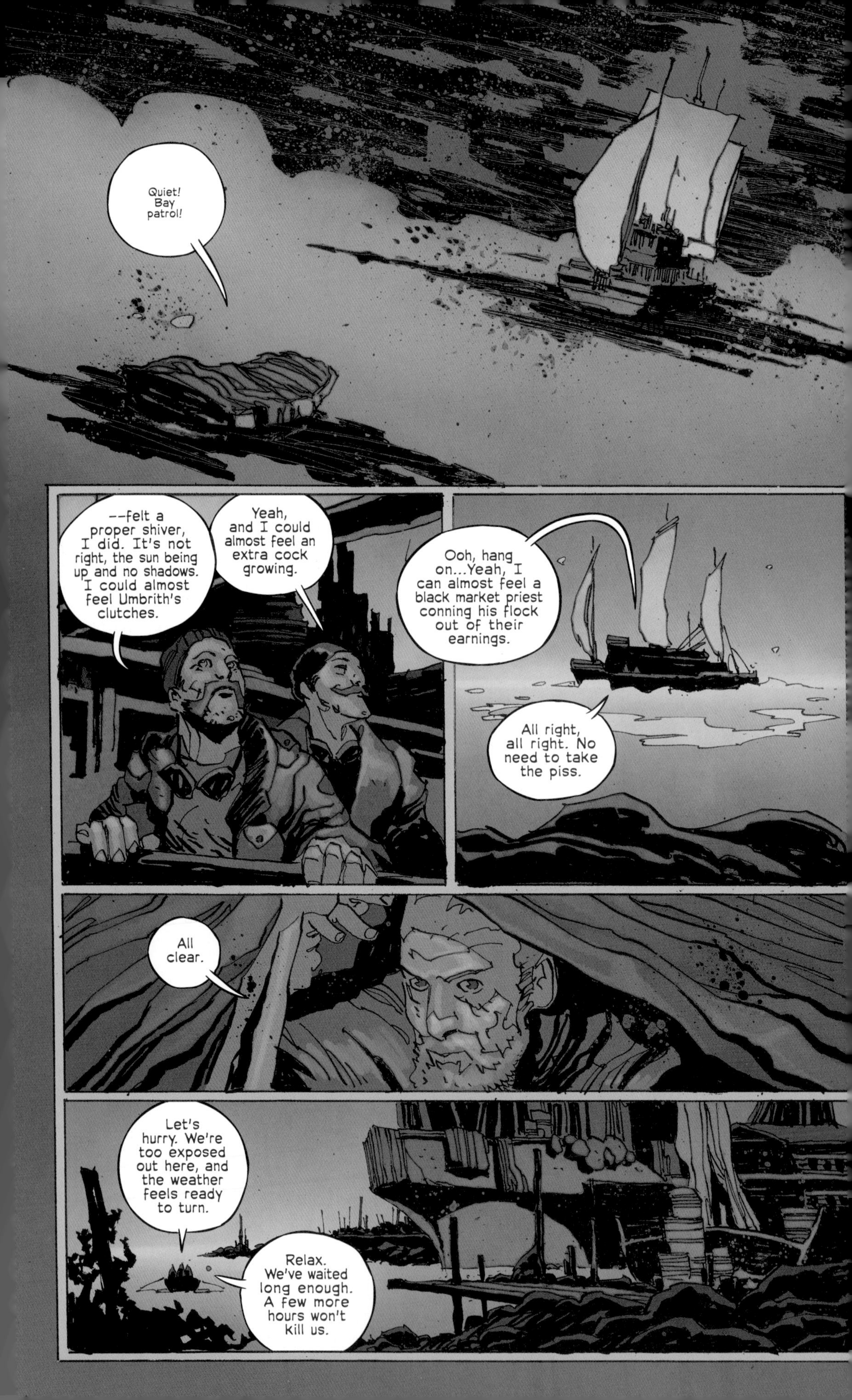
Quiet! Bay patrol!
--felt a proper shiver, I did. It's not right, the sun being up and no shadows. I could almost feel Umbrith's clutches.
Yeah, and I could almost feel an extra cock growing.
Ooh, hang on...Yeah, I can almost feel a black market priest conning his flock out of their earnings.
All right, all right. No need to take the piss.
All clear.
Let's hurry. We're too exposed out here, and the weather feels ready to turn.
Relax. We've waited long enough. A few more hours won't kill us.

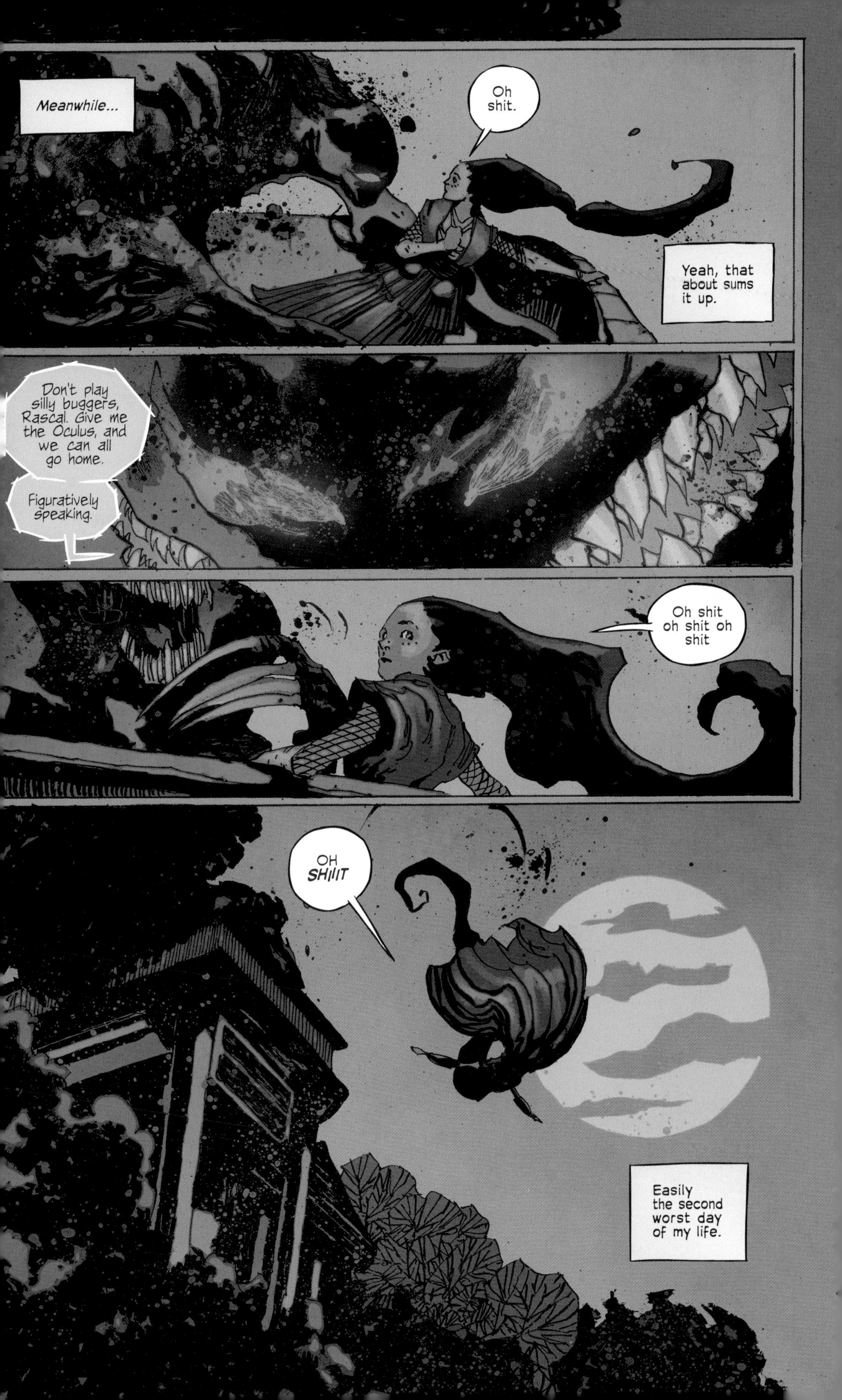

Meanwhile...
Oh shit.
Yeah, that about sums it up.
Don't play silly buggers, Rascal. Give me the Oculus, and we can all go home.
Figuratively speaking.
Oh shit oh shit oh shit
OH SHIIIT
Easily the second worst day of my life.

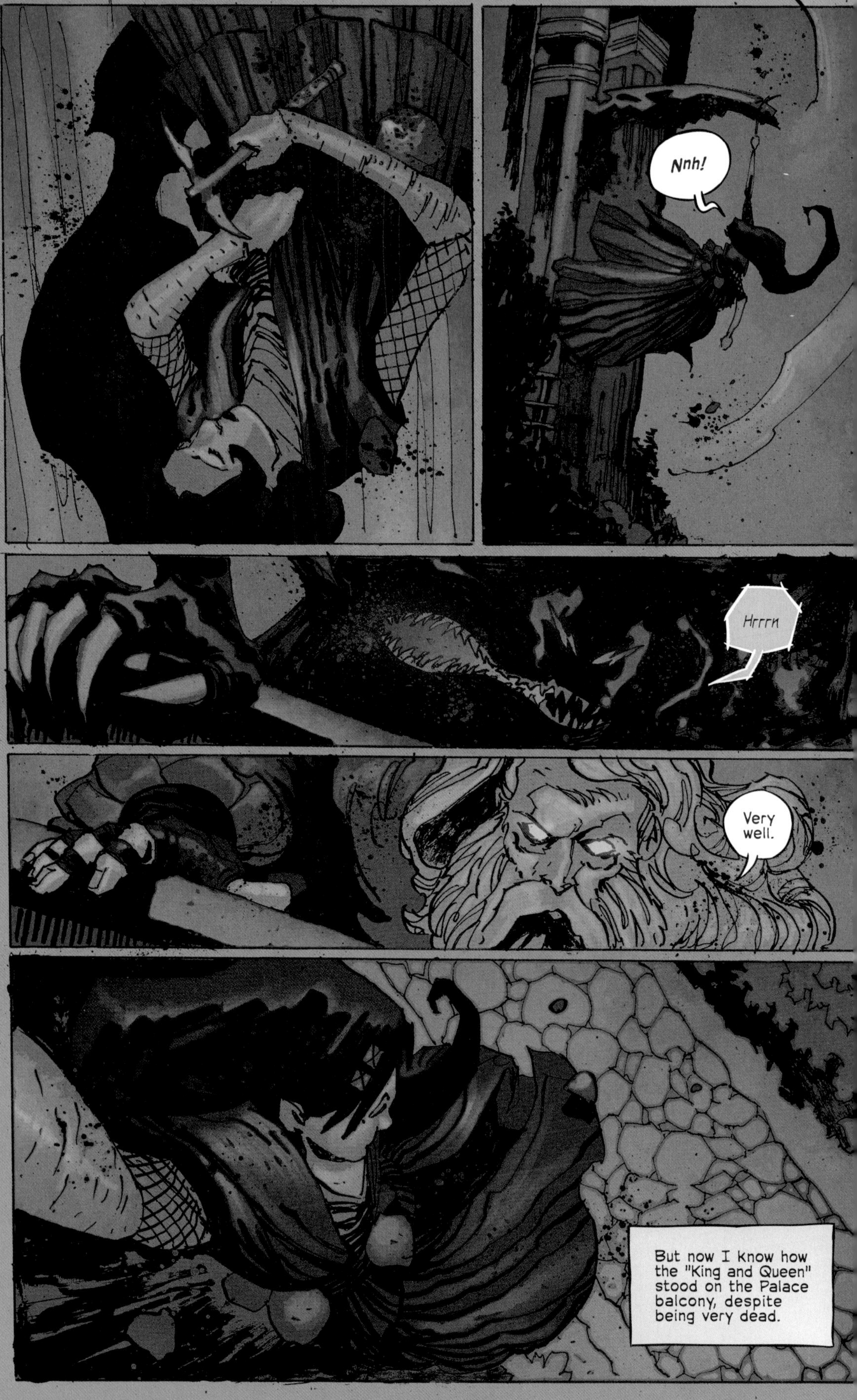
Nnh!
Hrrrn
Very well.
But now I know how the "King and Queen" stood on the Palace balcony, despite being very dead.

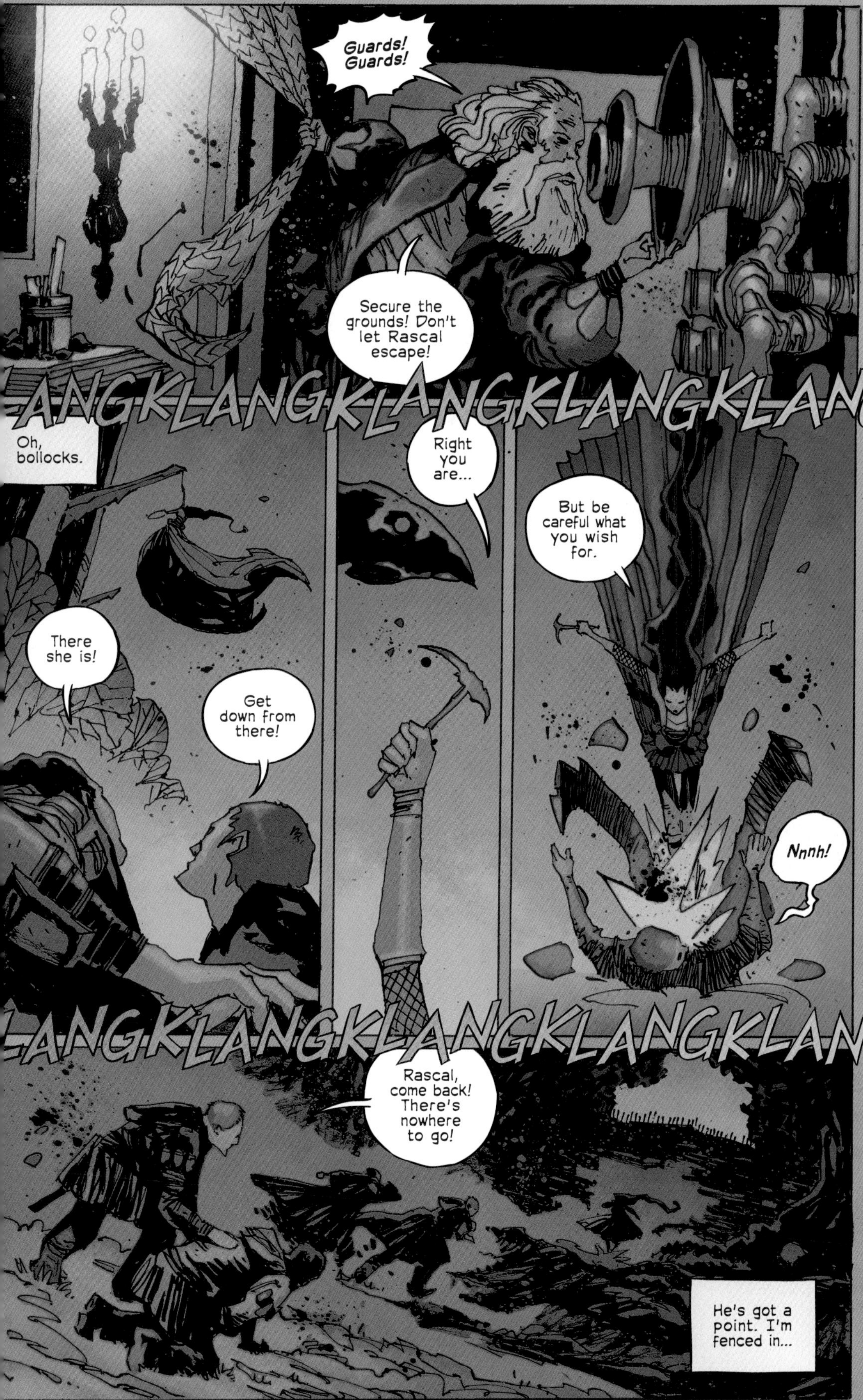
Guards! Guards!
Secure the grounds! Don't let Rascal escape!
KLANGKLANGKLANGKLANGKLANGKLANG
Oh, bollocks.
There she is!
Get down from there!
Right you are...
But be careful what you wish for.
Nnnh!
KLANGKLANGKLANGKLANGKLANGKLANG
Rascal, come back! There's nowhere to go!
He's got a point. I'm fenced in...

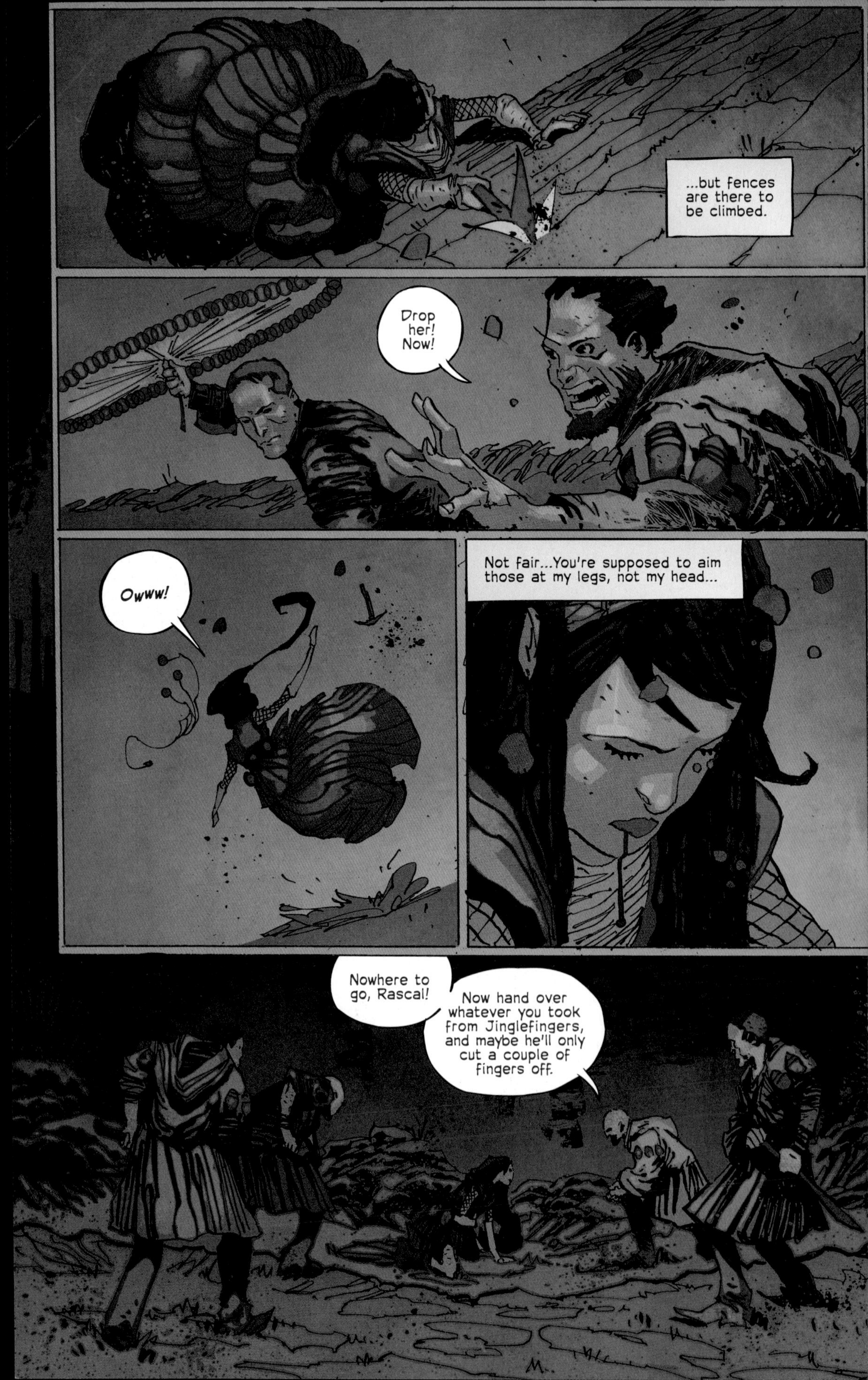
...but fences are there to be climbed.
Drop her! Now!
Owww!
Not fair...You're supposed to aim those at my legs, not my head...
Nowhere to go, Rascal!
Now hand over whatever you took from Jinglefingers, and maybe he'll only cut a couple of fingers off.

Why not just run me through, you bastards?! You didn't think twice about gutting poor Arthir!

So make it bloody quick, and then you can loot my corpse all you like!

What the hell are you babbling about? Did someone feed you a wad of sweetleaf?

I wish they had, it'd bloody well slow her down.

I dare say, miss...

...that these particular ruffians have no idea what you're talking about.

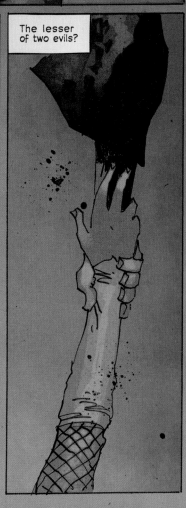

The lesser of two evils?

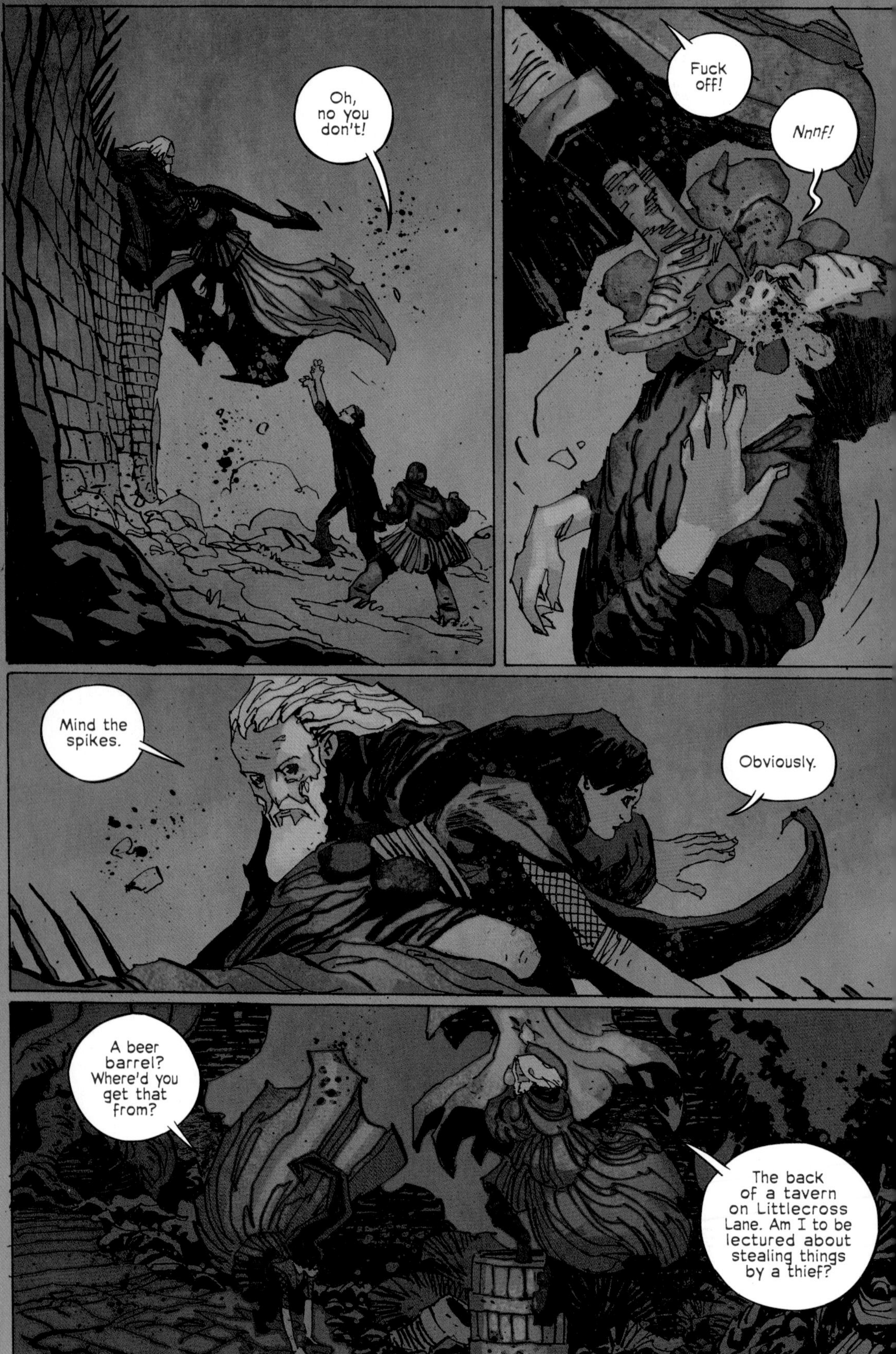
Oh, no you don't!
Fuck off!
Nnnf!
Mind the spikes.
Obviously.
A beer barrel? Where'd you get that from?
The back of a tavern on Littlecross Lane. Am I to be lectured about stealing things by a thief?

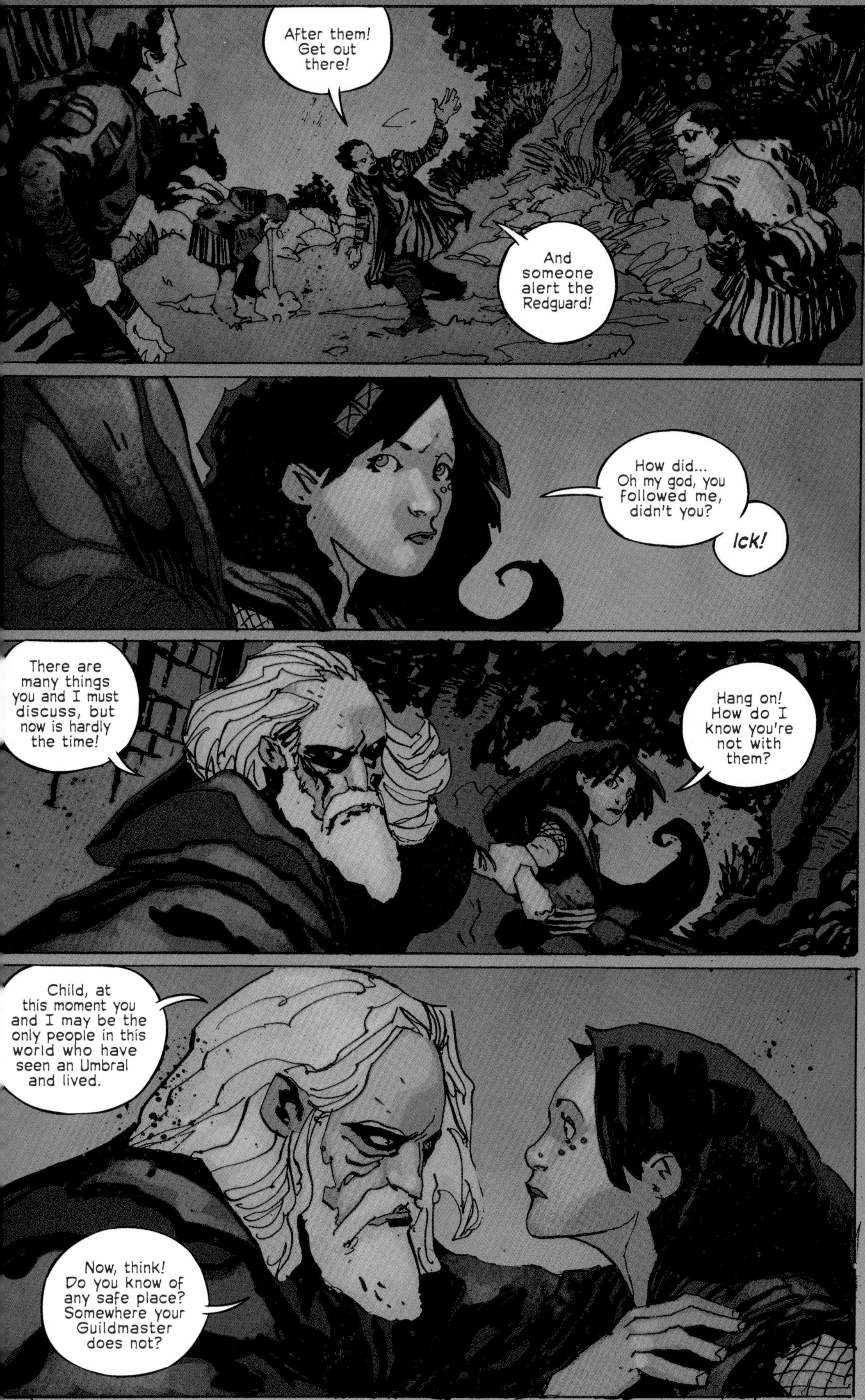
After them! Get out there!
And someone alert the Redguard!
How did... Oh my god, you followed me, didn't you?
Ick!
There are many things you and I must discuss, but now is hardly the time!
Hang on! How do I know you're not with them?
Child, at this moment you and I may be the only people in this world who have seen an Umbral and lived.
Now, think! Do you know of any safe place? Somewhere your Guildmaster does not?

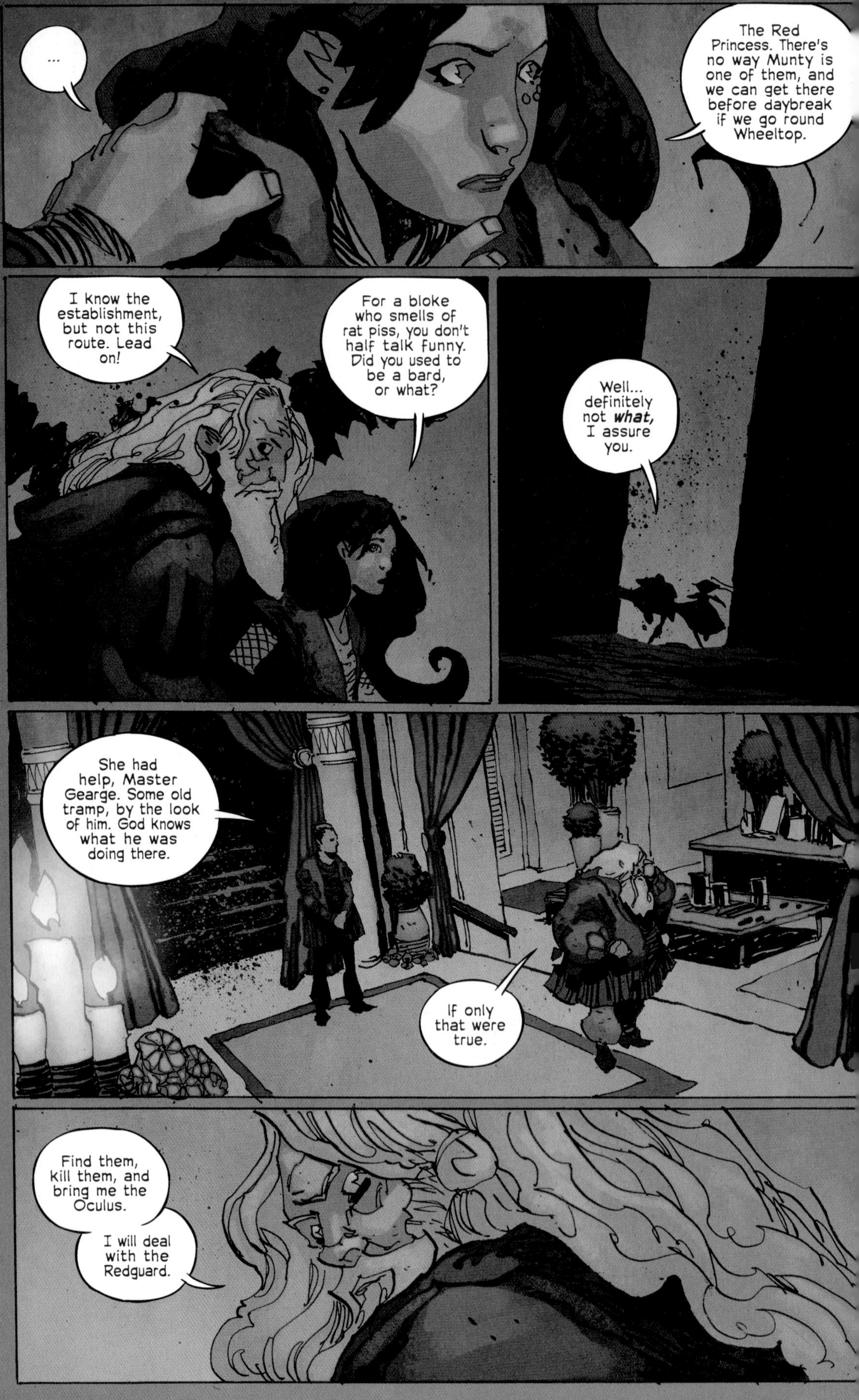
...
The Red Princess. There's no way Munty is one of them, and we can get there before daybreak if we go round Wheeltop.
I know the establishment, but not this route. Lead on!
For a bloke who smells of rat piss, you don't half talk funny. Did you used to be a bard, or what?
Well... definitely not *what,* I assure you.
She had help, Master Gearge. Some old tramp, by the look of him. God knows what he was doing there.
If only that were true.
Find them, kill them, and bring me the Oculus.
I will deal with the Redguard.

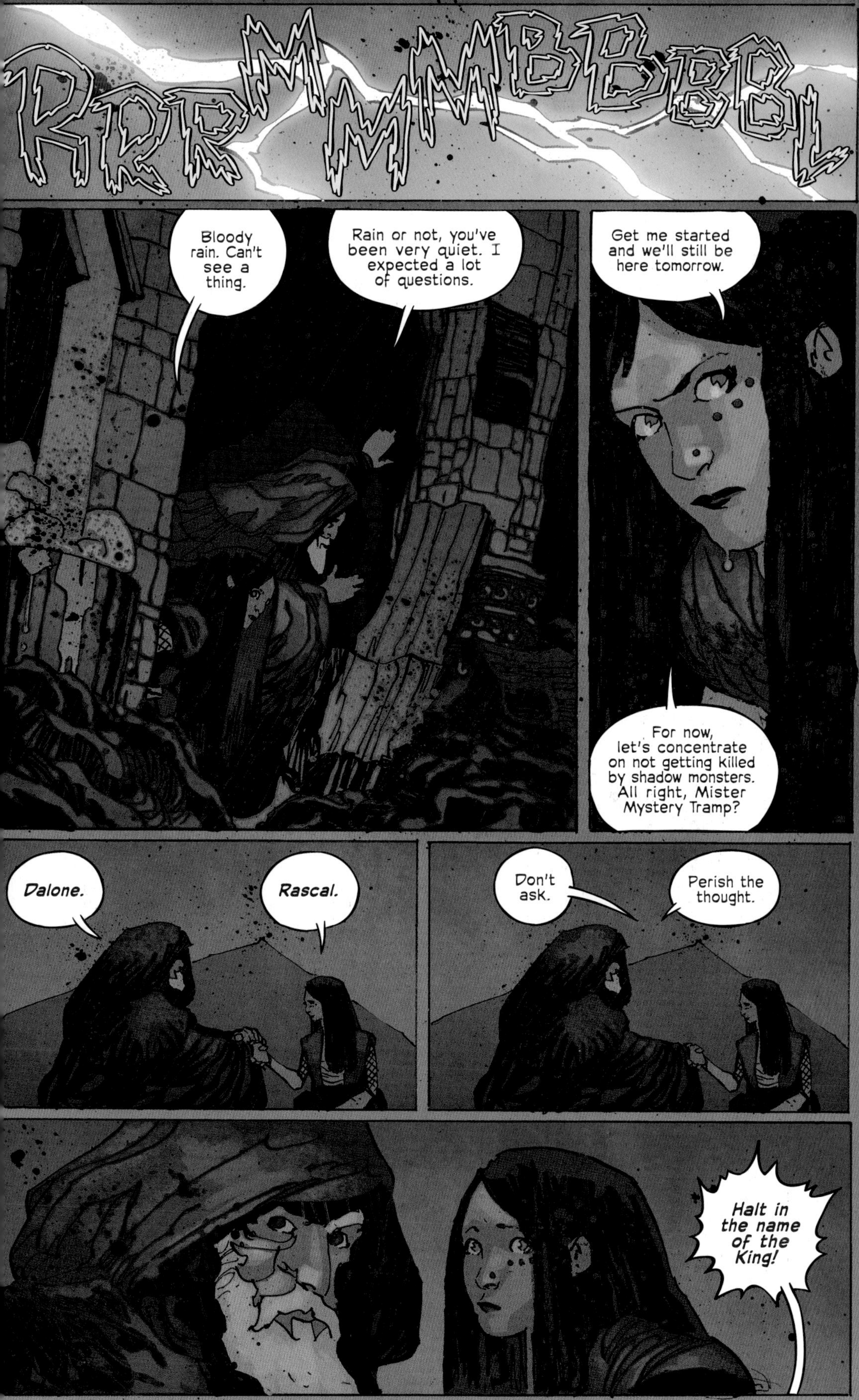
RRRMMMBBBBL
Bloody rain. Can't see a thing.
Rain or not, you've been very quiet. I expected a lot of questions.
Get me started and we'll still be here tomorrow.
For now, let's concentrate on not getting killed by shadow monsters. All right, Mister Mystery Tramp?
Dalone.
Rascal.
Don't ask.
Perish the thought.
Halt in the name of the King!

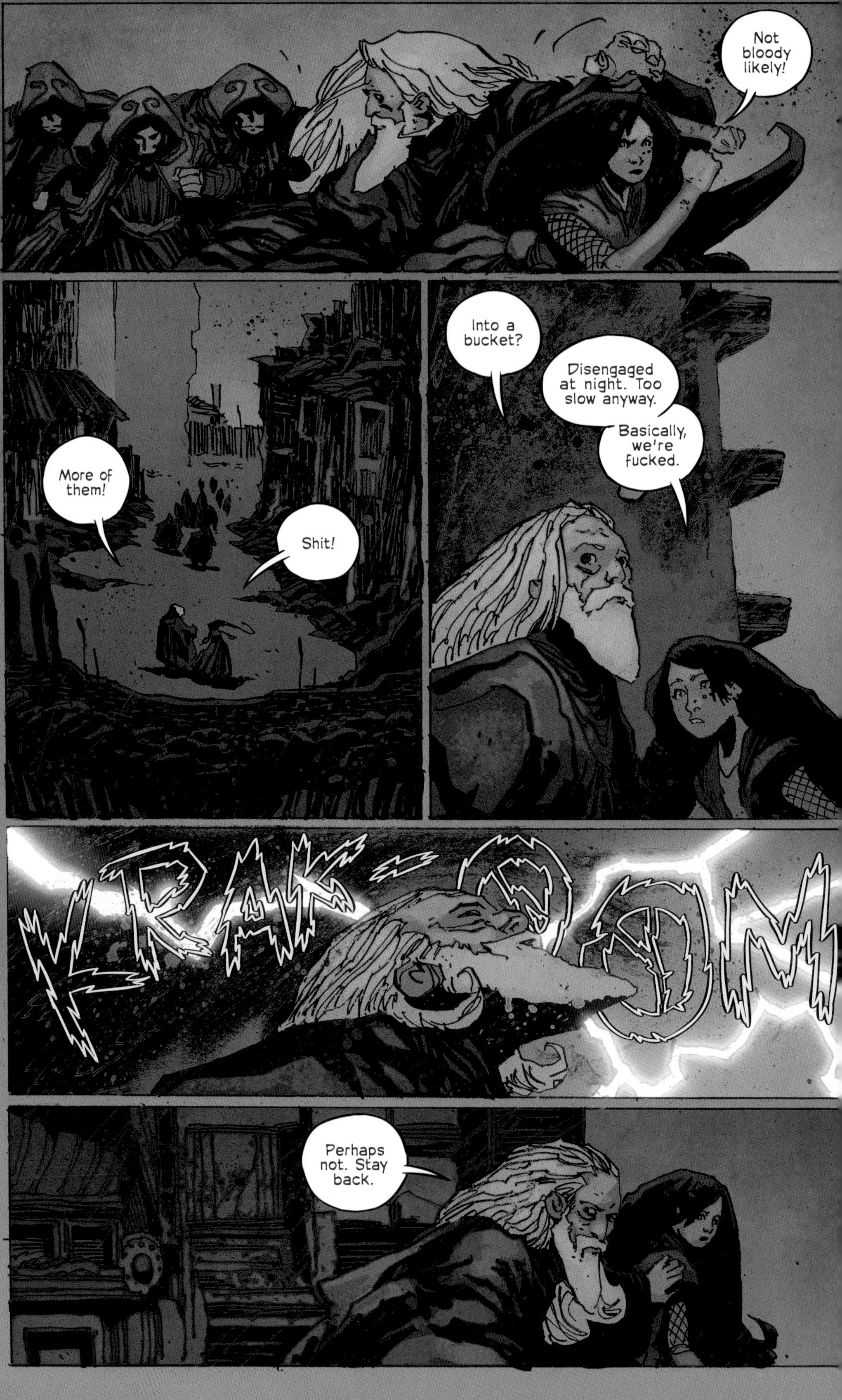

Not bloody likely!
More of them!
Shit!
Into a bucket?
Disengaged at night. Too slow anyway.
Basically, we're fucked.
KRAK-BOOM
Perhaps not. Stay back.

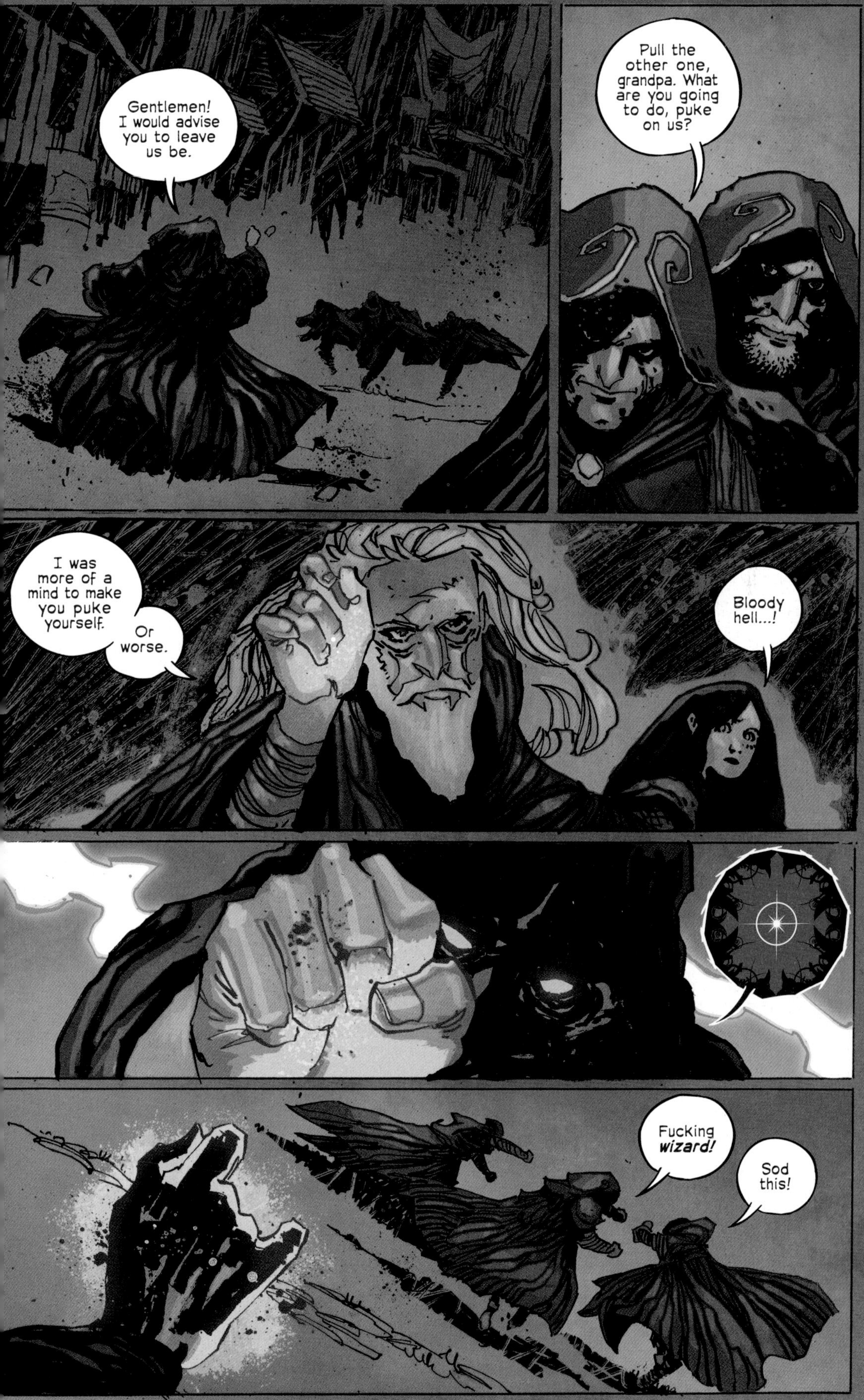
Gentlemen! I would advise you to leave us be.
Pull the other one, grandpa. What are you going to do, puke on us?
I was more of a mind to make you puke yourself.
Or worse.
Bloody hell...!
Fucking *wizard!*
Sod this!

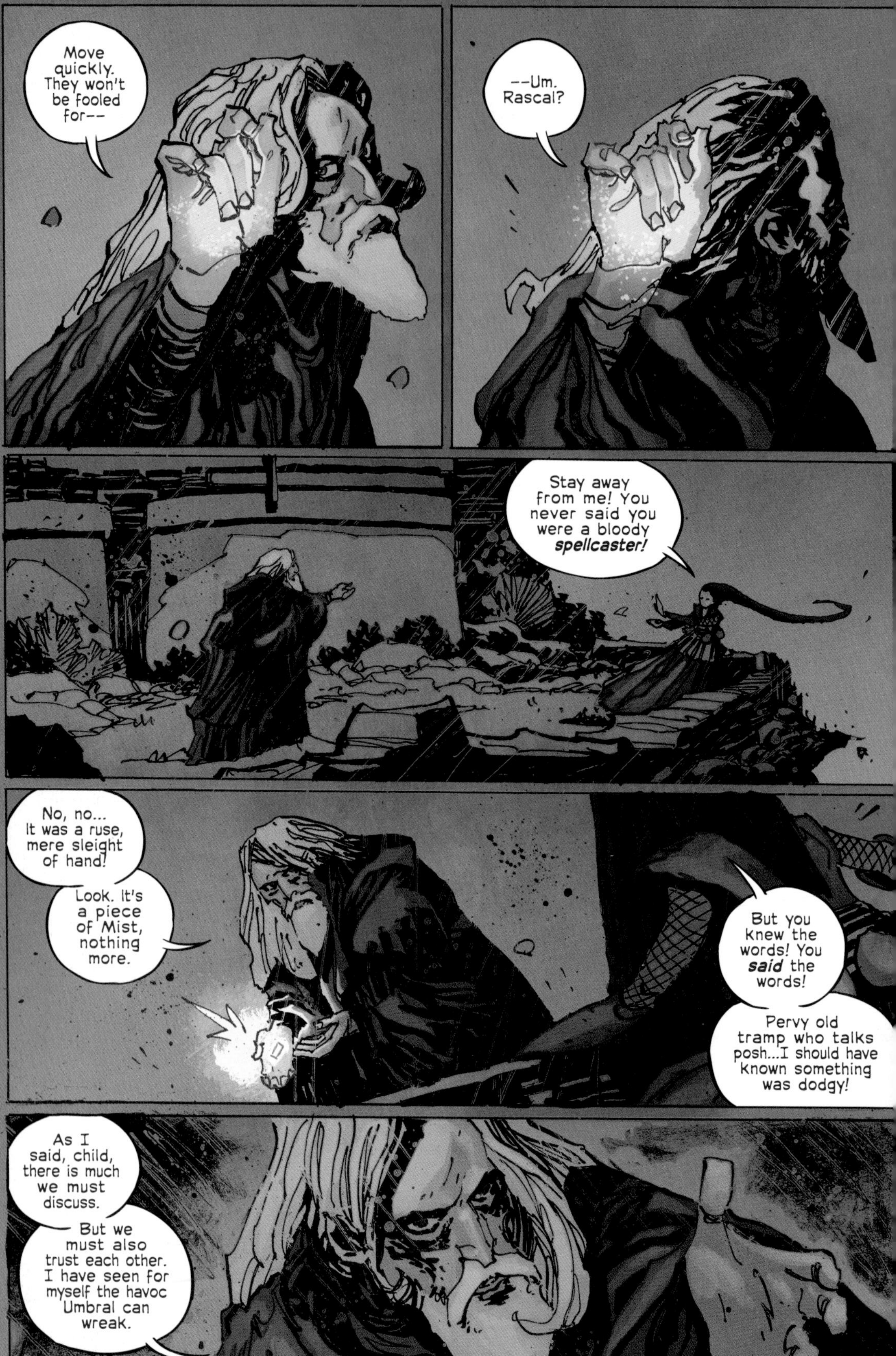
Move quickly. They won't be fooled for--
--Um. Rascal?
Stay away from me! You never said you were a bloody *spellcaster!*
No, no... It was a ruse, mere sleight of hand!
Look. It's a piece of Mist, nothing more.
But you knew the words! You *said* the words!
Pervy old tramp who talks posh...I should have known something was dodgy!
As I said, child, there is much we must discuss.
But we must also trust each other. I have seen for myself the havoc Umbral can wreak.

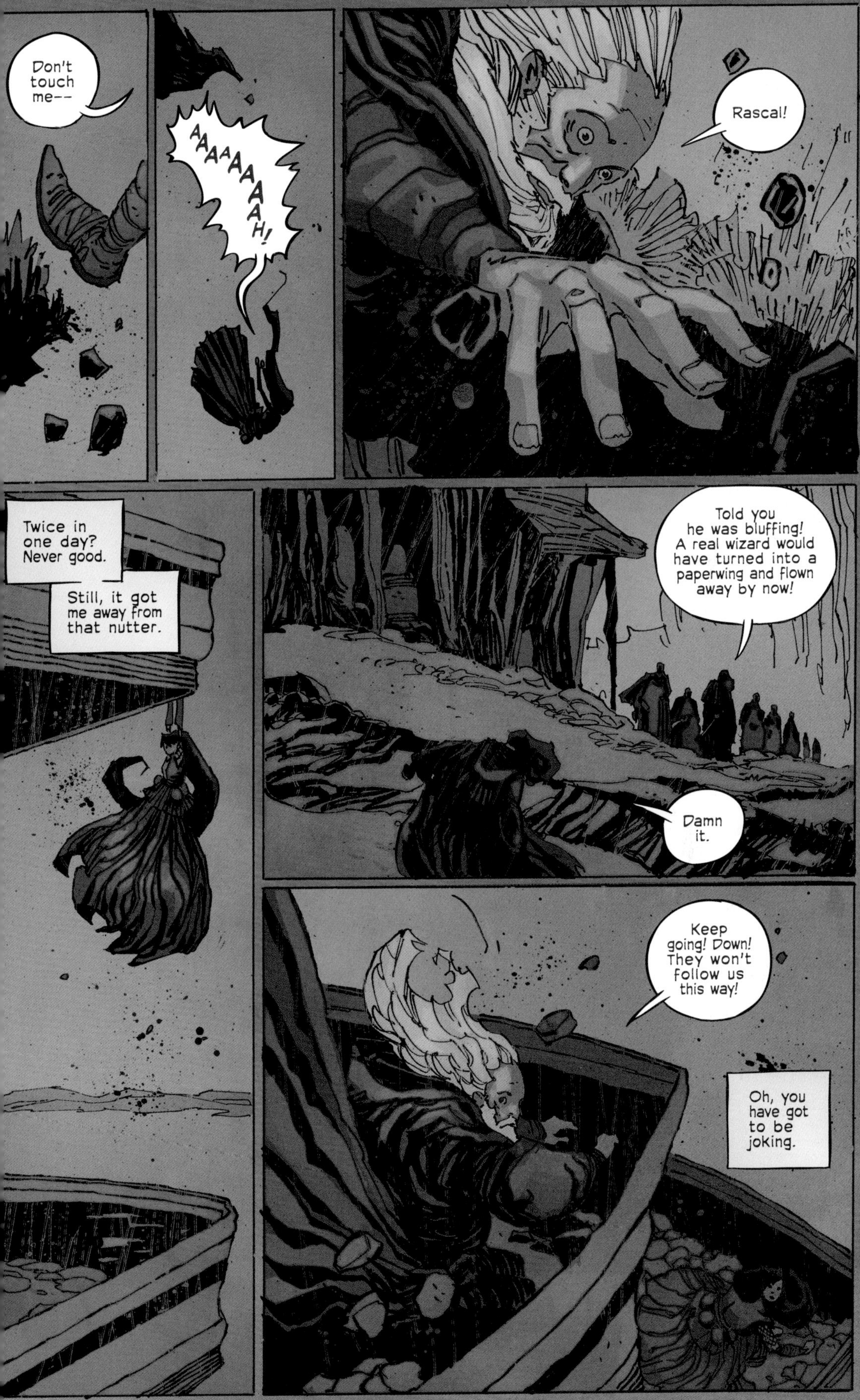
Don't touch me--
AAAAAAAAAH!
Rascal!
Twice in one day? Never good.
Still, it got me away from that nutter.
Told you he was bluffing! A real wizard would have turned into a paperwing and flown away by now!
Damn it.
Keep going! Down! They won't follow us this way!
Oh, you have got to be joking.

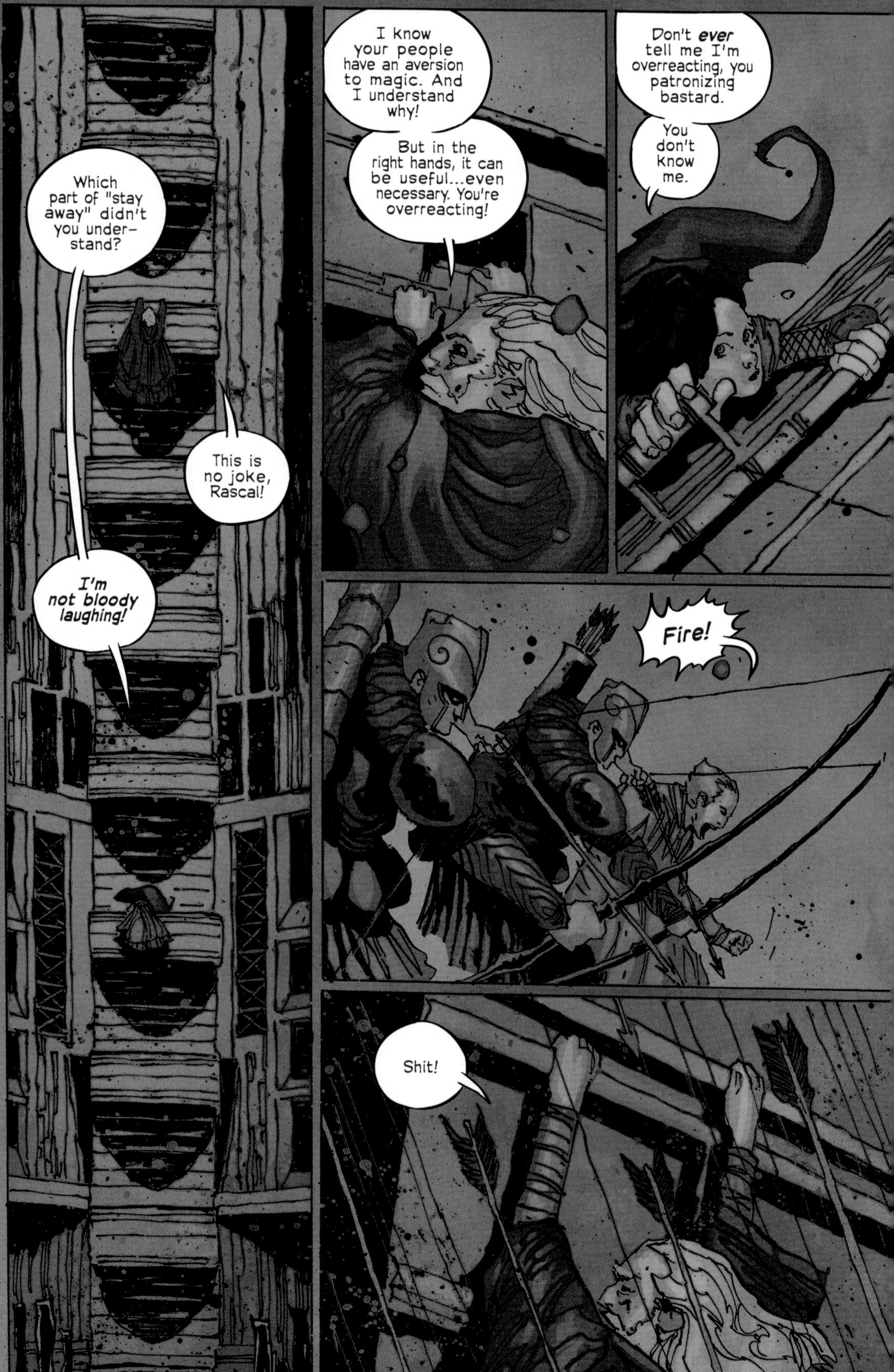

Which part of "stay away" didn't you under-stand?
This is no joke, Rascal!
I'm not bloody laughing!
I know your people have an aversion to magic. And I understand why!
But in the right hands, it can be useful...even necessary. You're overreacting!
Don't ever tell me I'm overreacting, you patronizing bastard.
You don't know me.
Fire!
Shit!

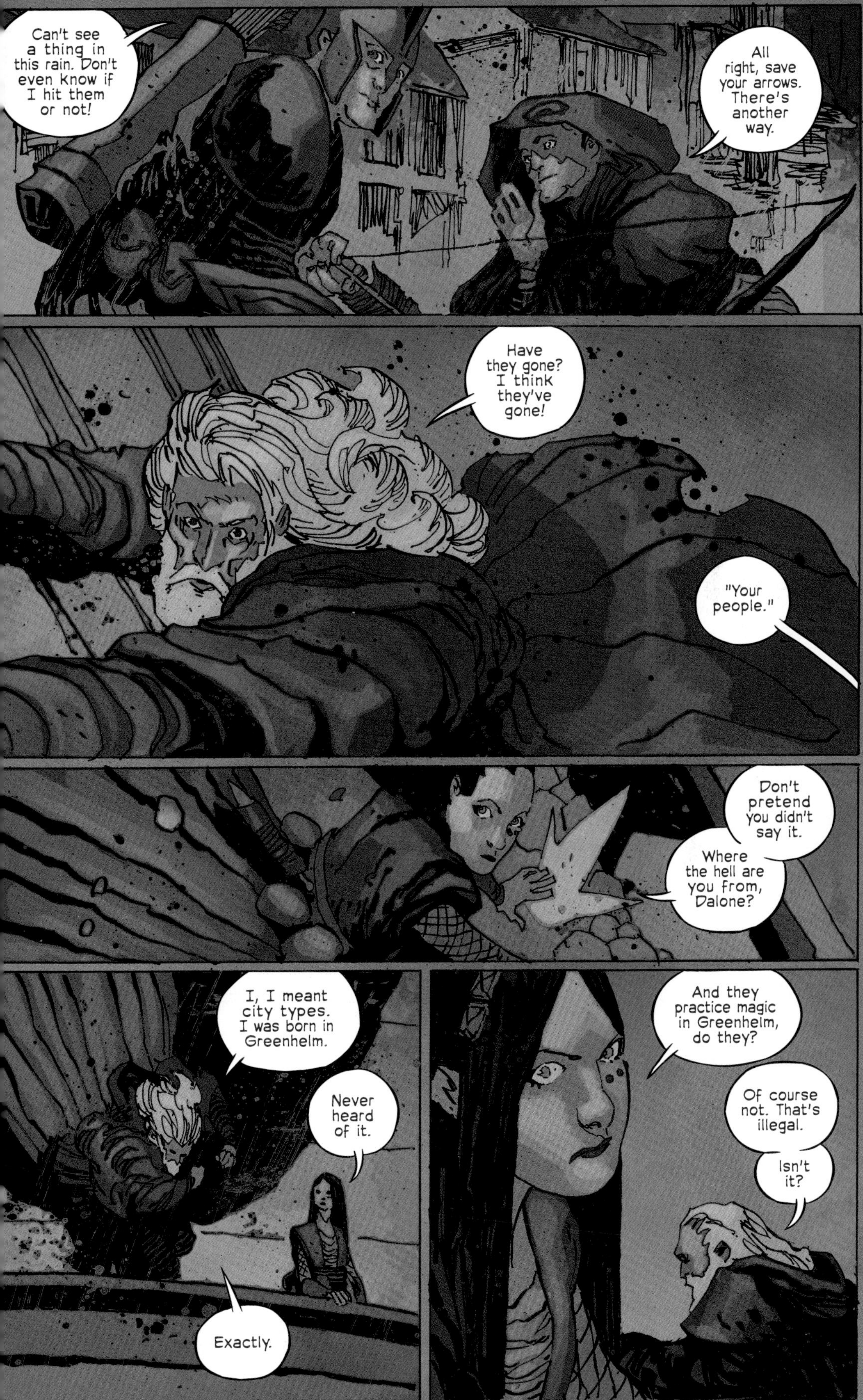
Can't see a thing in this rain. Don't even know if I hit them or not!
All right, save your arrows. There's another way.
Have they gone? I think they've gone!
"Your people."
Don't pretend you didn't say it.
Where the hell are you from, Dalone?
I, I meant city types. I was born in Greenhelm.
Never heard of it.
Exactly.
And they practice magic in Greenhelm, do they?
Of course not. That's illegal.
Isn't it?

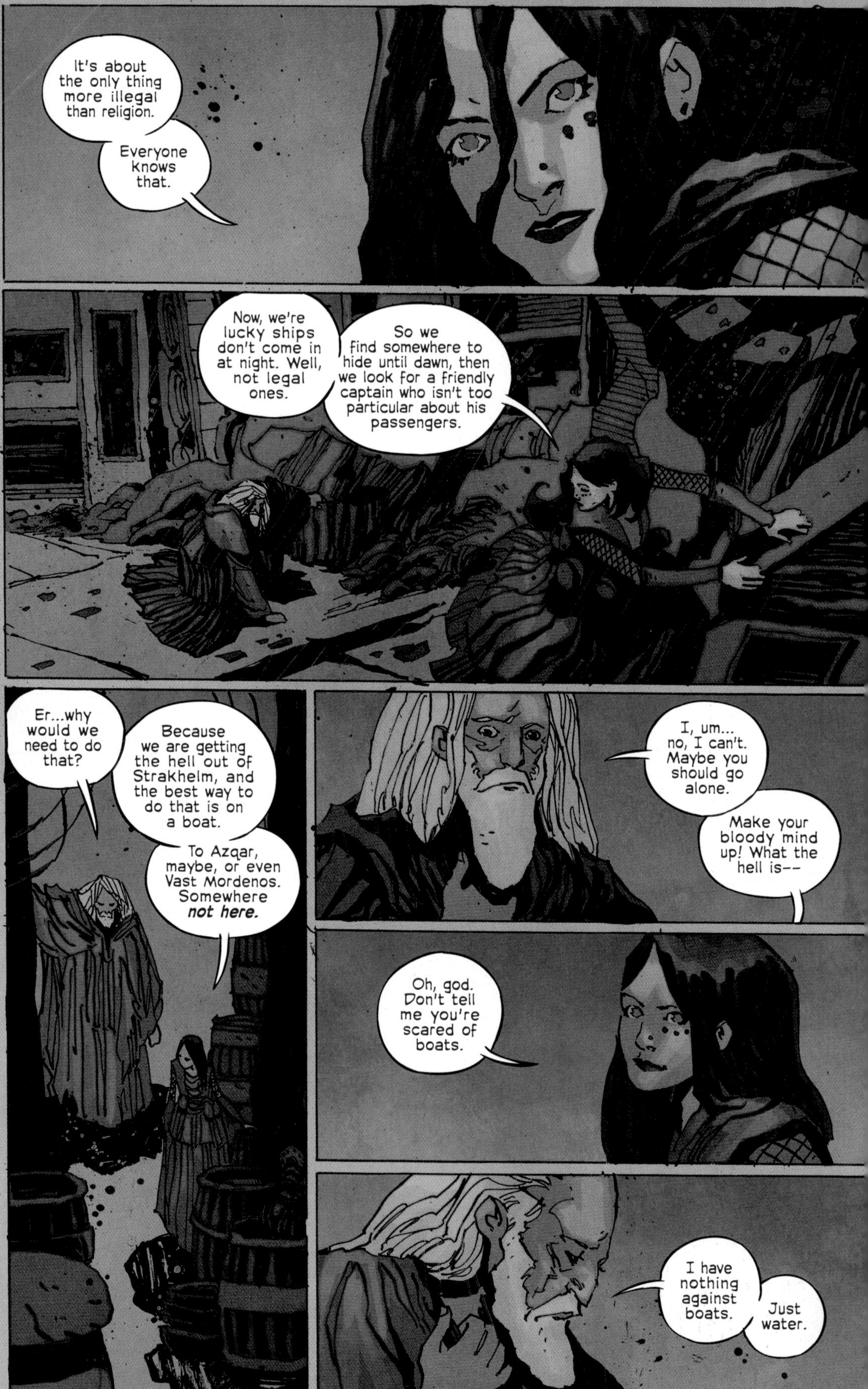
It's about the only thing more illegal than religion.
Everyone knows that.
Now, we're lucky ships don't come in at night. Well, not legal ones.
So we find somewhere to hide until dawn, then we look for a friendly captain who isn't too particular about his passengers.
Er...why would we need to do that?
Because we are getting the hell out of Strakhelm, and the best way to do that is on a boat.
To Azqar, maybe, or even Vast Mordenos. Somewhere *not here.*
I, um... no, I can't. Maybe you should go alone.
Make your bloody mind up! What the hell is--
Oh, god. Don't tell me you're scared of boats.
I have nothing against boats.
Just water.

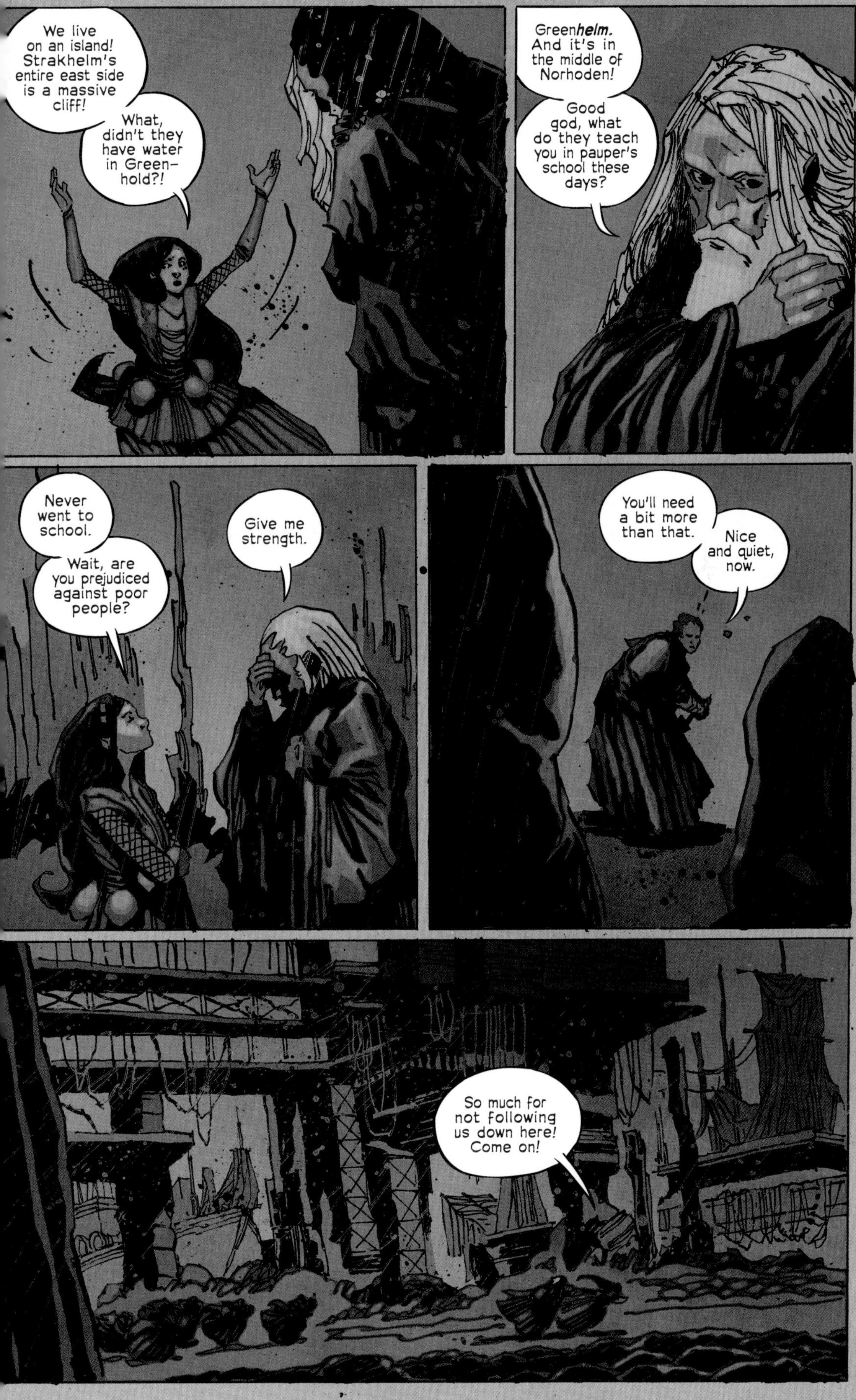
We live on an island! Strakhelm's entire east side is a massive cliff!
What, didn't they have water in Greenhold?!
Greenhelm. And it's in the middle of Norhoden!
Good god, what do they teach you in pauper's school these days?
Never went to school.
Wait, are you prejudiced against poor people?
Give me strength.
You'll need a bit more than that.
Nice and quiet, now.
So much for not following us down here! Come on!

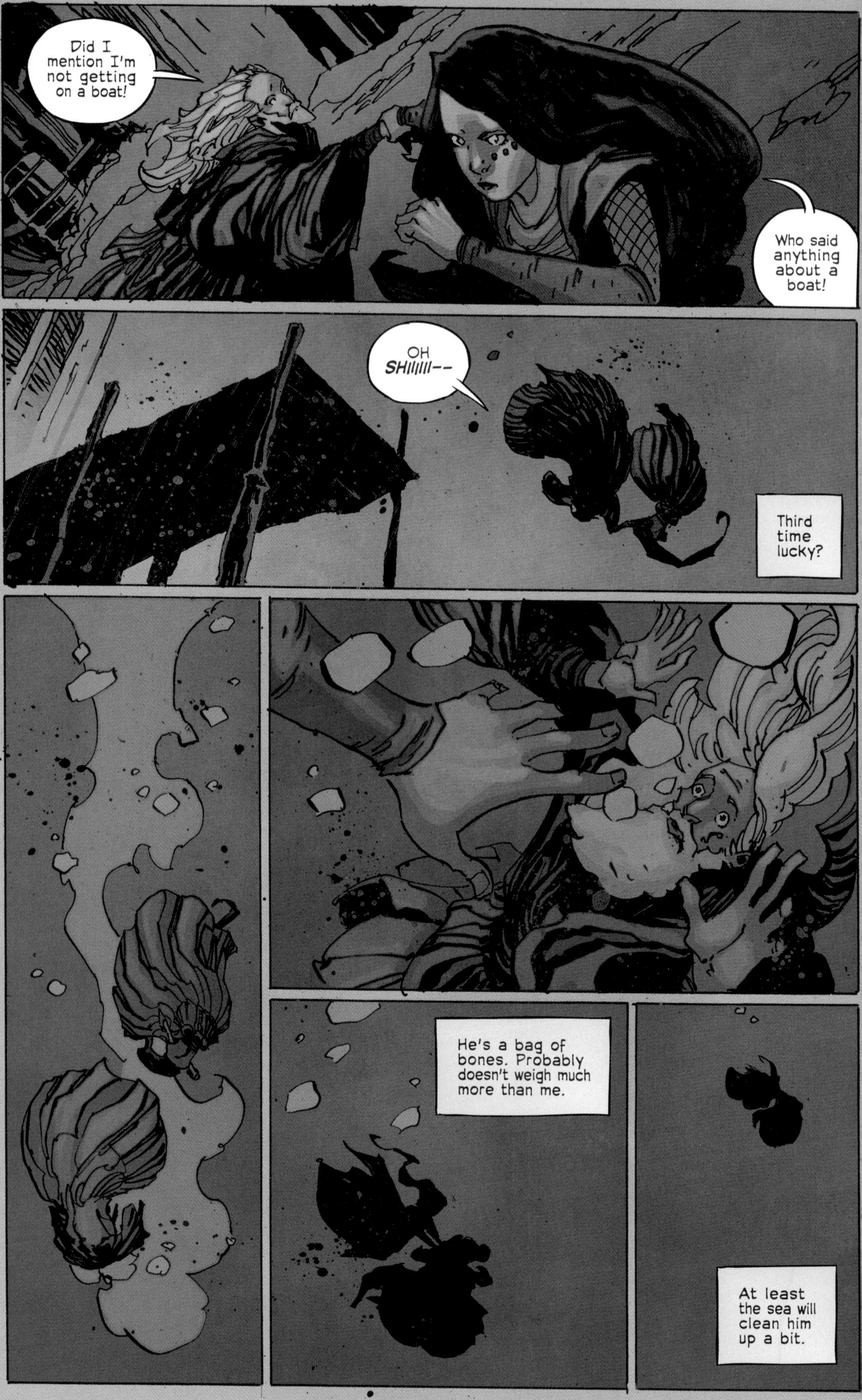
Did I mention I'm not getting on a boat!
Who said anything about a boat!
OH SHIIIIII--
Third time lucky?
He's a bag of bones. Probably doesn't weigh much more than me.
At least the sea will clean him up a bit.

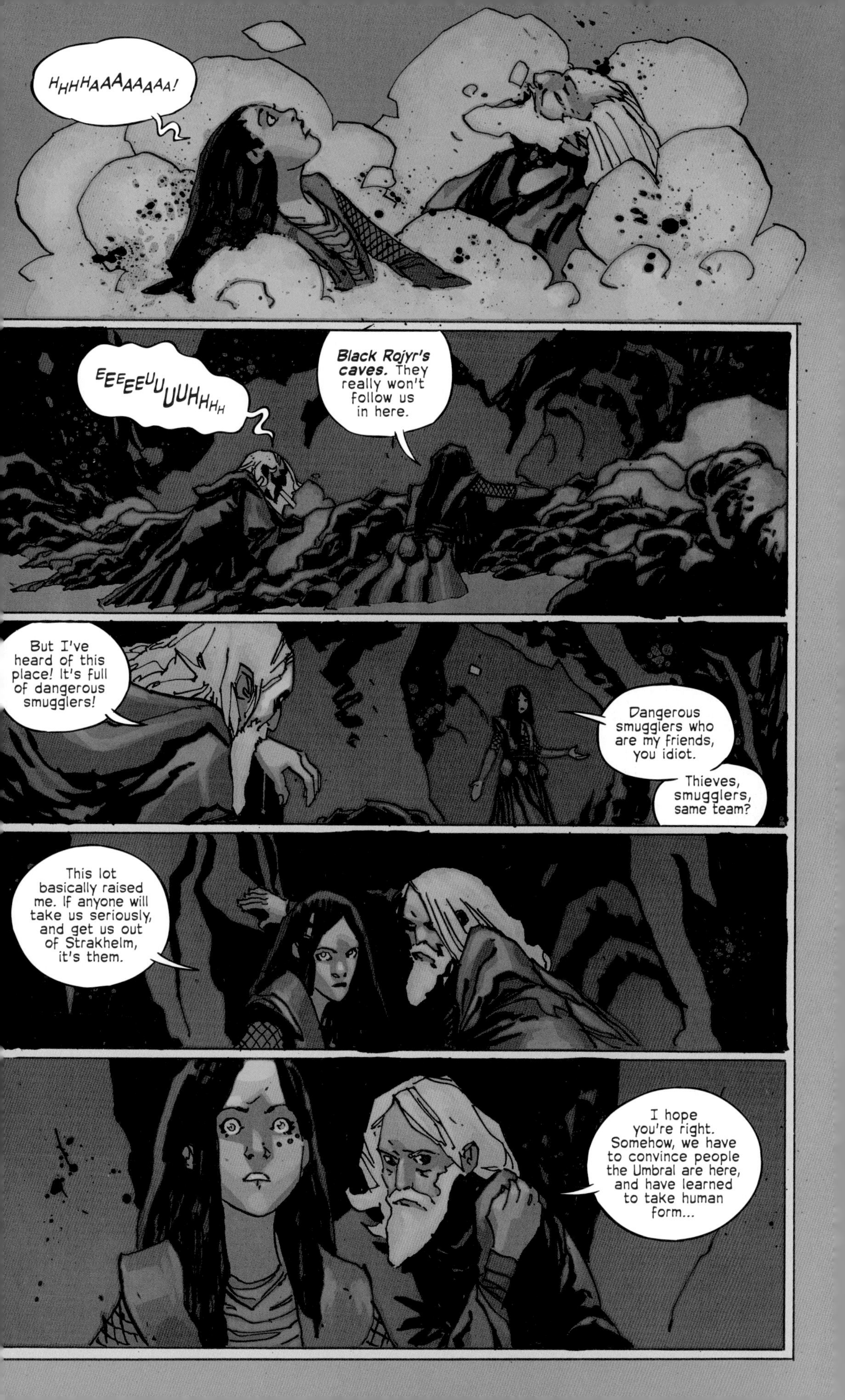
HHHHAAAAAAAA!
EEEEEUUUUHHHH
Black Rojyr's caves. They really won't follow us in here.
But I've heard of this place! It's full of dangerous smugglers!
Dangerous smugglers who are my friends, you idiot.
Thieves, smugglers, same team?
This lot basically raised me. If anyone will take us seriously, and get us out of Strakhelm, it's them.
I hope you're right. Somehow, we have to convince people the Umbral are here, and have learned to take human form...

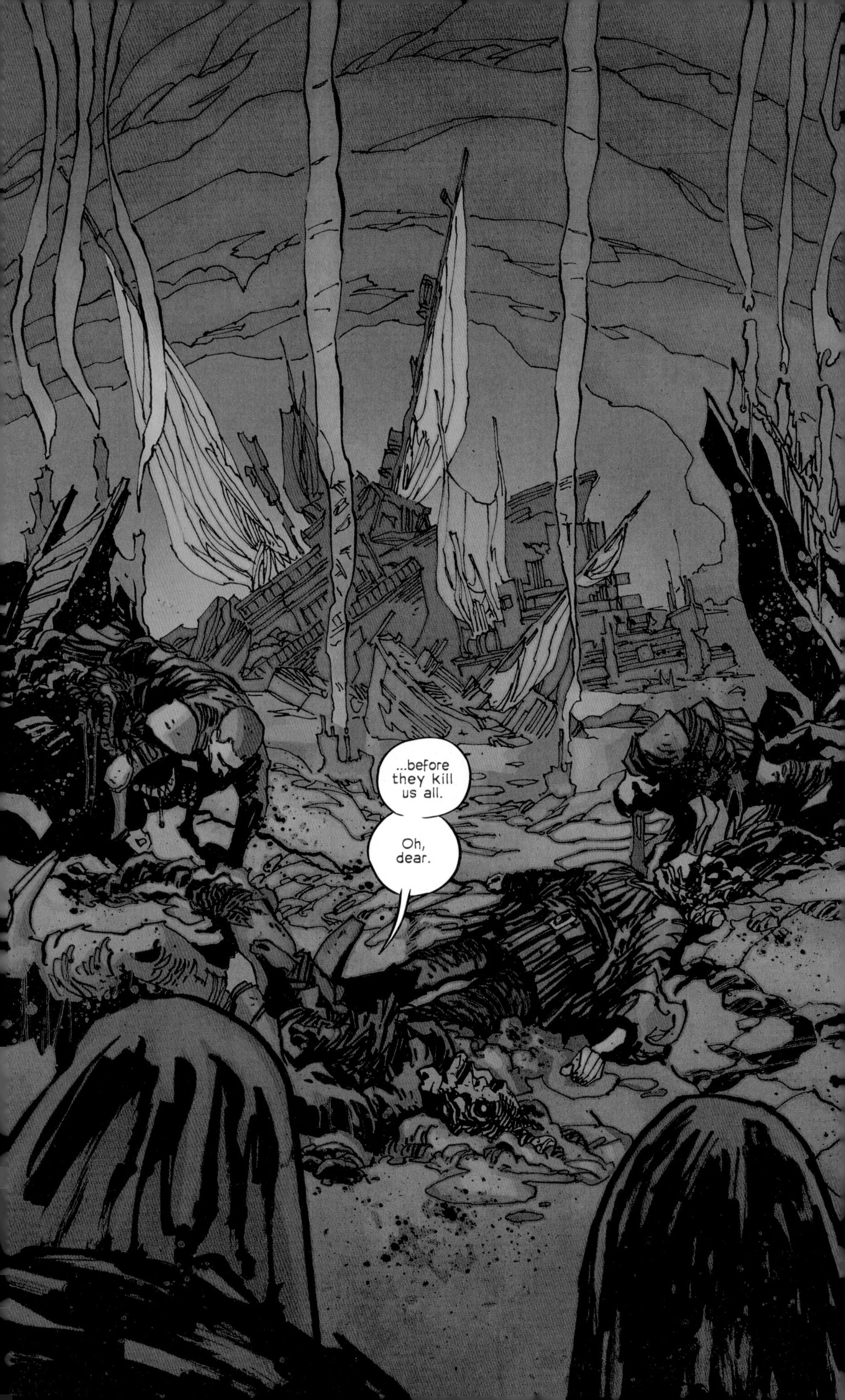
...before they kill us all.
Oh, dear.

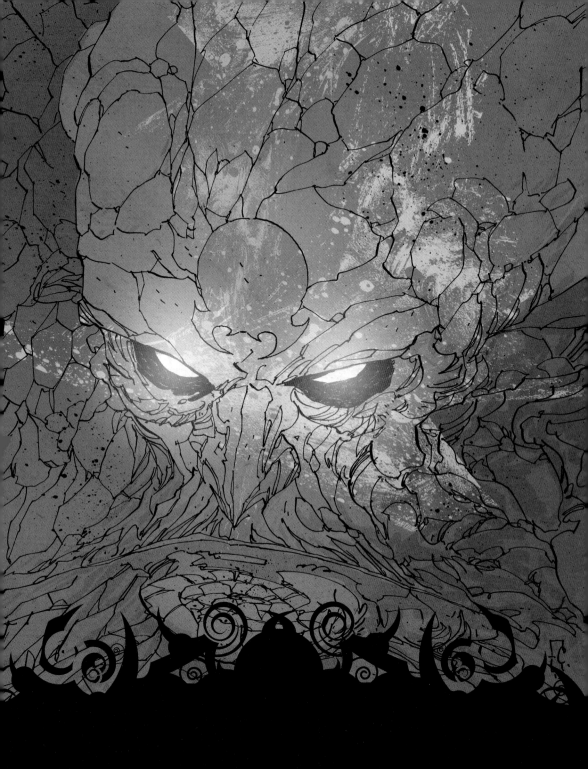

BLOOD FROM A STONE

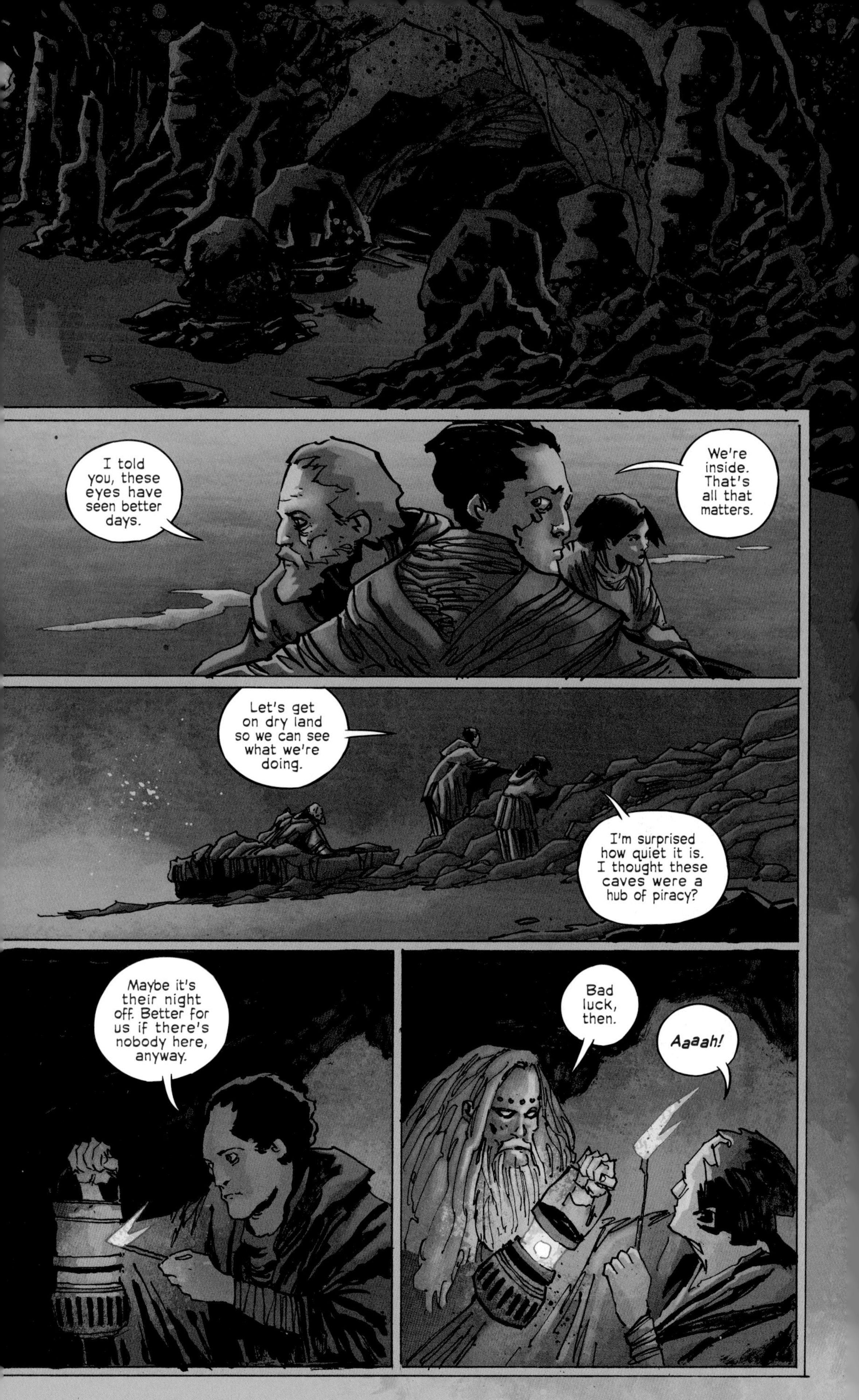
I told you, these eyes have seen better days.
We're inside. That's all that matters.
Let's get on dry land so we can see what we're doing.
I'm surprised how quiet it is. I thought these caves were a hub of piracy?
Maybe it's their night off. Better for us if there's nobody here, anyway.
Bad luck, then.
Aaaah!

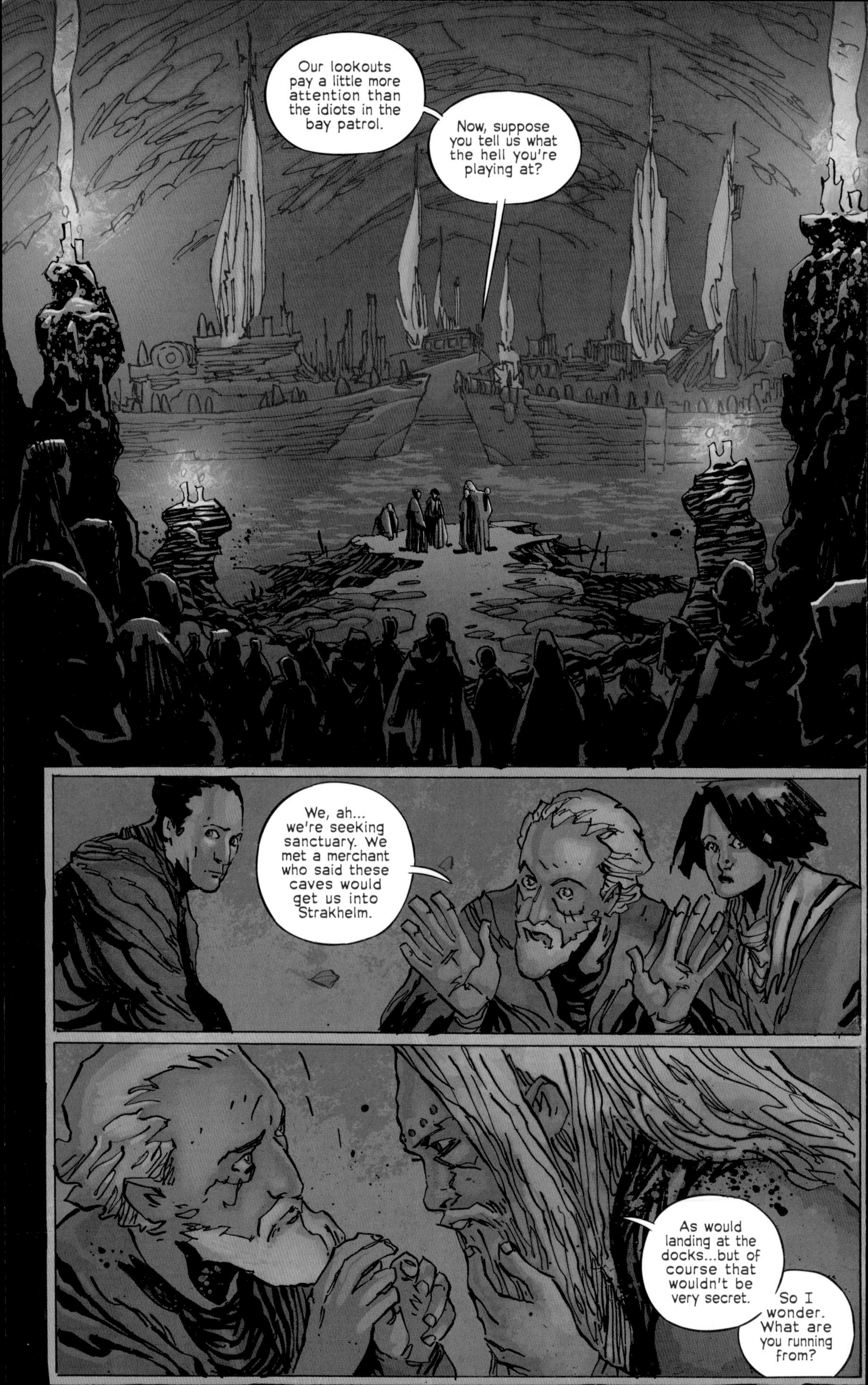
Our lookouts pay a little more attention than the idiots in the bay patrol.
Now, suppose you tell us what the hell you're playing at?
We, ah... we're seeking sanctuary. We met a merchant who said these caves would get us into Strakhelm.
As would landing at the docks...but of course that wouldn't be very secret.
So I wonder. What are you running from?

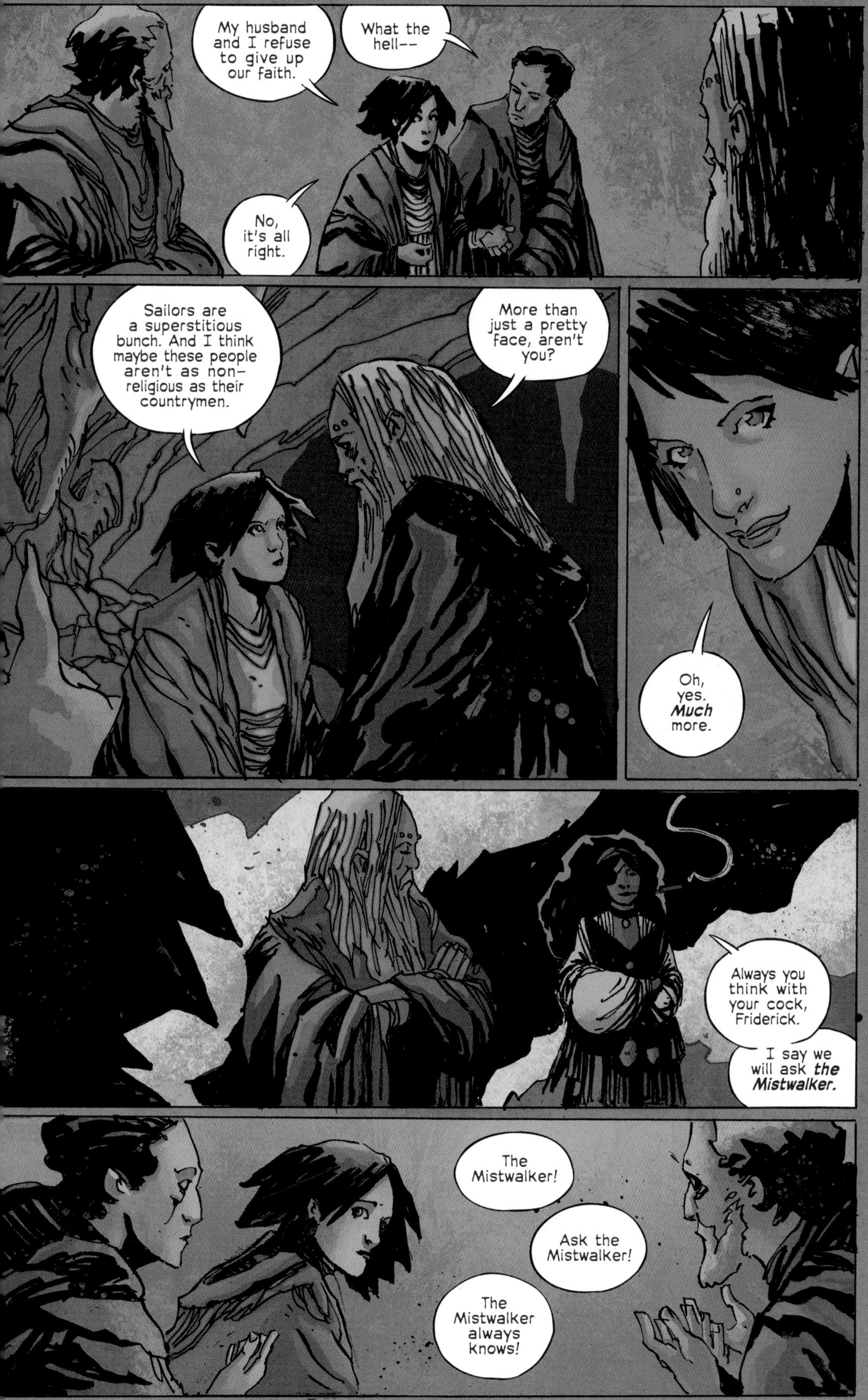

My husband and I refuse to give up our faith.
What the hell--
No, it's all right.
Sailors are a superstitious bunch. And I think maybe these people aren't as non-religious as their countrymen.
More than just a pretty face, aren't you?
Oh, yes. *Much* more.
Always you think with your cock, Friderick.
I say we will ask *the Mistwalker.*
The Mistwalker!
Ask the Mistwalker!
The Mistwalker always knows!

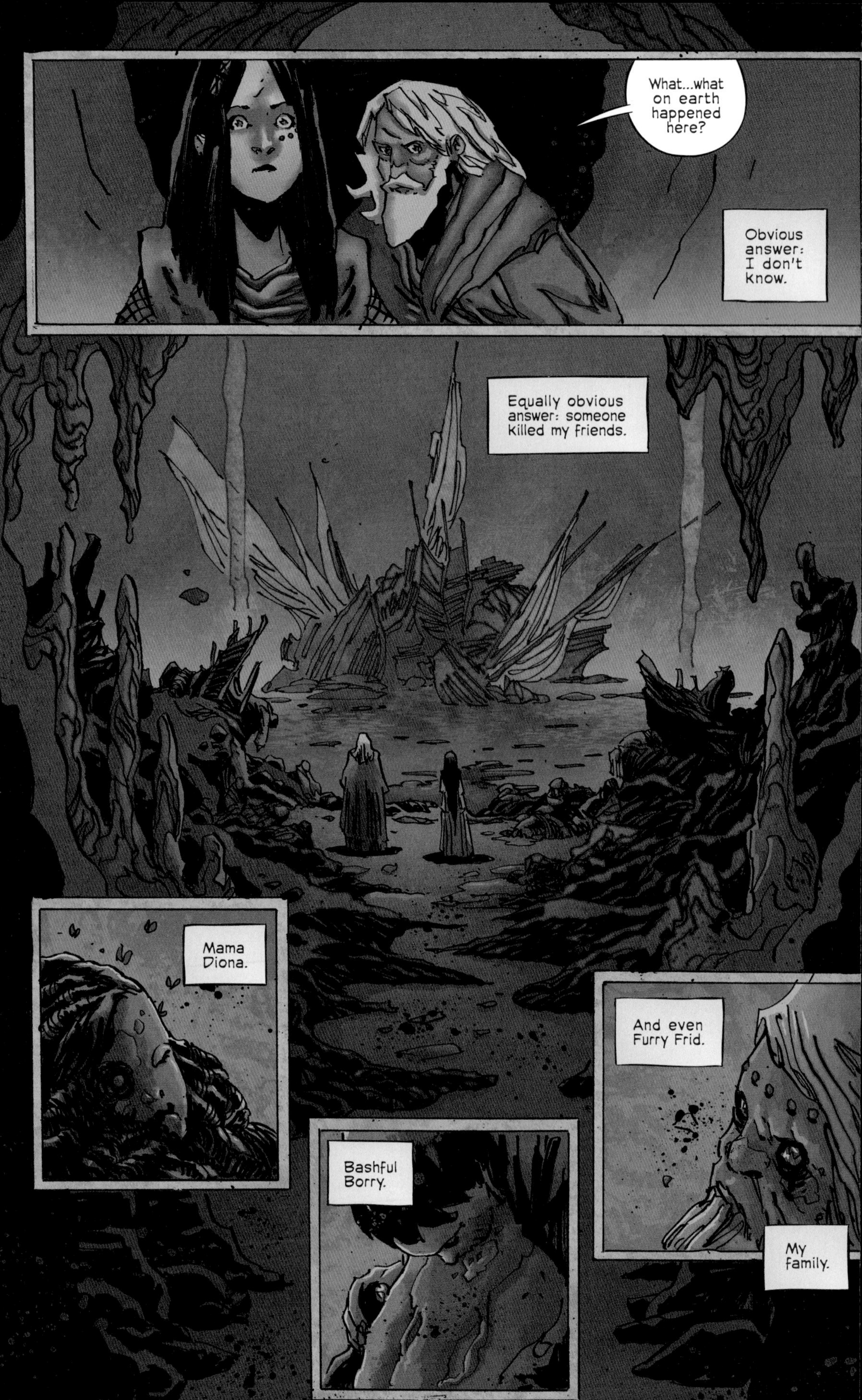
What...what on earth happened here?
Obvious answer: I don't know.
Equally obvious answer: someone killed my friends.
Mama Diona.
Bashful Borry.
And even Furry Frid.
My family.

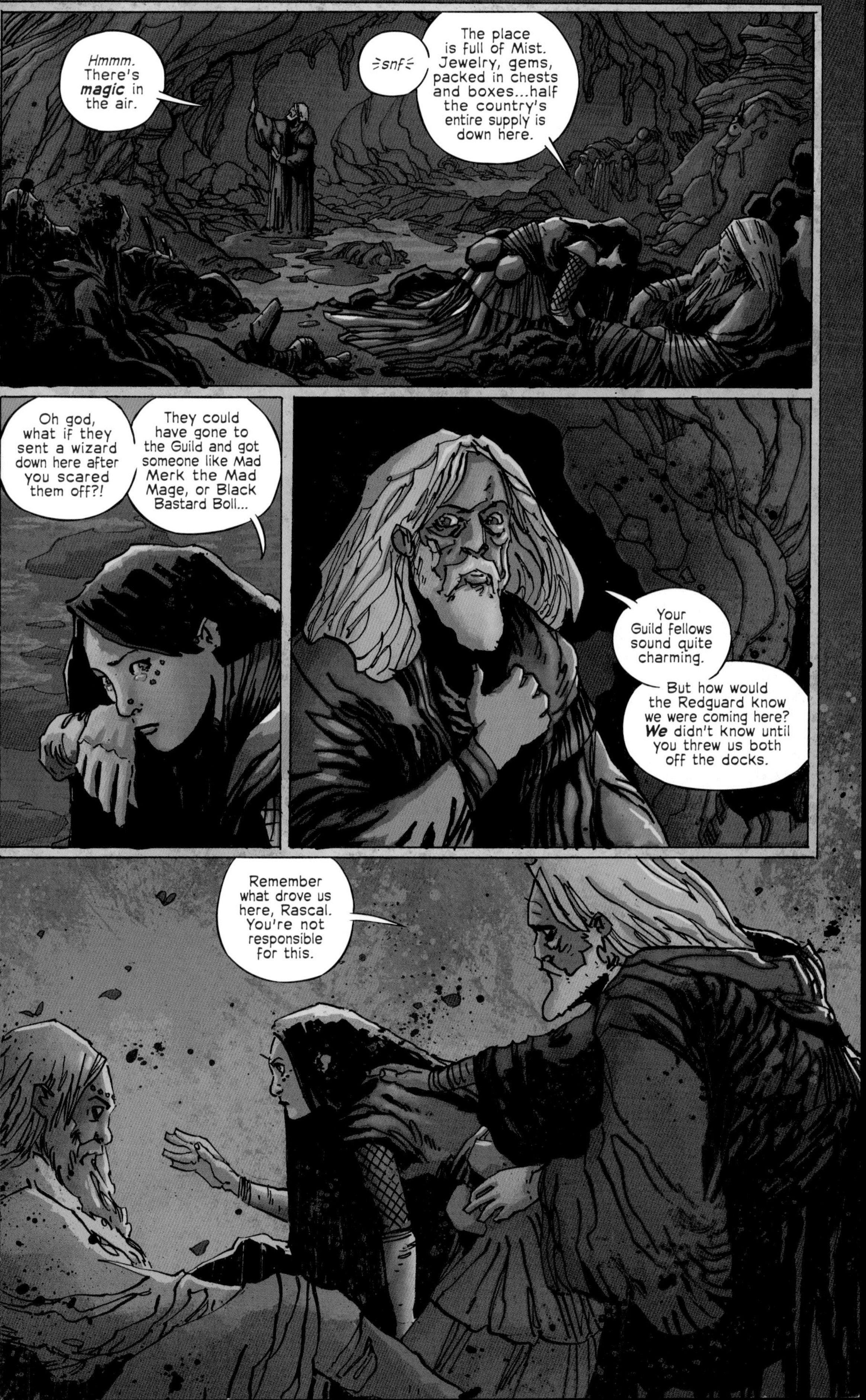
Hmmm. There's magic in the air.
snf
The place is full of Mist. Jewelry, gems, packed in chests and boxes...half the country's entire supply is down here.
Oh god, what if they sent a wizard down here after you scared them off?!
They could have gone to the Guild and got someone like Mad Merk the Mad Mage, or Black Bastard Boll...
Your Guild fellows sound quite charming.
But how would the Redguard know we were coming here? We didn't know until you threw us both off the docks.
Remember what drove us here, Rascal. You're not responsible for this.

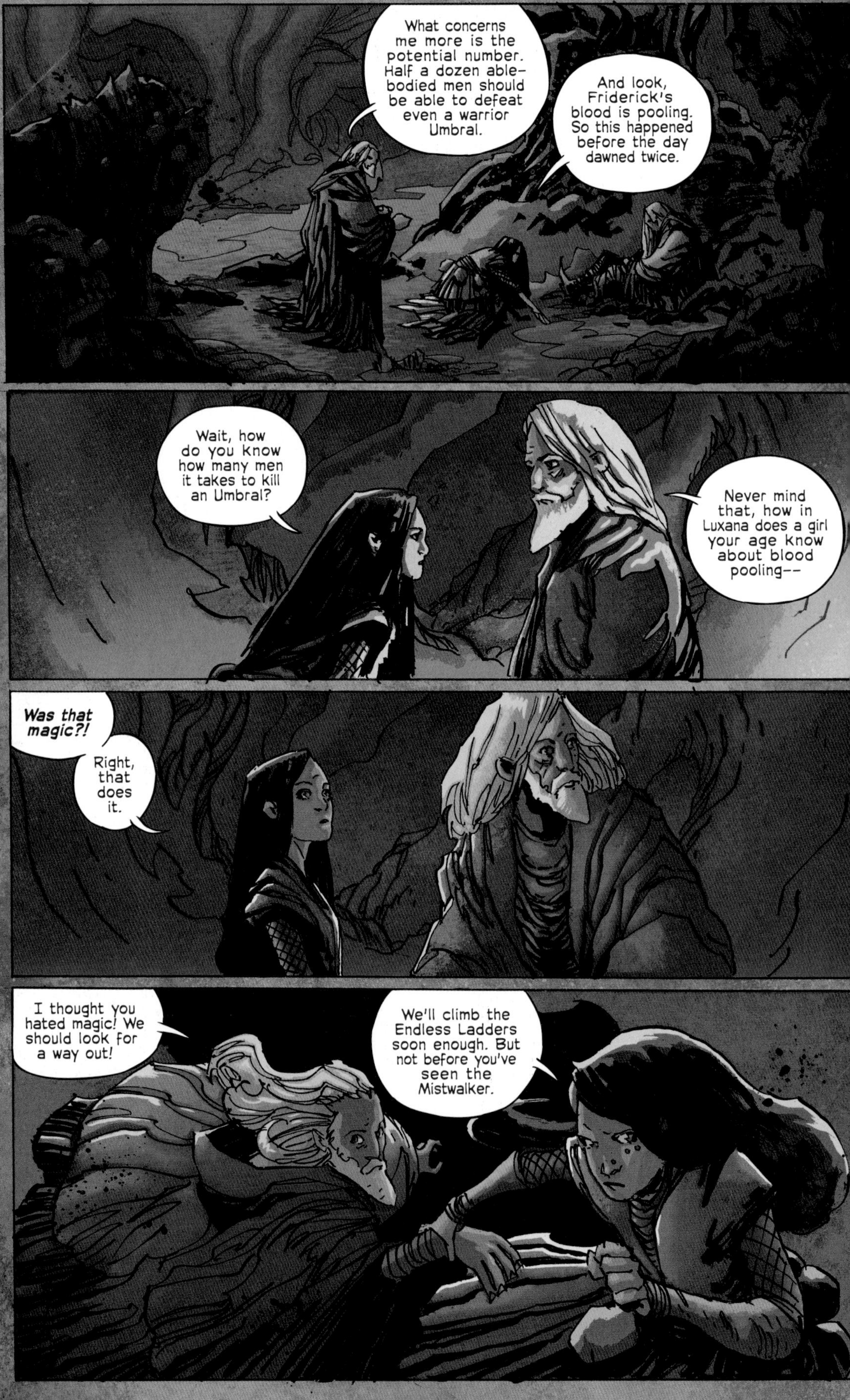
What concerns me more is the potential number. Half a dozen able-bodied men should be able to defeat even a warrior Umbral.
And look, Friderick's blood is pooling. So this happened before the day dawned twice.
Wait, how do you know how many men it takes to kill an Umbral?
Never mind that, how in Luxana does a girl your age know about blood pooling--
Was that magic?!
Right, that does it.
I thought you hated magic! We should look for a way out!
We'll climb the Endless Ladders soon enough. But not before you've seen the Mistwalker.

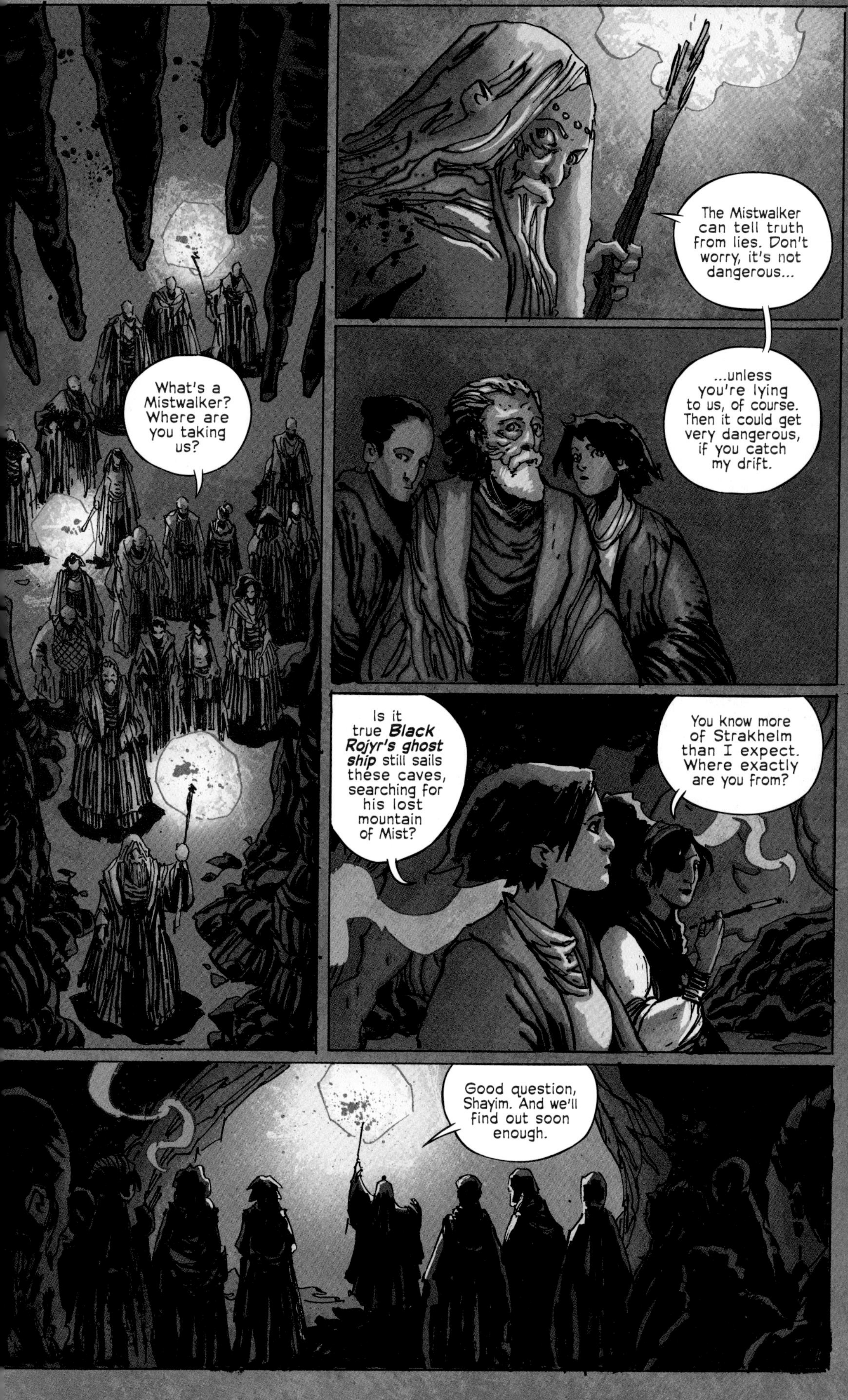
What's a Mistwalker? Where are you taking us?
The Mistwalker can tell truth from lies. Don't worry, it's not dangerous...
...unless you're lying to us, of course. Then it could get very dangerous, if you catch my drift.
Is it true **Black Rojyr's ghost ship** still sails these caves, searching for his lost mountain of Mist?
You know more of Strakhelm than I expect. Where exactly are you from?
Good question, Shayim. And we'll find out soon enough.

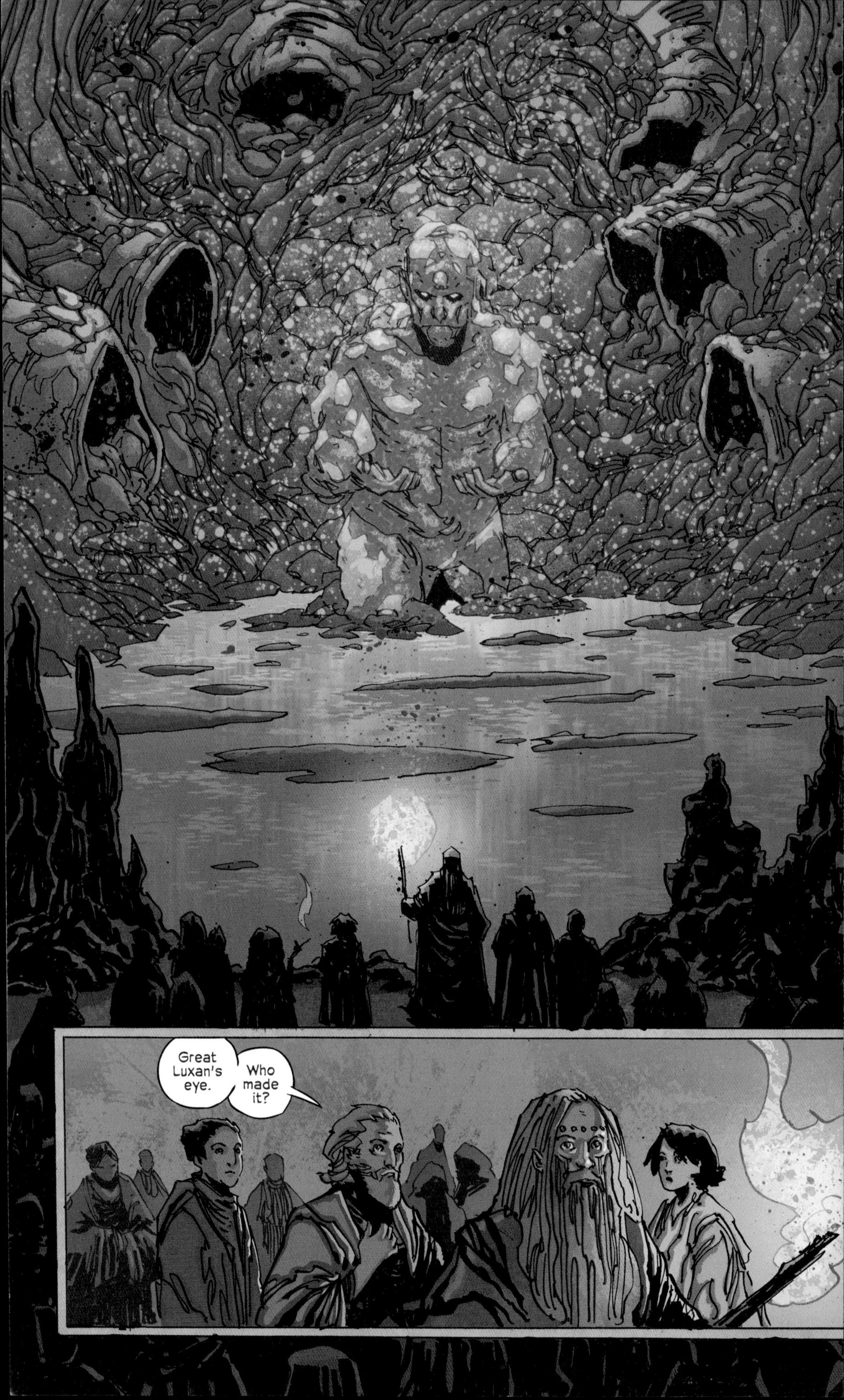
Great Luxan's eye.
Who made it?

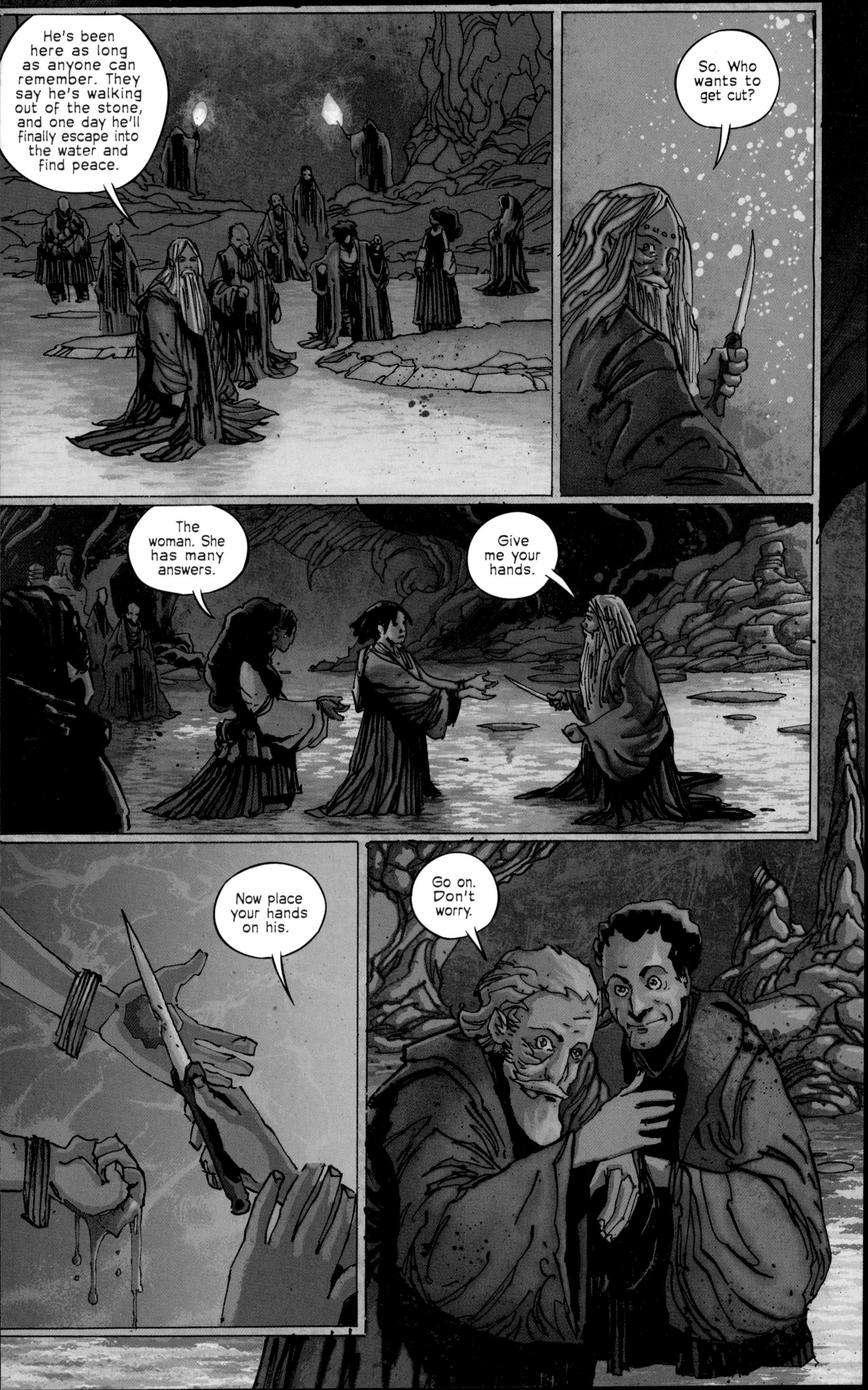
He's been here as long as anyone can remember. They say he's walking out of the stone, and one day he'll finally escape into the water and find peace.
So. Who wants to get cut?
The woman. She has many answers.
Give me your hands.
Now place your hands on his.
Go on. Don't worry.

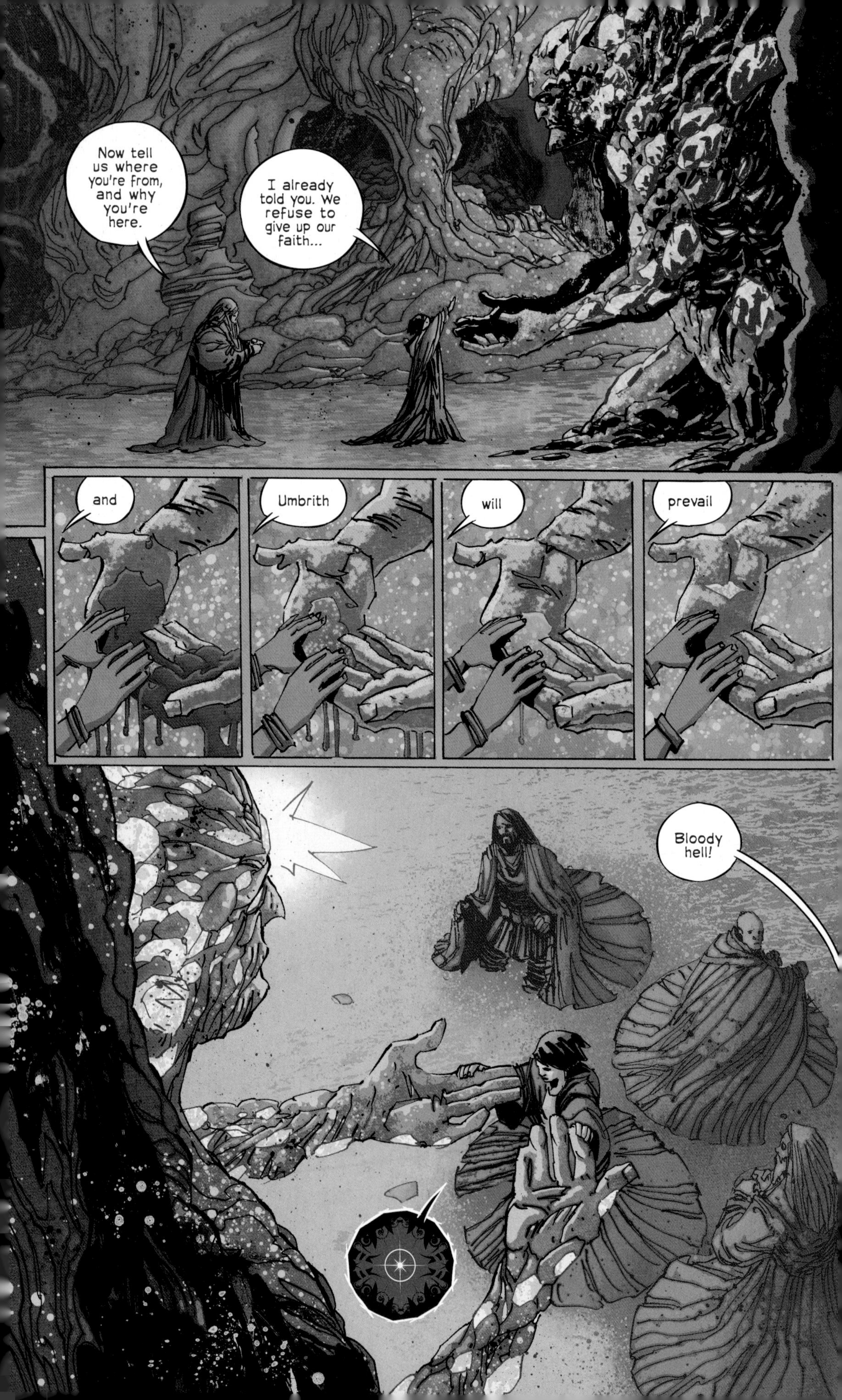

Now tell us where you're from, and why you're here.
I already told you. We refuse to give up our faith...
and
Umbrith
will
prevail
Bloody hell!

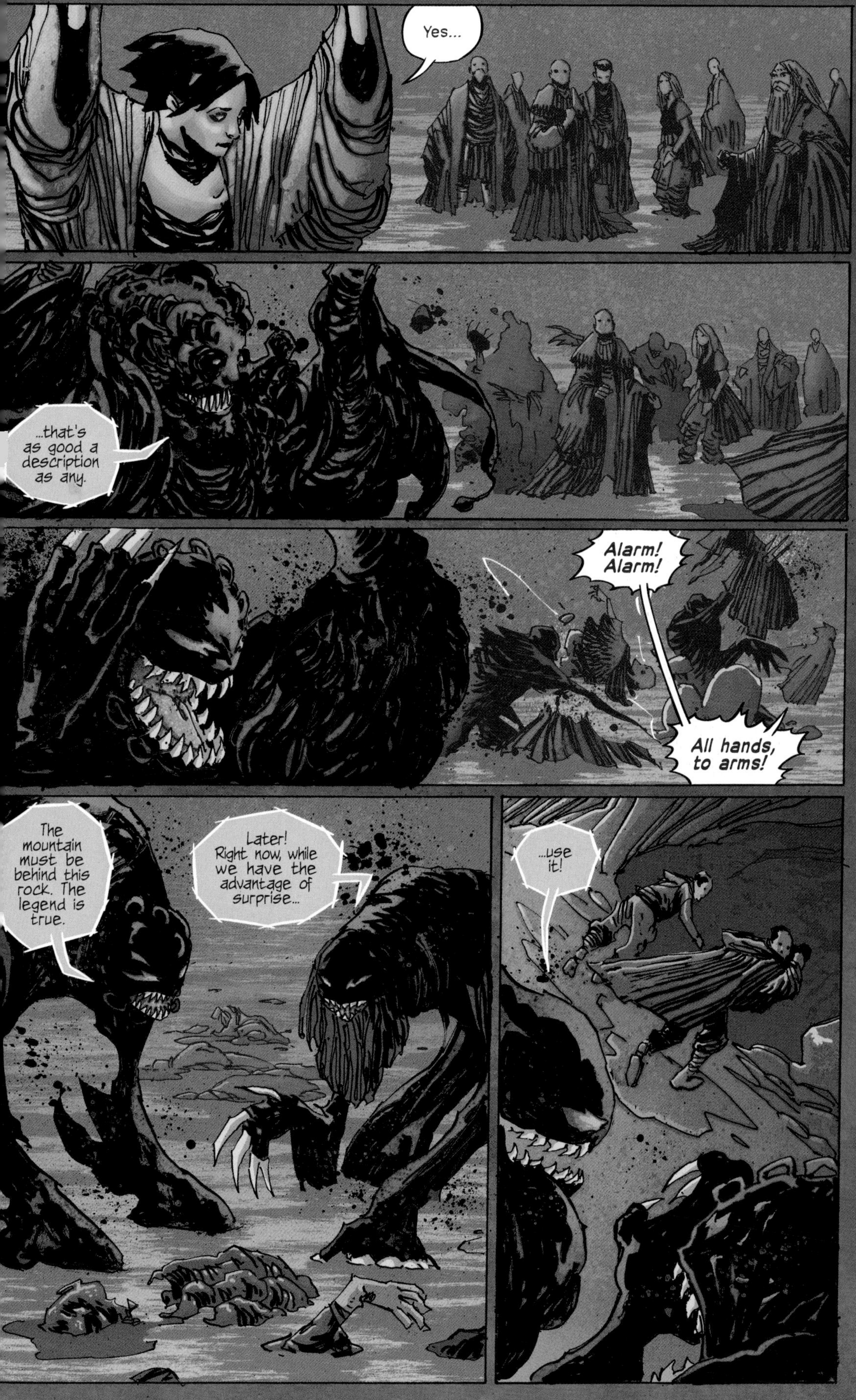
Yes...
...that's as good a description as any.
Alarm! Alarm!
All hands, to arms!
The mountain must be behind this rock. The legend is true.
Later! Right now, while we have the advantage of surprise...
...use it!

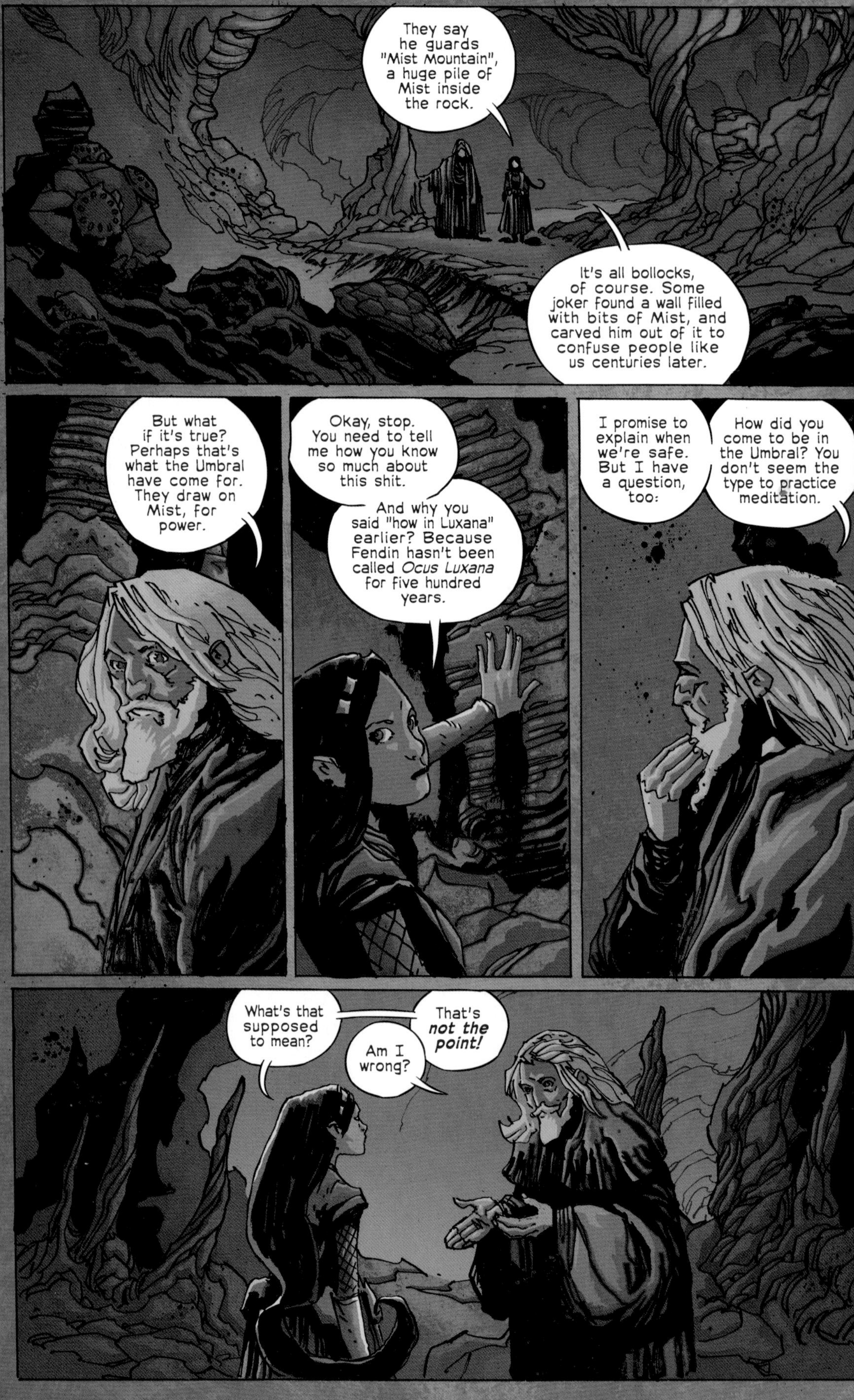
They say he guards "Mist Mountain", a huge pile of Mist inside the rock.
It's all bollocks, of course. Some joker found a wall filled with bits of Mist, and carved him out of it to confuse people like us centuries later.
But what if it's true? Perhaps that's what the Umbral have come for. They draw on Mist, for power.
Okay, stop. You need to tell me how you know so much about this shit.
And why you said "how in Luxana" earlier? Because Fendin hasn't been called *Ocus Luxana* for five hundred years.
I promise to explain when we're safe. But I have a question, too:
How did you come to be in the Umbral? You don't seem the type to practice meditation.
What's that supposed to mean?
That's **not the point!**
Am I wrong?

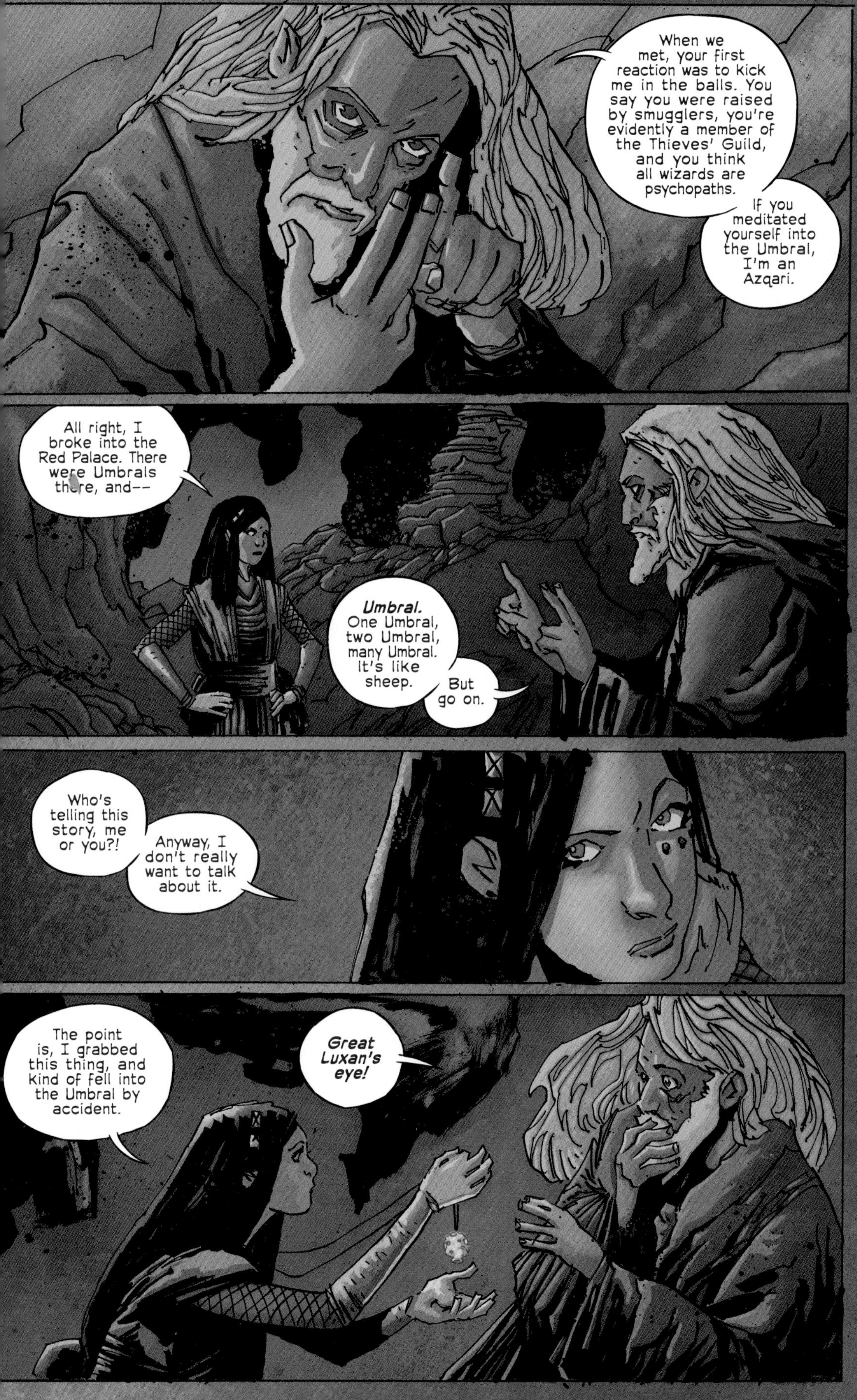
When we met, your first reaction was to kick me in the balls. You say you were raised by smugglers, you're evidently a member of the Thieves' Guild, and you think all wizards are psychopaths.
If you meditated yourself into the Umbral, I'm an Azqari.
All right, I broke into the Red Palace. There were Umbrals there, and--
Umbral. One Umbral, two Umbral, many Umbral. It's like sheep.
But go on.
Who's telling this story, me or you?!
Anyway, I don't really want to talk about it.
The point is, I grabbed this thing, and kind of fell into the Umbral by accident.
Great Luxan's eye!

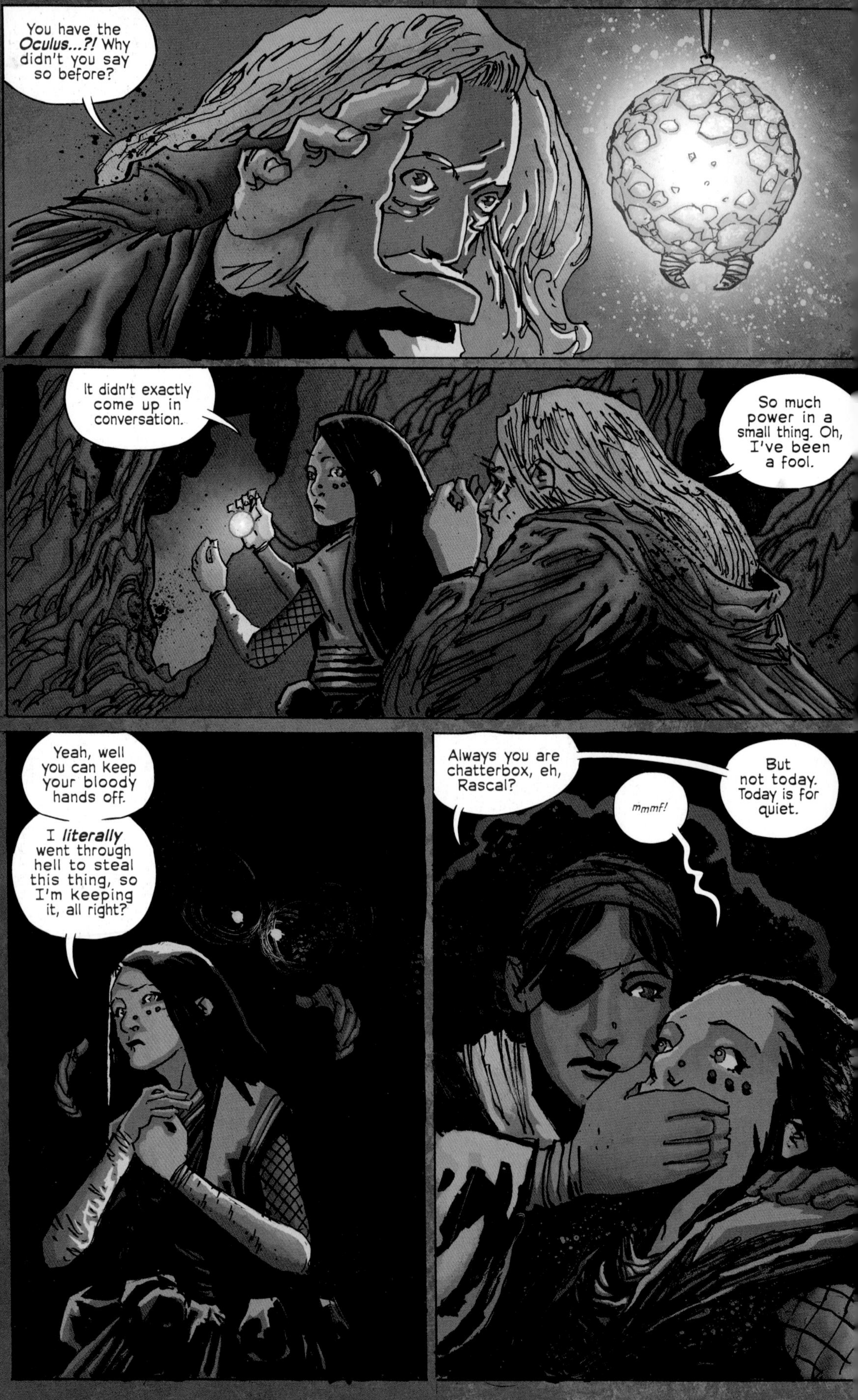

You have the *Oculus...?!* Why didn't you say so before?
It didn't exactly come up in conversation.
So much power in a small thing. Oh, I've been a fool.
Yeah, well you can keep your bloody hands off.
I *literally* went through hell to steal this thing, so I'm keeping it, all right?
Always you are chatterbox, eh, Rascal?
But not today. Today is for quiet.
mmmf!

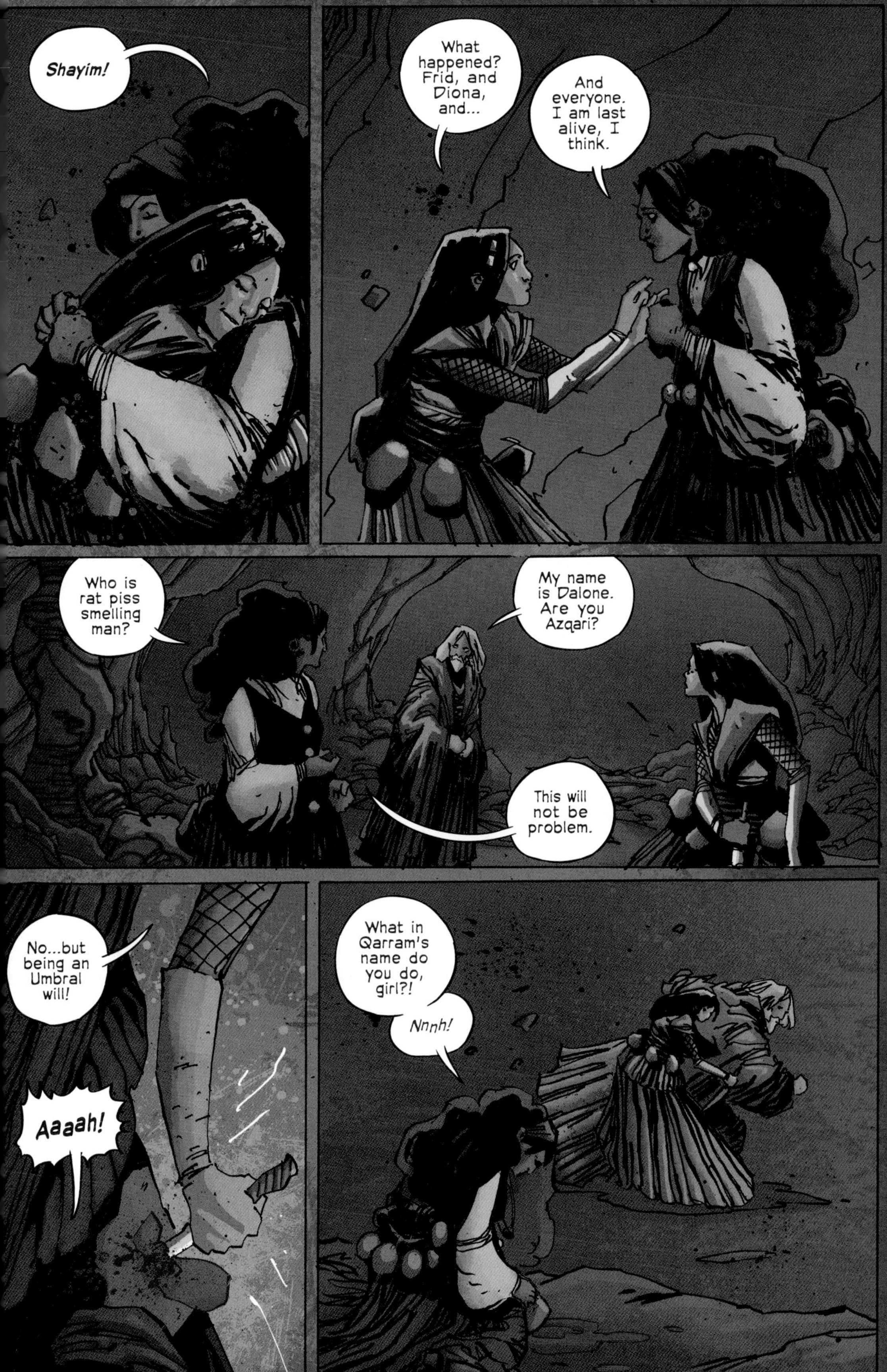
Shayim!
What happened? Frid, and Diona, and...
And everyone. I am last alive, I think.
Who is rat piss smelling man?
My name is Dalone. Are you Azqari?
This will not be problem.
No...but being an Umbral will!
Aaaah!
What in Qarram's name do you do, girl?!
Nnnh!

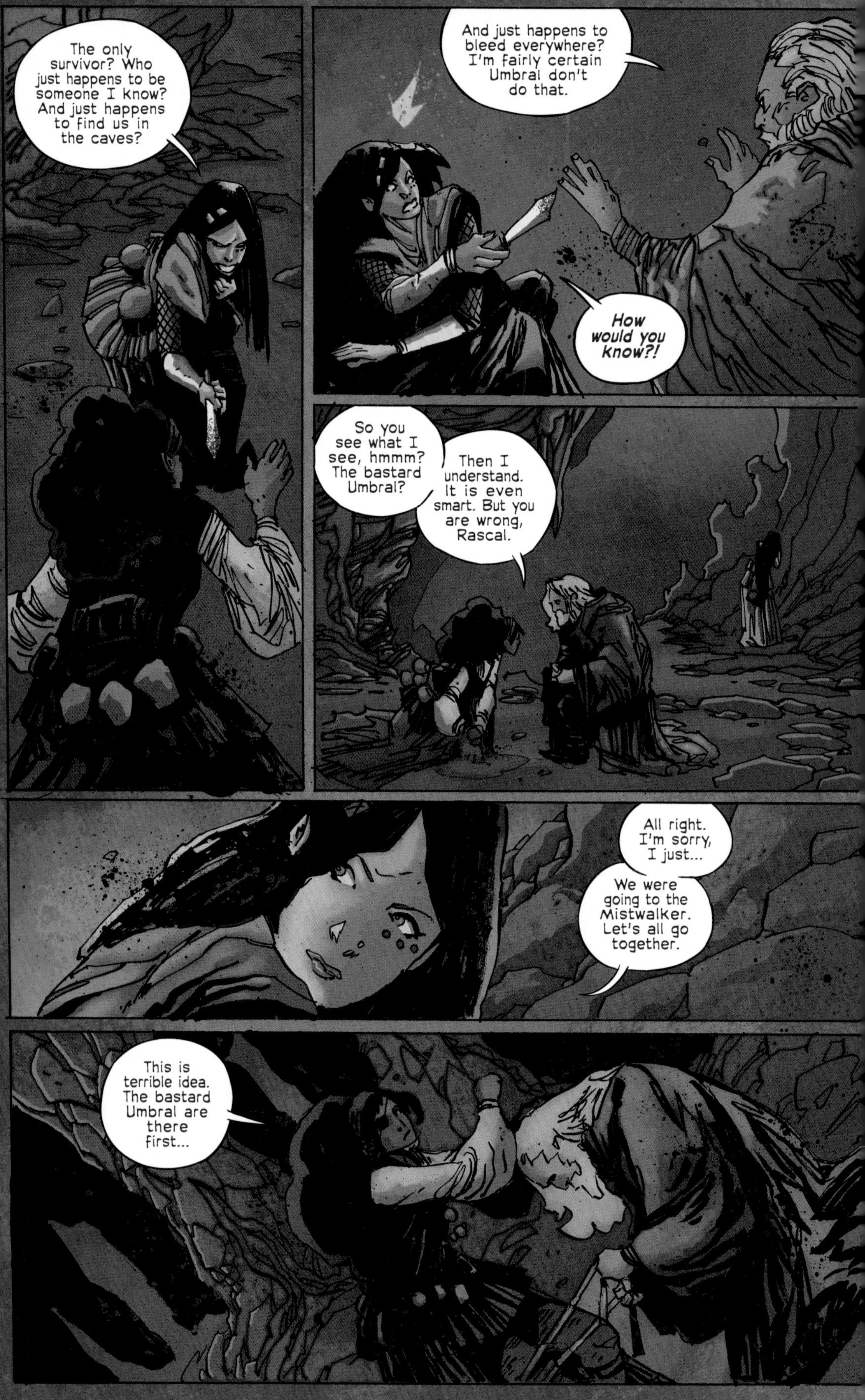
The only survivor? Who just happens to be someone I know? And just happens to find us in the caves?
And just happens to bleed everywhere? I'm fairly certain Umbral don't do that.
How would you know?!
So you see what I see, hmmm? The bastard Umbral?
Then I understand. It is even smart. But you are wrong, Rascal.
All right. I'm sorry, I just...
We were going to the Mistwalker. Let's all go together.
This is terrible idea. The bastard Umbral are there first...

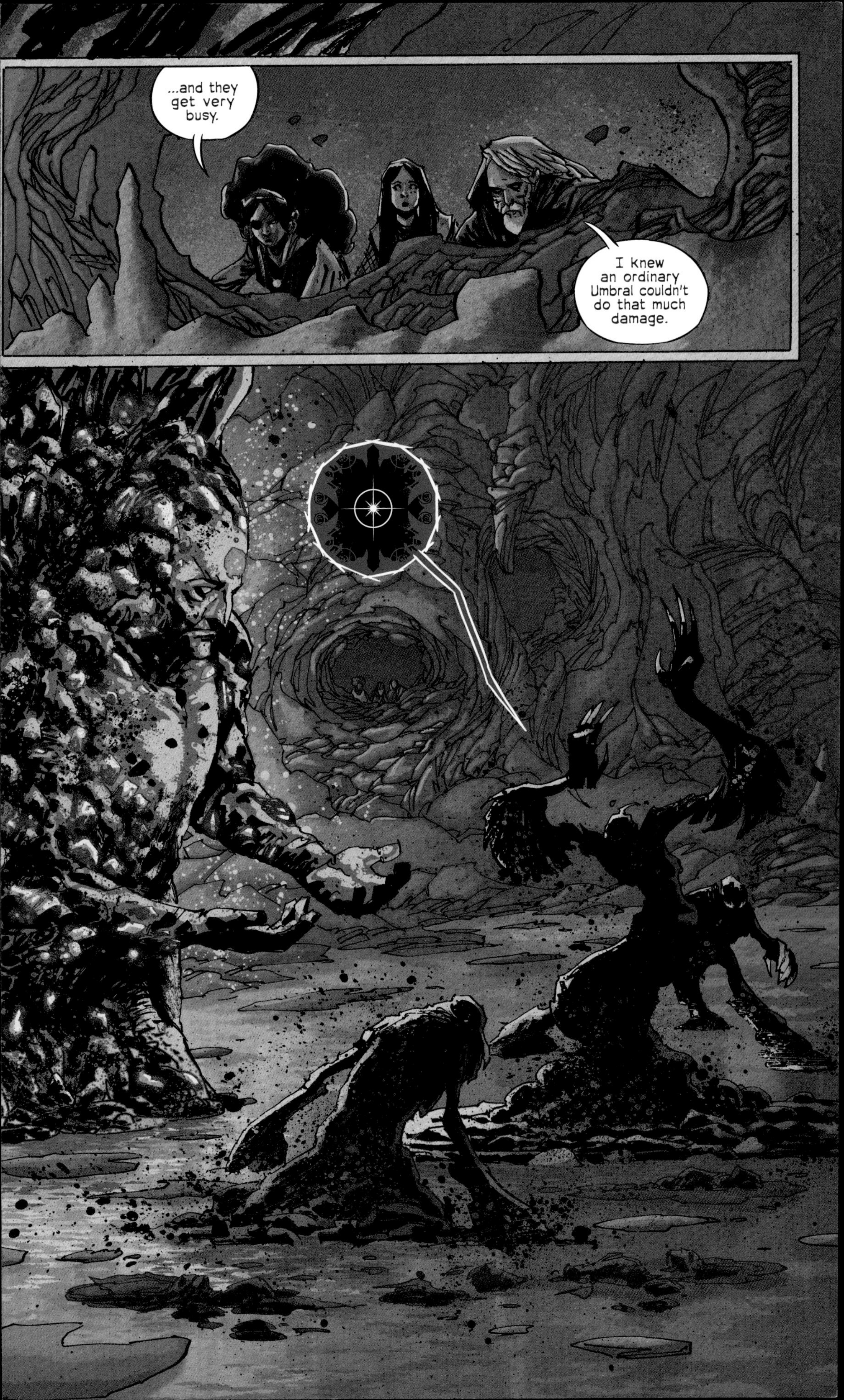
...and they get very busy.
I knew an ordinary Umbral couldn't do that much damage.

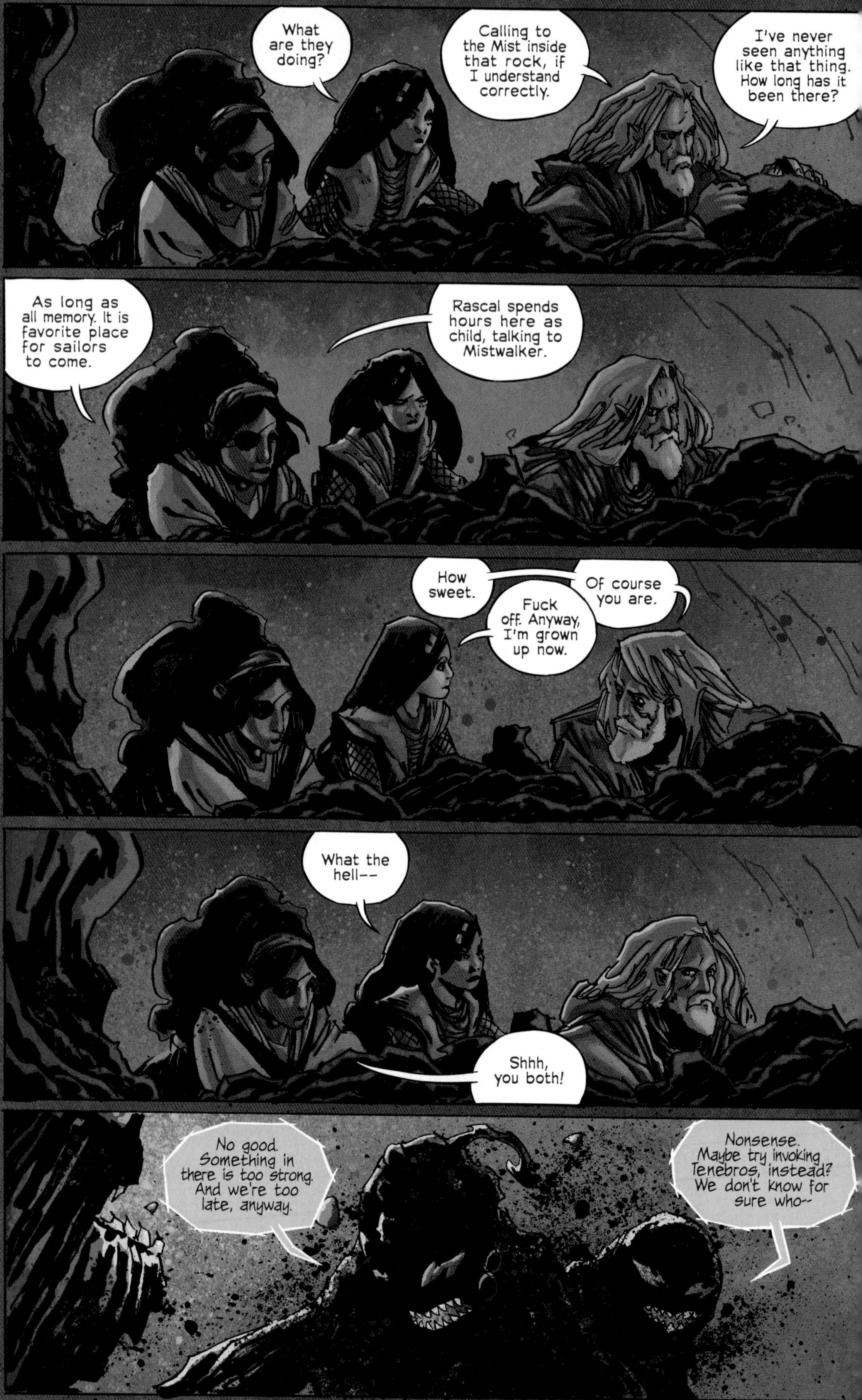

What are they doing?
Calling to the Mist inside that rock, if I understand correctly.
I've never seen anything like that thing. How long has it been there?
As long as all memory. It is favorite place for sailors to come.
Rascal spends hours here as child, talking to Mistwalker.
How sweet.
Of course you are.
Fuck off. Anyway, I'm grown up now.
What the hell--
Shhh, you both!
No good. Something in there is too strong. And we're too late, anyway.
Nonsense. Maybe try invoking Tenebros, instead? We don't know for sure who--

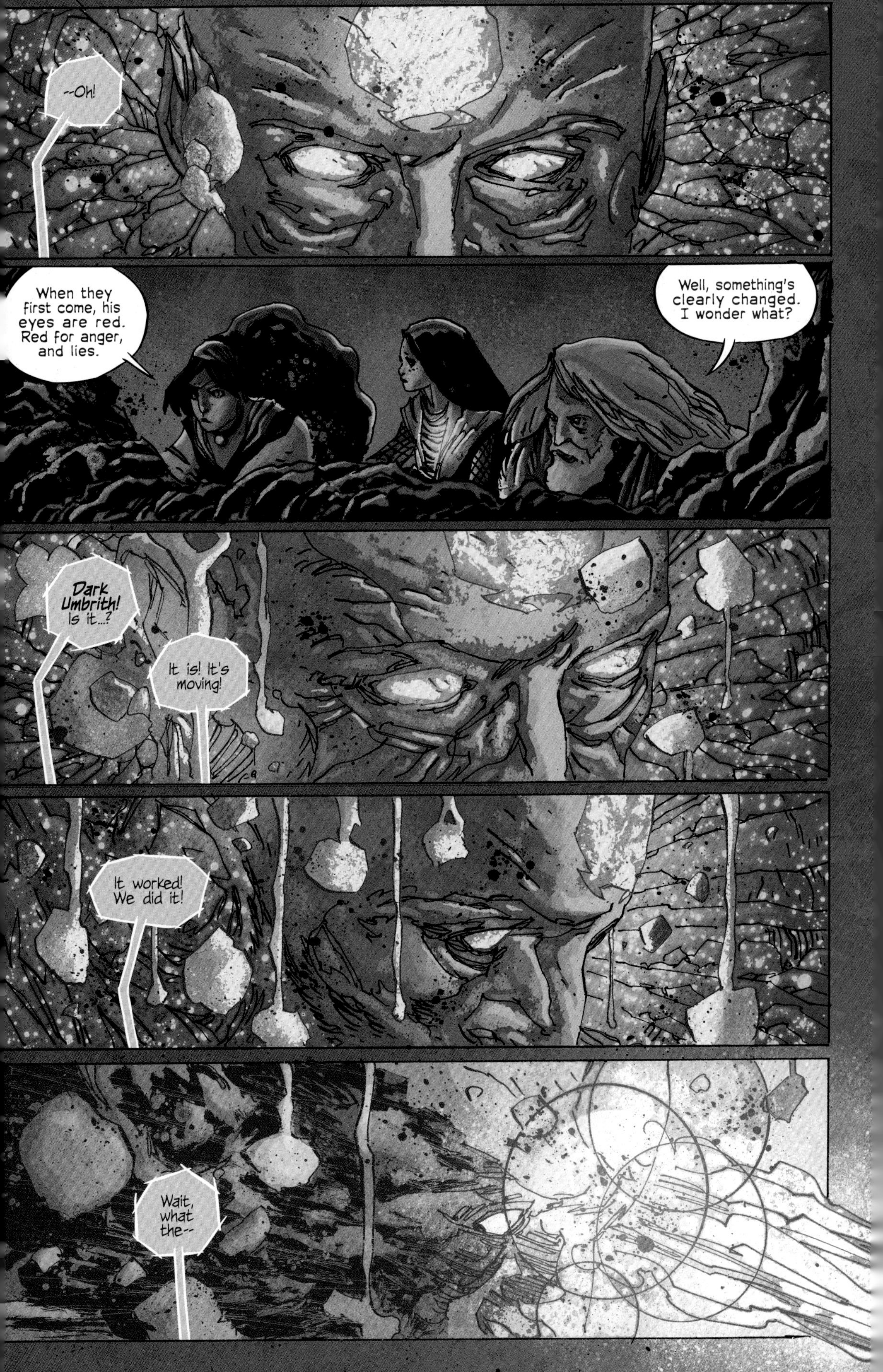
--Oh!
When they first come, his eyes are red. Red for anger, and lies.
Well, something's clearly changed. I wonder what?
Dark Umbrith! Is it...?
It is! It's moving!
It worked! We did it!
Wait, what the--

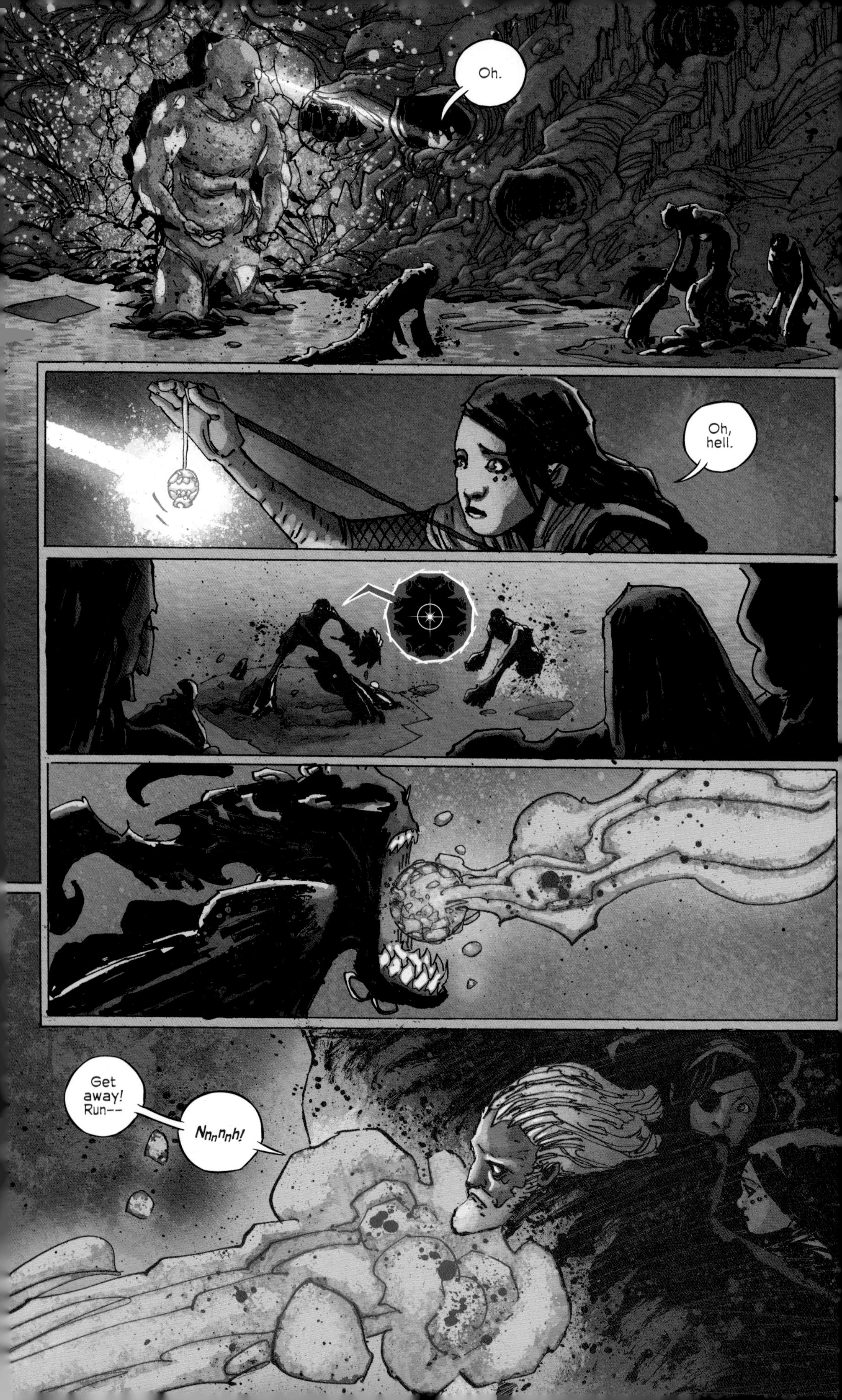
Oh.
Oh, hell.
Get away! Run--
Nnnnnh!

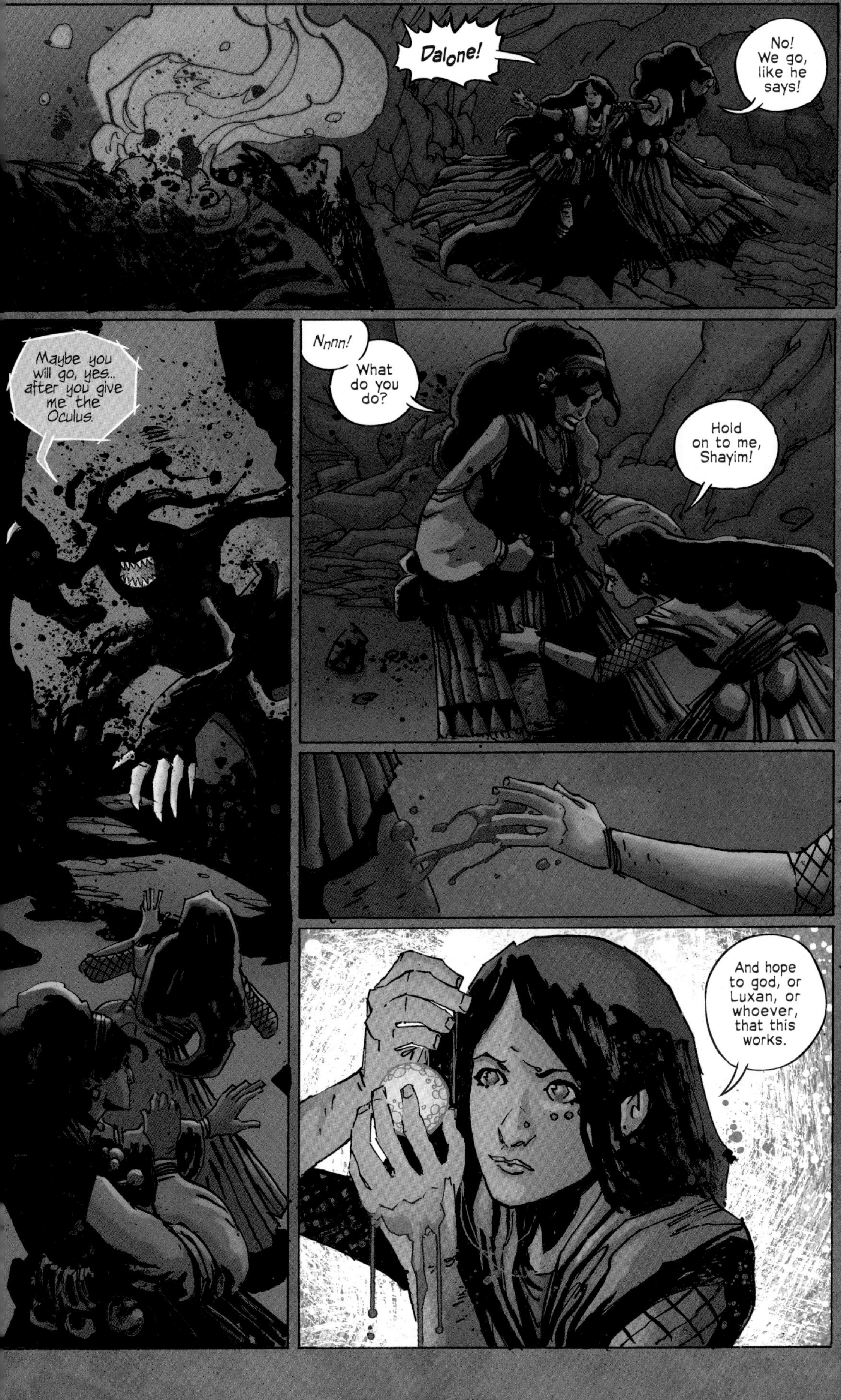
Dalone!
No! We go, like he says!
Maybe you will go, yes... after you give me the Oculus.
Nnnn!
What do you do?
Hold on to me, Shayim!
And hope to god, or Luxan, or whoever, that this works.

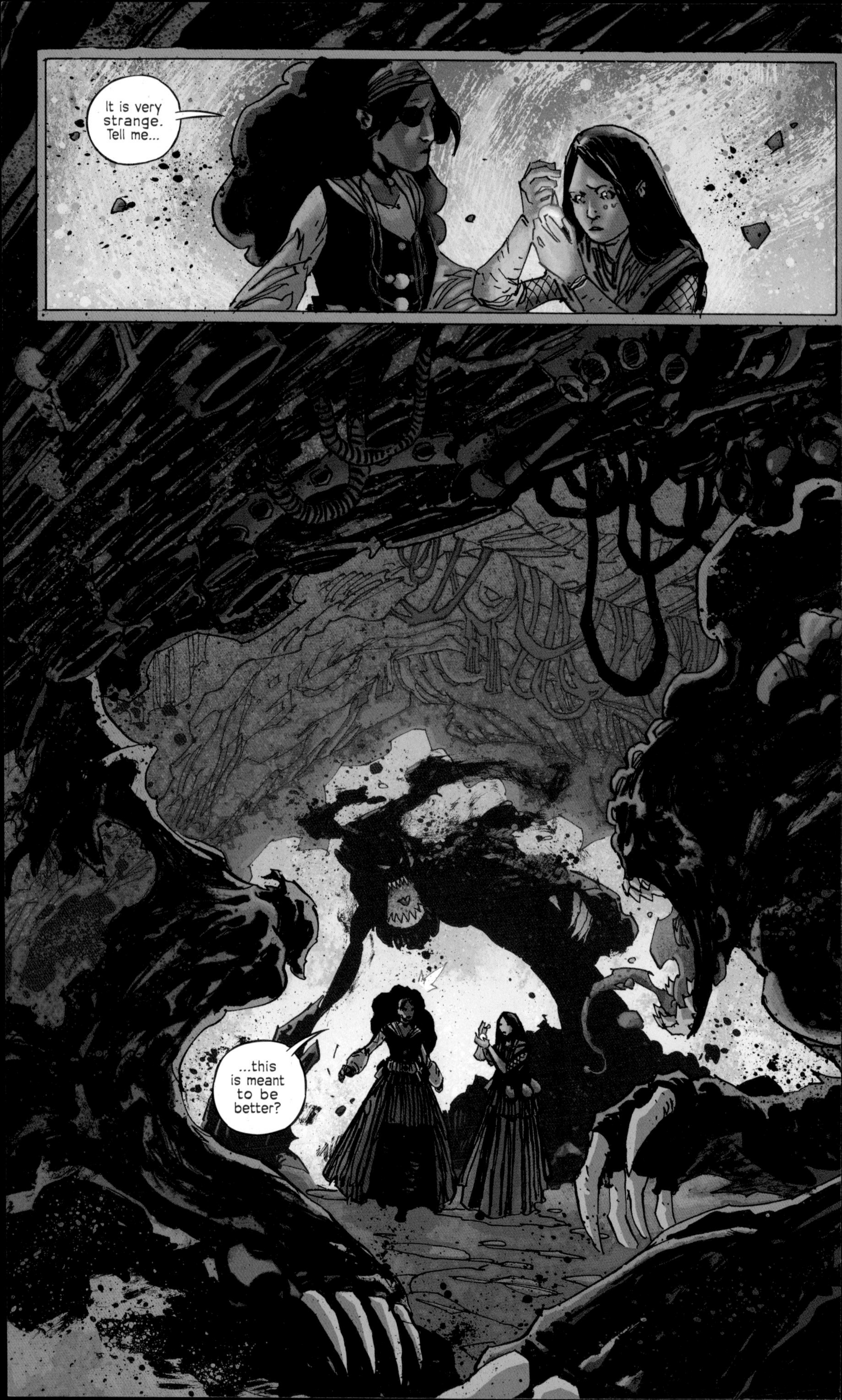
It is very strange. Tell me...
...this is meant to be better?

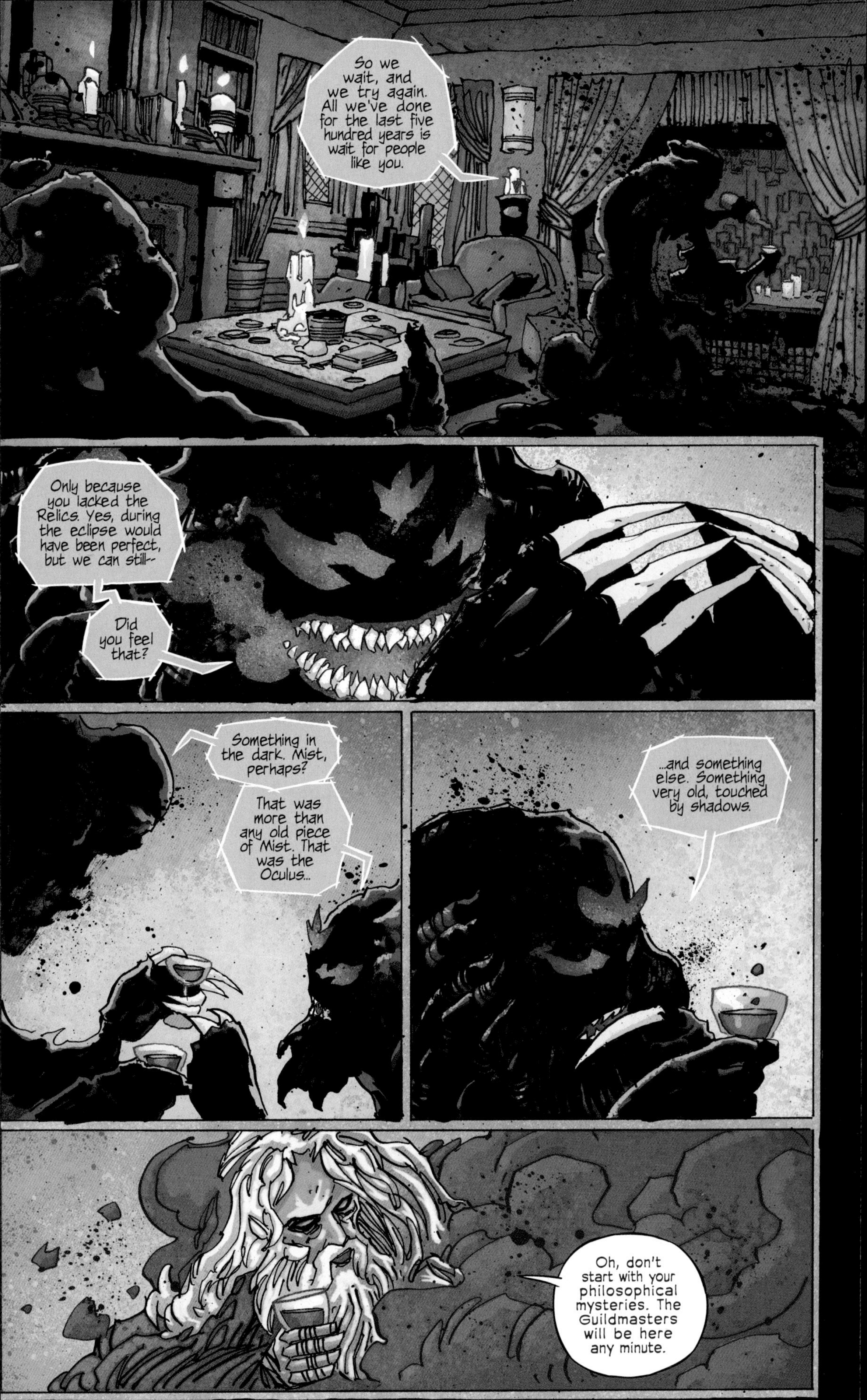
So we wait, and we try again. All we've done for the last five hundred years is wait for people like you.
Only because you lacked the Relics. Yes, during the eclipse would have been perfect, but we can still--
Did you feel that?
Something in the dark. Mist, perhaps?
That was more than any old piece of Mist. That was the Oculus...
...and something else. Something very old, touched by shadows.
Oh, don't start with your philosophical mysteries. The Guildmasters will be here any minute.

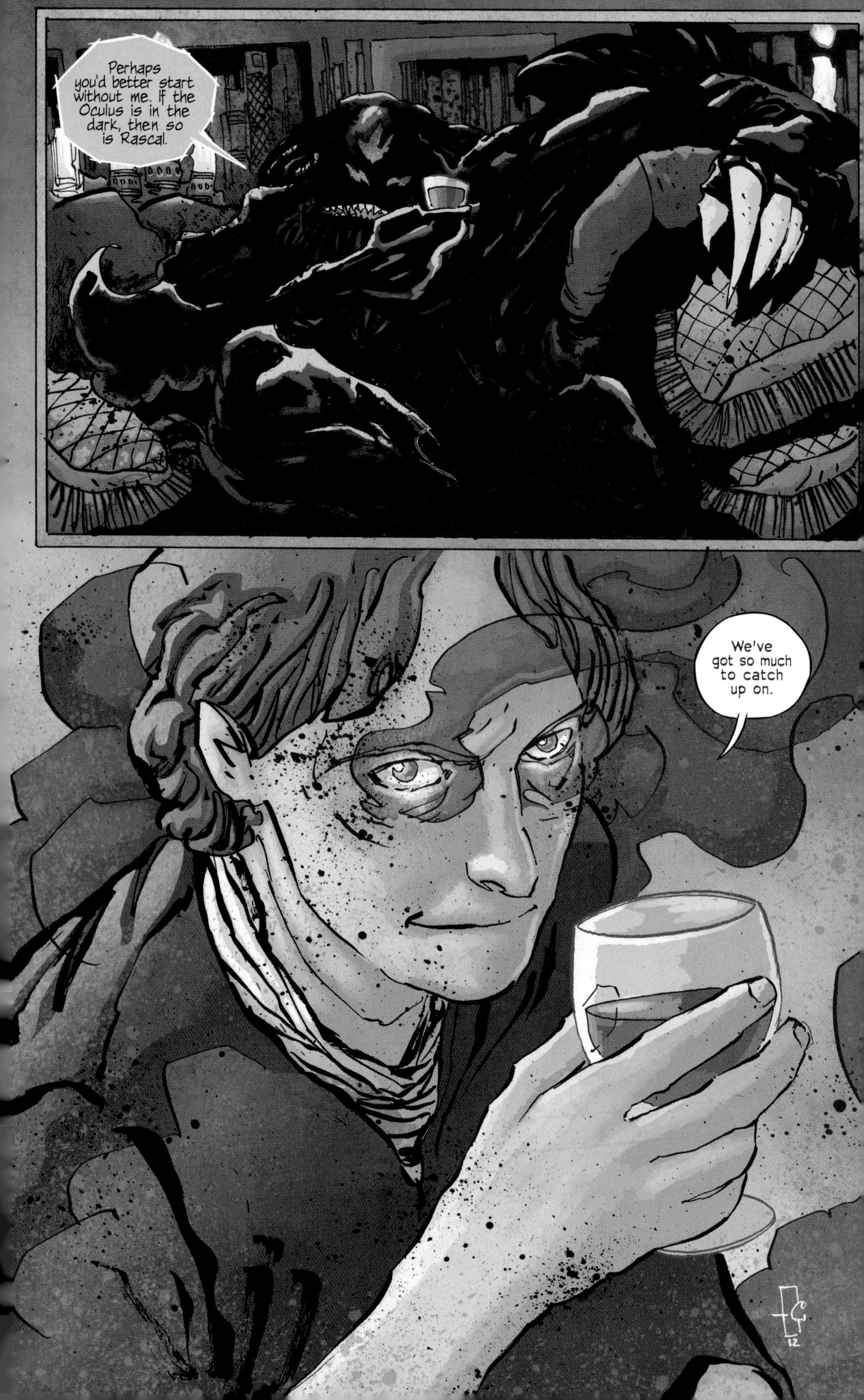
Perhaps you'd better start without me. If the Oculus is in the dark, then so is Rascal.
We've got so much to catch up on.

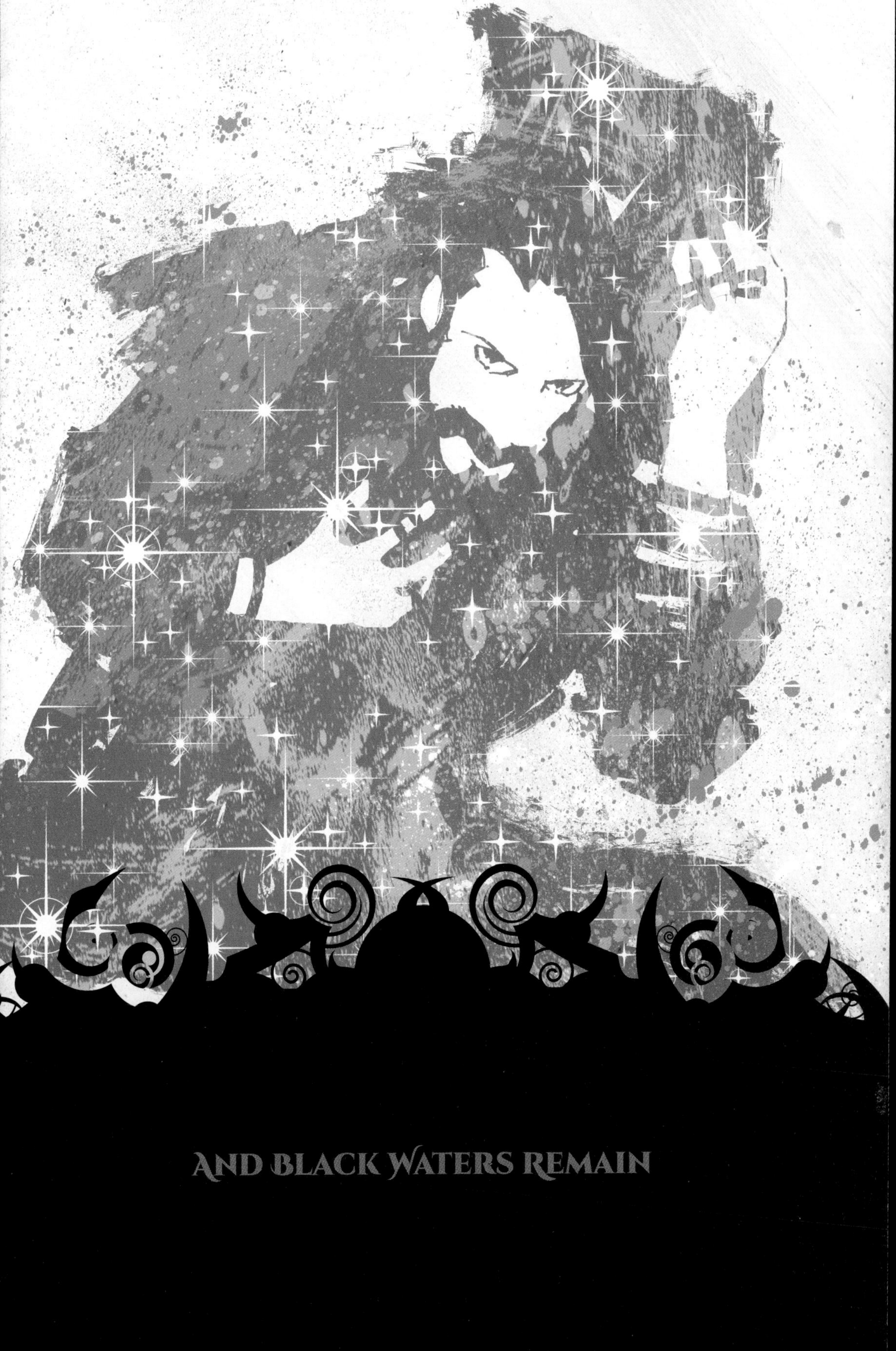

AND BLACK WATERS REMAIN

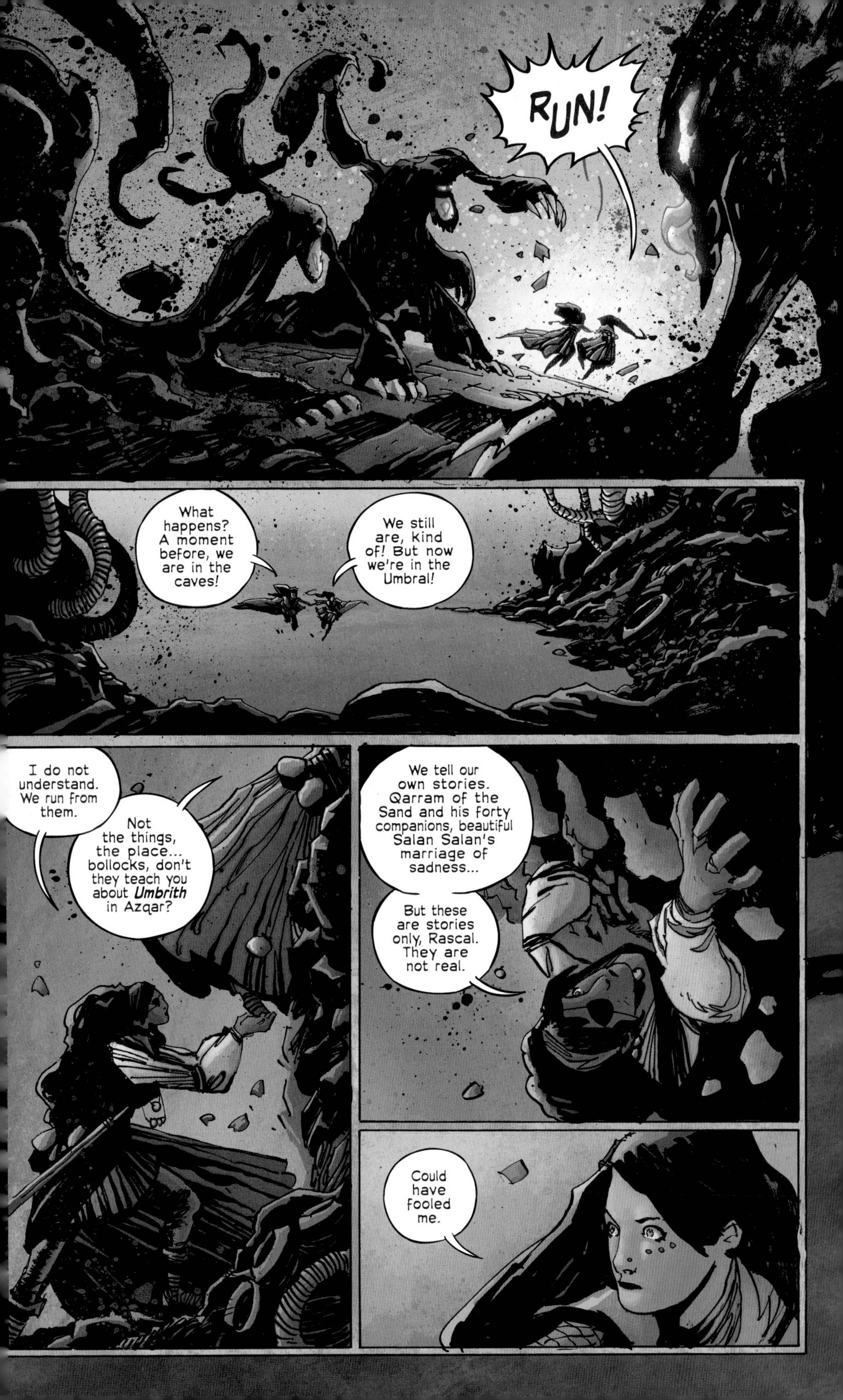
RUN!
What happens? A moment before, we are in the caves!
We still are, kind of! But now we're in the Umbral!
I do not understand. We run from them.
Not the things, the place... bollocks, don't they teach you about *Umbrith* in Azqar?
We tell our own stories. Qarram of the Sand and his forty companions, beautiful Salan Salan's marriage of sadness...
But these are stories only, Rascal. They are not real.
Could have fooled me.

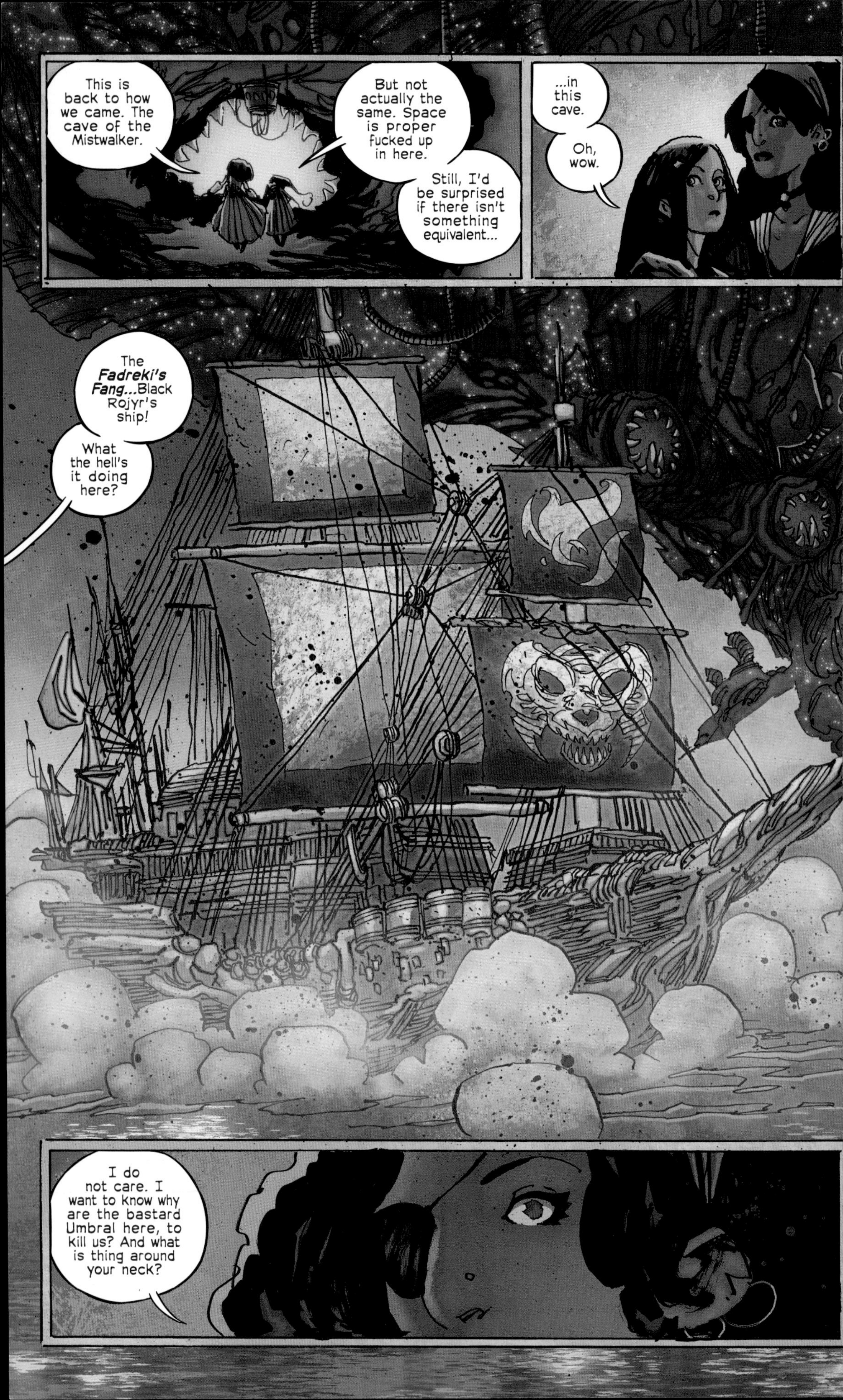
This is back to how we came. The cave of the Mistwalker.
But not actually the same. Space is proper fucked up in here.
Still, I'd be surprised if there isn't something equivalent...
...in this cave.
Oh, wow.
The *Fadreki's Fang*...Black Rojyr's ship!
What the hell's it doing here?
I do not care. I want to know why are the bastard Umbral here, to kill us? And what is thing around your neck?

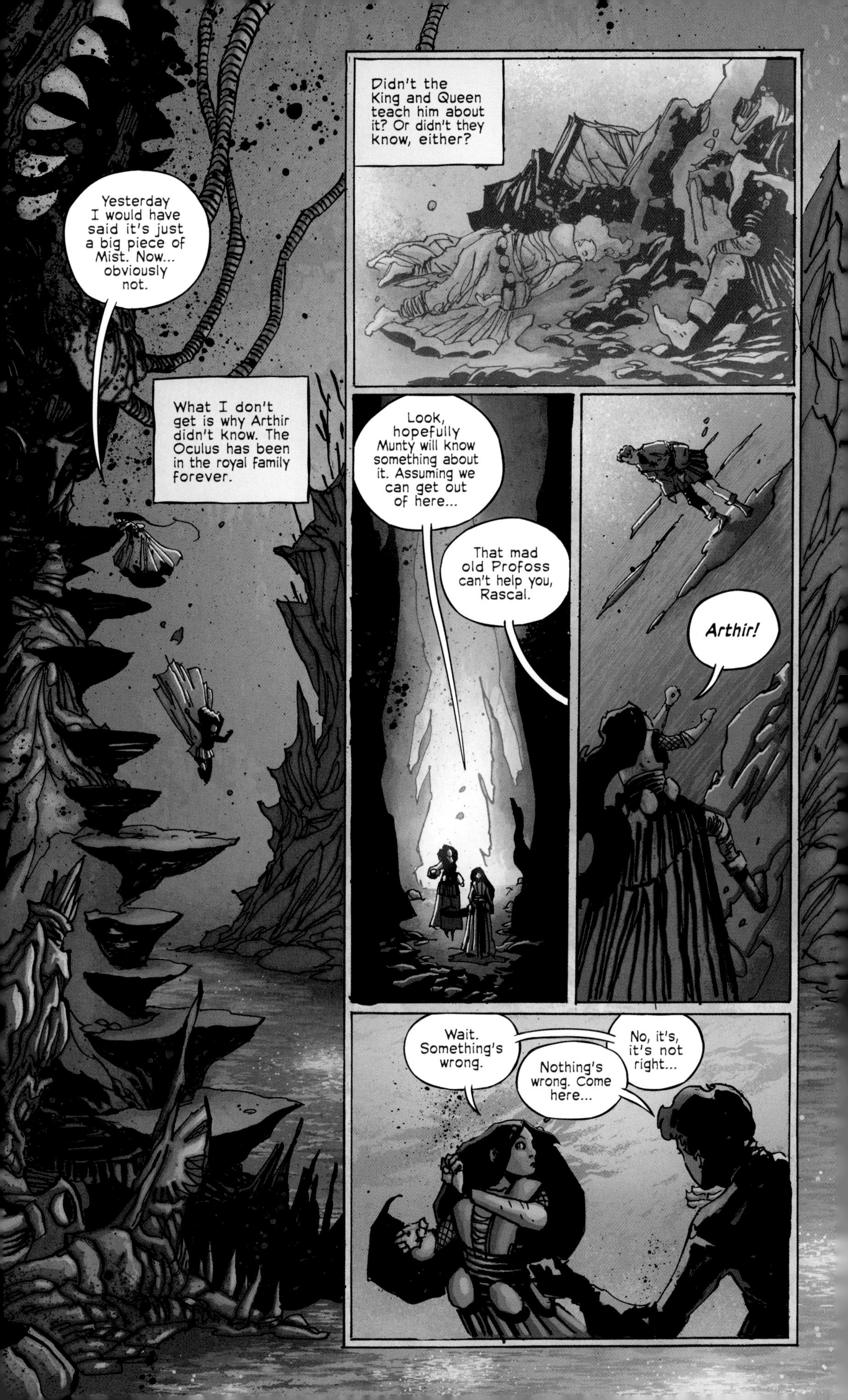
Yesterday I would have said it's just a big piece of Mist. Now... obviously not.
What I don't get is why Arthir didn't know. The Oculus has been in the royal family forever.
Didn't the King and Queen teach him about it? Or didn't they know, either?
Look, hopefully Munty will know something about it. Assuming we can get out of here...
That mad old Profoss can't help you, Rascal.
Arthir!
Wait. Something's wrong.
Nothing's wrong. Come here...
No, it's, it's not right...

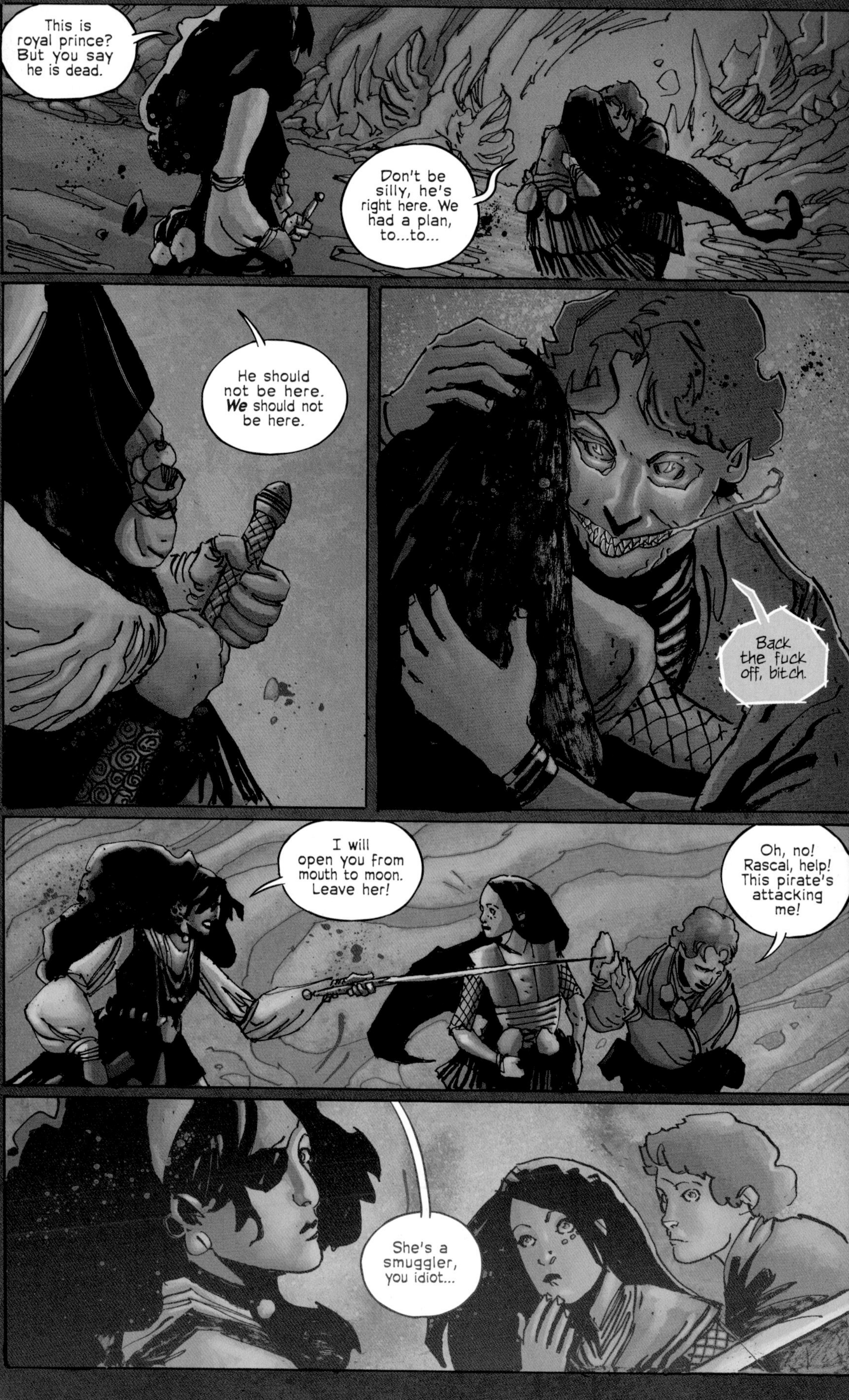
This is royal prince? But you say he is dead.
Don't be silly, he's right here. We had a plan, to...to...
He should not be here. *We* should not be here.
Back the fuck off, bitch.
I will open you from mouth to moon. Leave her!
Oh, no! Rascal, help! This pirate's attacking me!
She's a smuggler, you idiot...

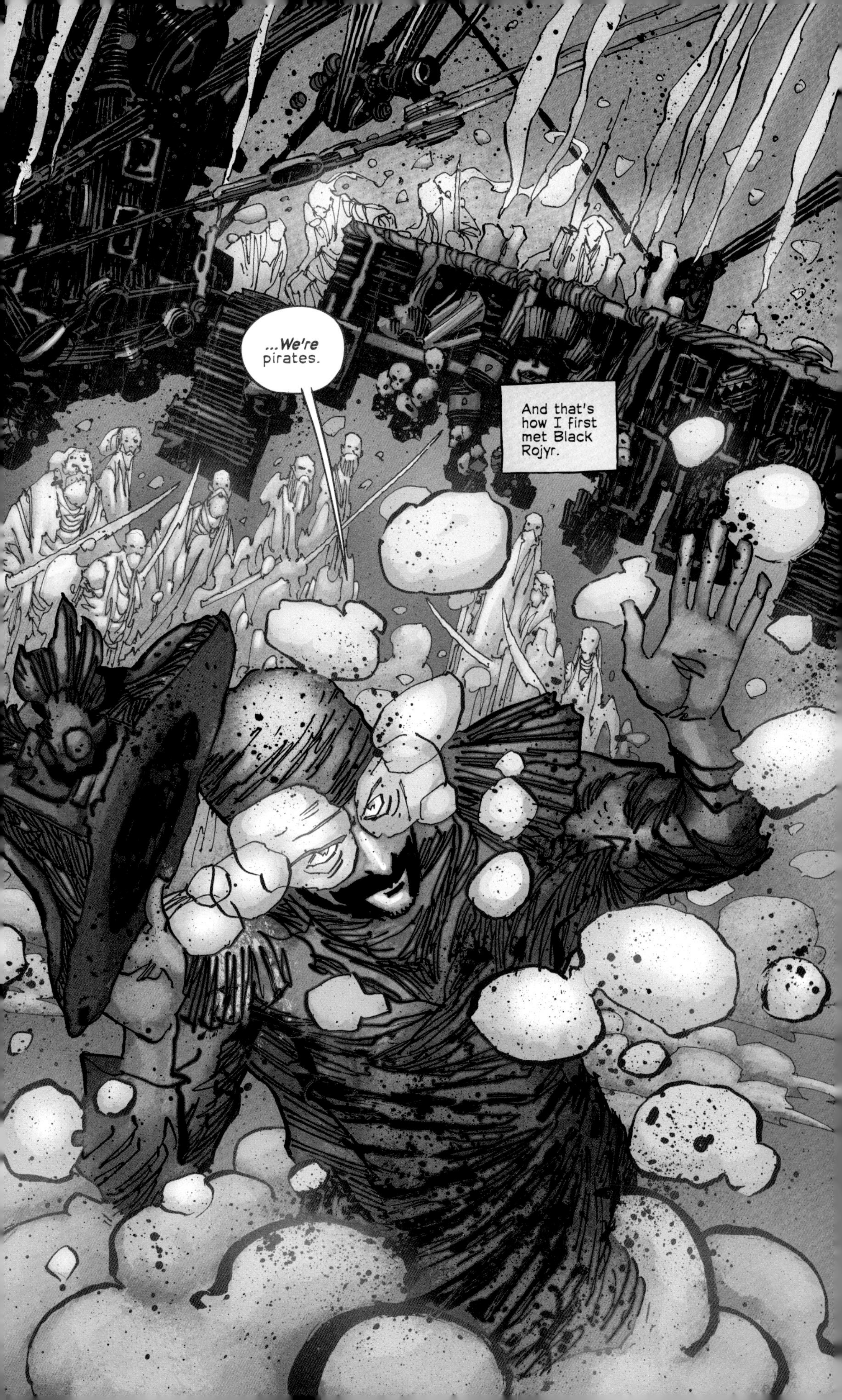
...We're pirates.
And that's how I first met Black Rojyr.

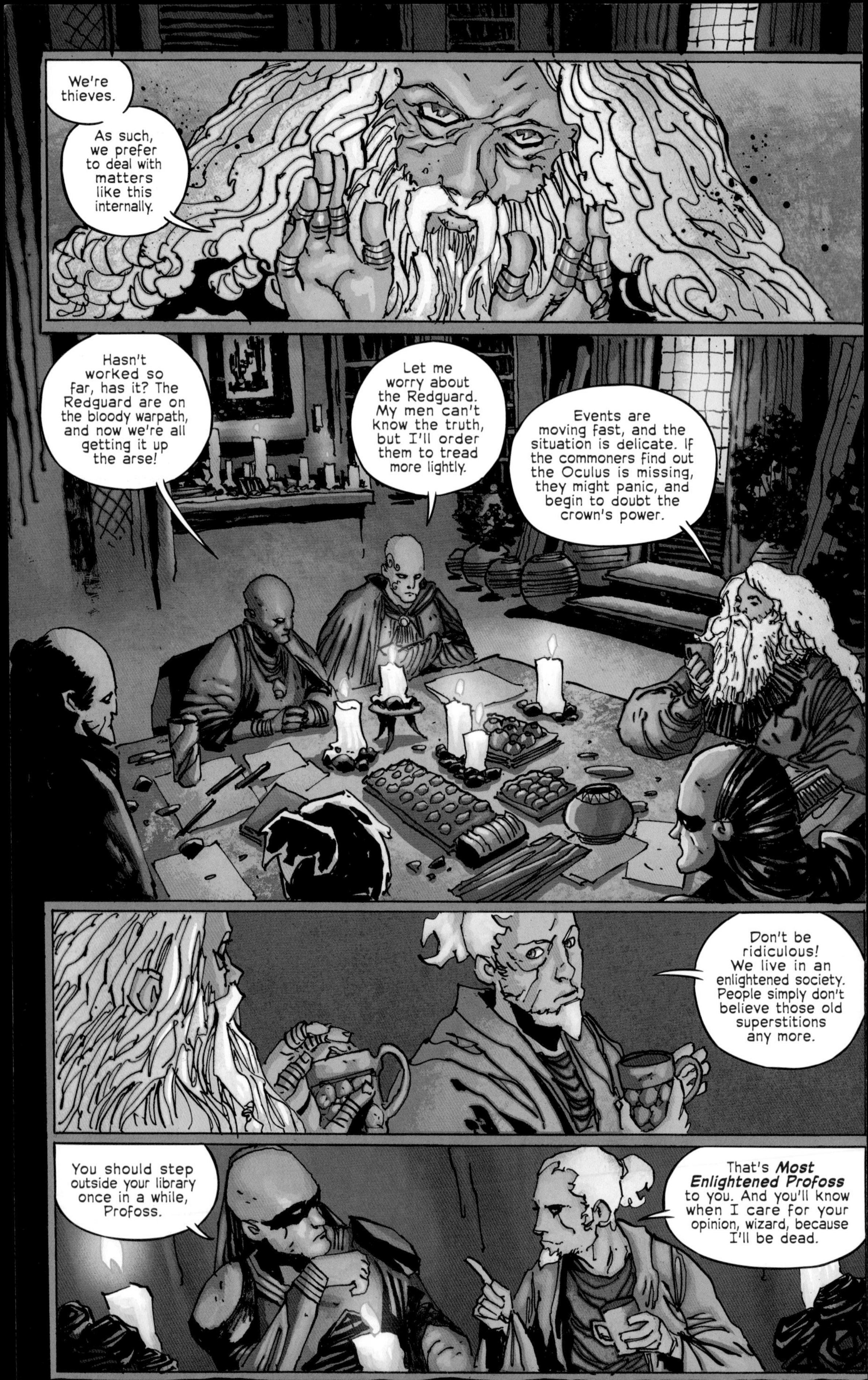

We're thieves.
As such, we prefer to deal with matters like this internally.
Hasn't worked so far, has it? The Redguard are on the bloody warpath, and now we're all getting it up the arse!
Let me worry about the Redguard. My men can't know the truth, but I'll order them to tread more lightly.
Events are moving fast, and the situation is delicate. If the commoners find out the Oculus is missing, they might panic, and begin to doubt the crown's power.
Don't be ridiculous! We live in an enlightened society. People simply don't believe those old superstitions any more.
You should step outside your library once in a while, Profoss.
That's ***Most Enlightened Profoss*** to you. And you'll know when I care for your opinion, wizard, because I'll be dead.

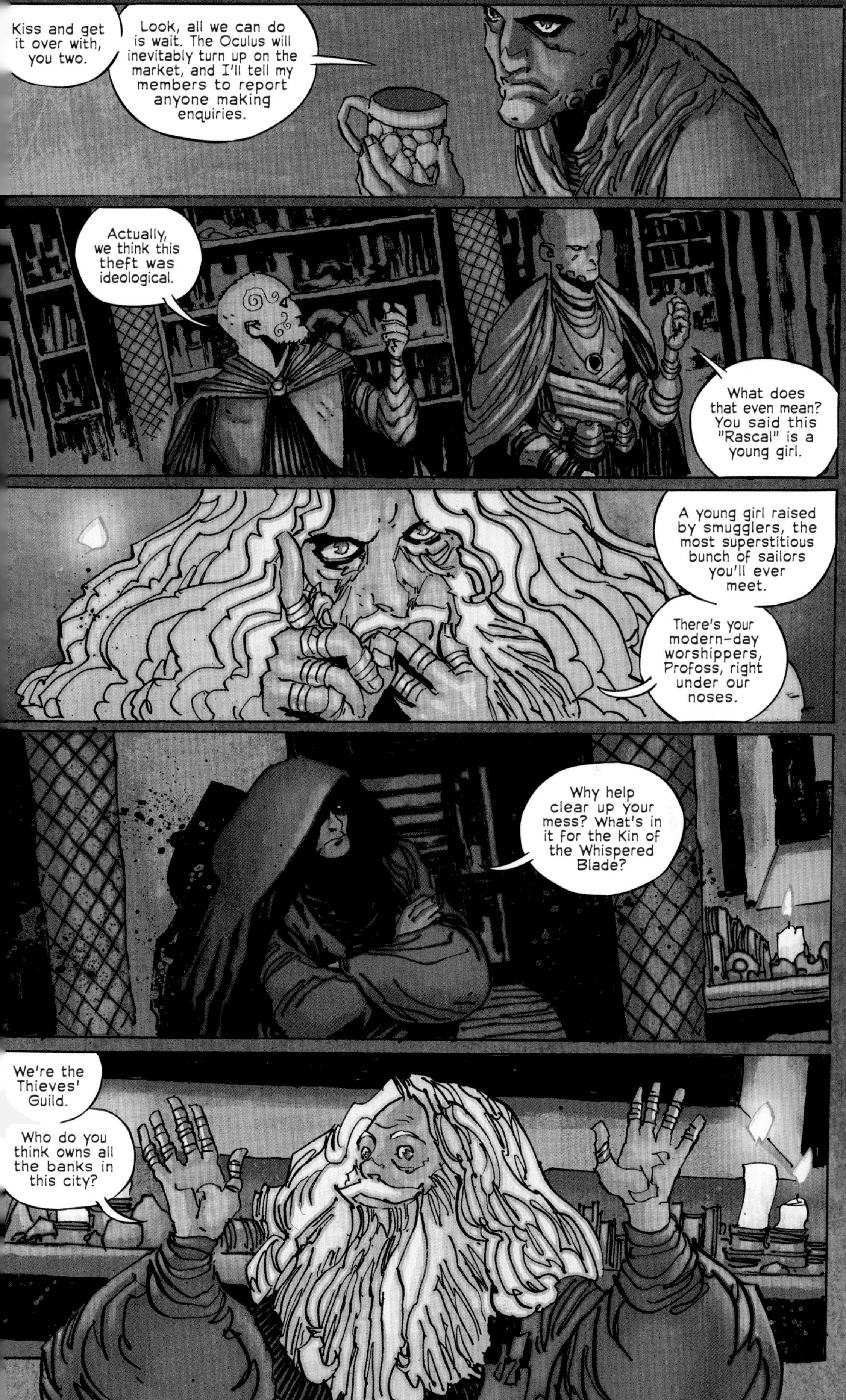
Kiss and get it over with, you two.
Look, all we can do is wait. The Oculus will inevitably turn up on the market, and I'll tell my members to report anyone making enquiries.
Actually, we think this theft was ideological.
What does that even mean? You said this "Rascal" is a young girl.
A young girl raised by smugglers, the most superstitious bunch of sailors you'll ever meet.
There's your modern-day worshippers, Profoss, right under our noses.
Why help clear up your mess? What's in it for the Kin of the Whispered Blade?
We're the Thieves' Guild.
Who do you think owns all the banks in this city?

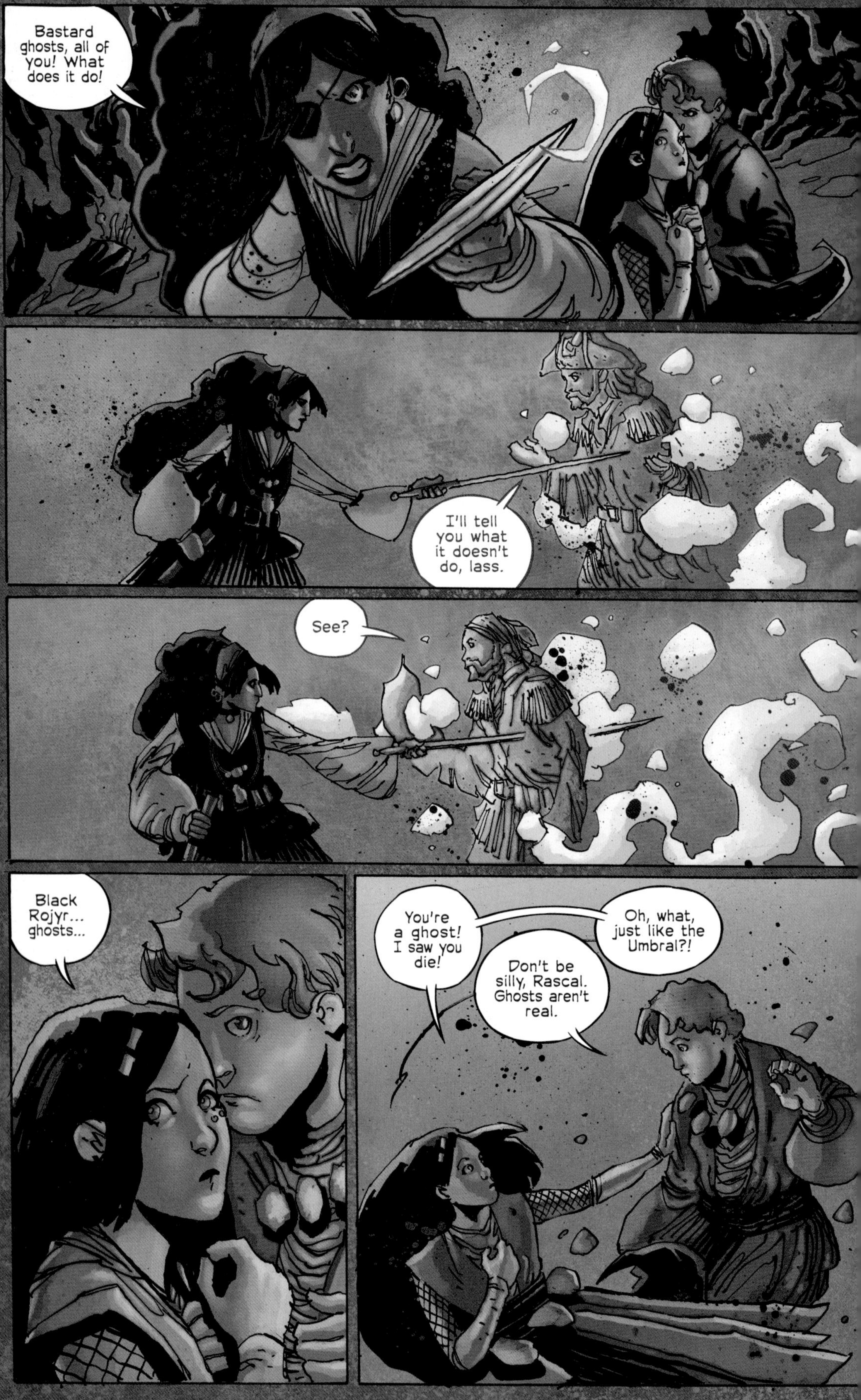
Bastard ghosts, all of you! What does it do!
I'll tell you what it doesn't do, lass.
See?
Black Rojyr... ghosts...
You're a ghost! I saw you die!
Oh, what, just like the Umbral?!
Don't be silly, Rascal. Ghosts aren't real.

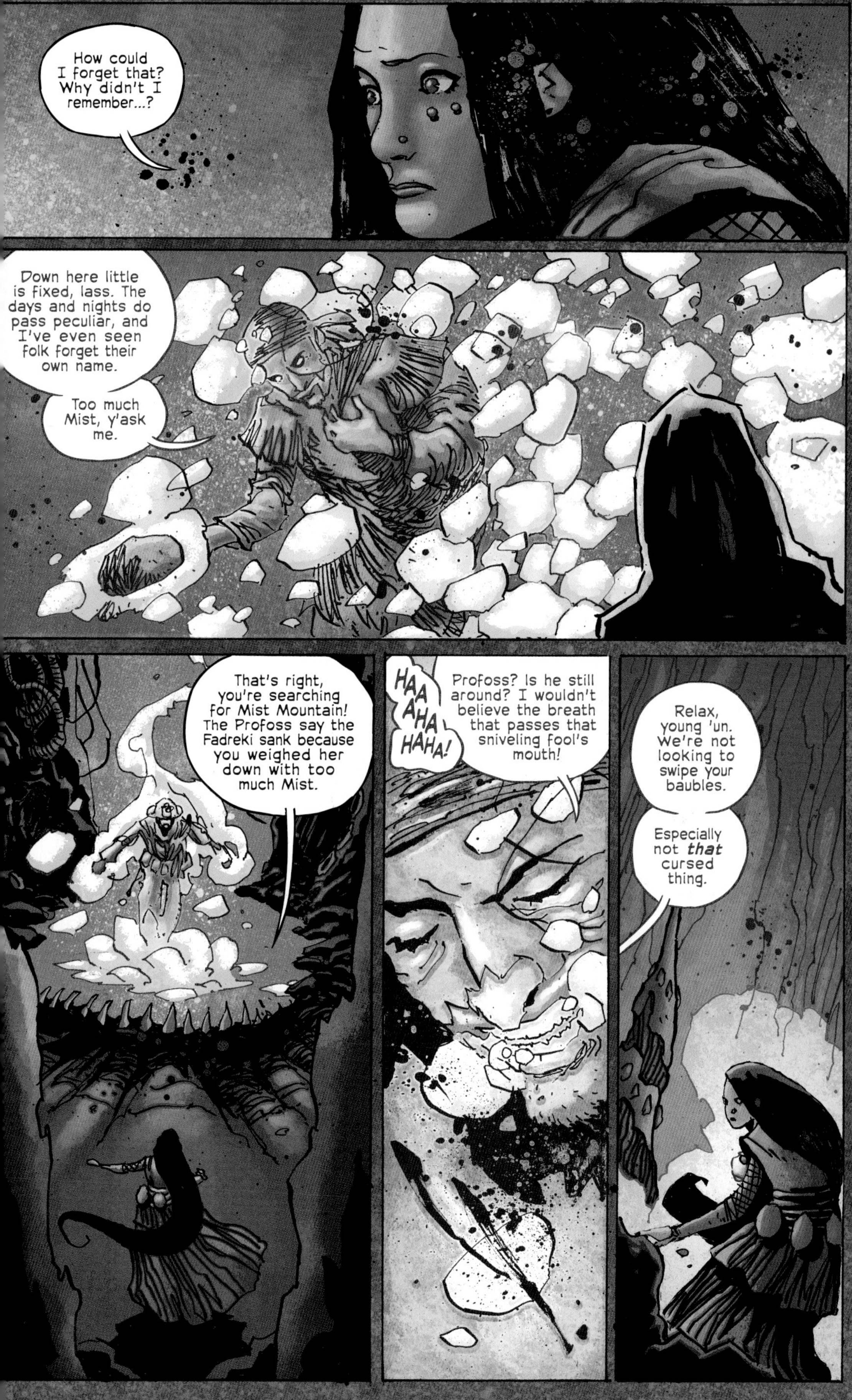
How could I forget that? Why didn't I remember...?
Down here little is fixed, lass. The days and nights do pass peculiar, and I've even seen folk forget their own name.
Too much Mist, y'ask me.
That's right, you're searching for Mist Mountain! The Profoss say the Fadreki sank because you weighed her down with too much Mist.
HAA AHA HAHA!
Profoss? Is he still around? I wouldn't believe the breath that passes that sniveling fool's mouth!
Relax, young 'un. We're not looking to swipe your baubles.
Especially not *that* cursed thing.

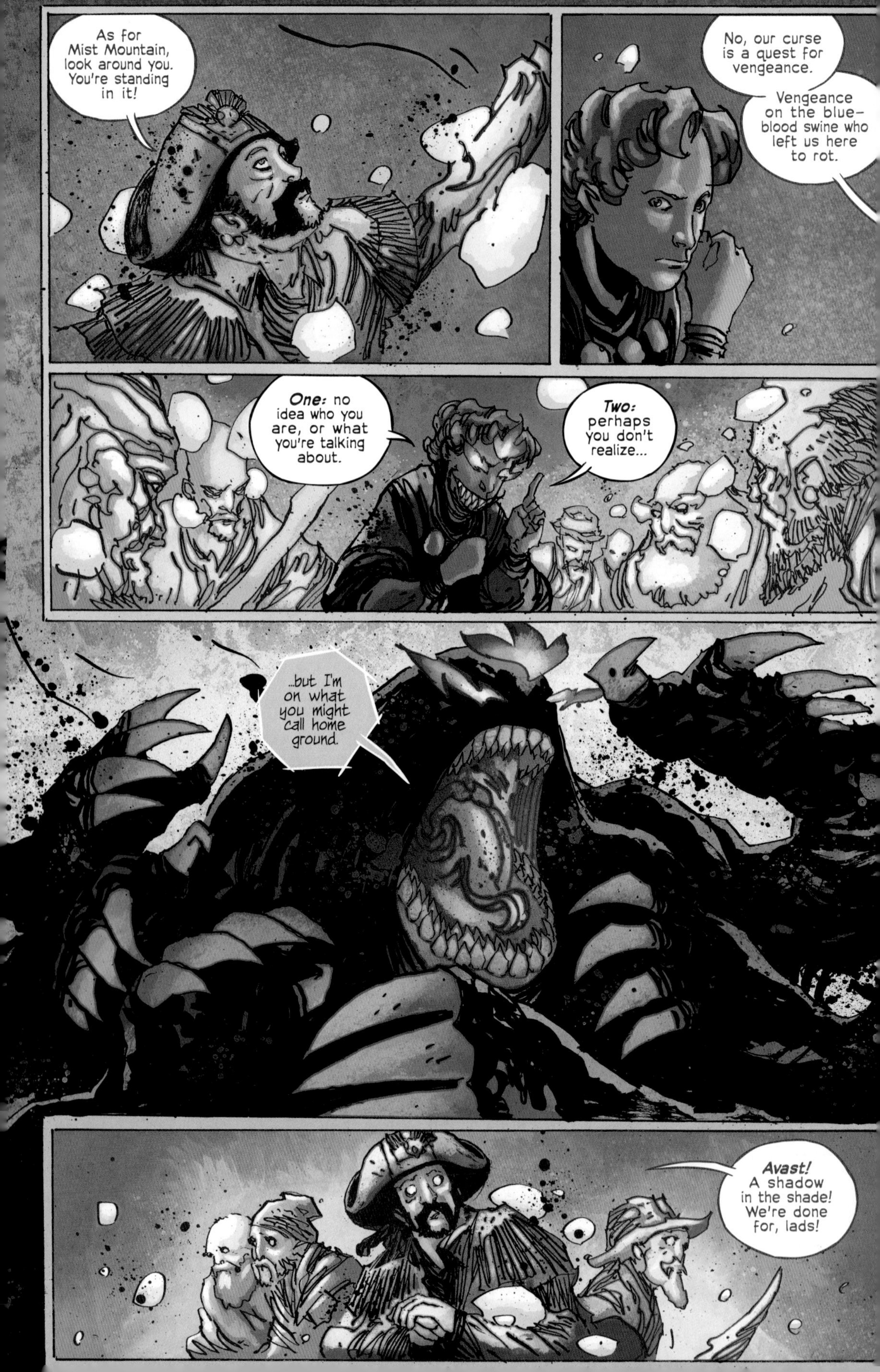
As for Mist Mountain, look around you. You're standing in it!
No, our curse is a quest for vengeance.
Vengeance on the blue-blood swine who left us here to rot.
One: no idea who you are, or what you're talking about.
Two: perhaps you don't realize...
...but I'm on what you might call home ground.
Avast! A shadow in the shade! We're done for, lads!

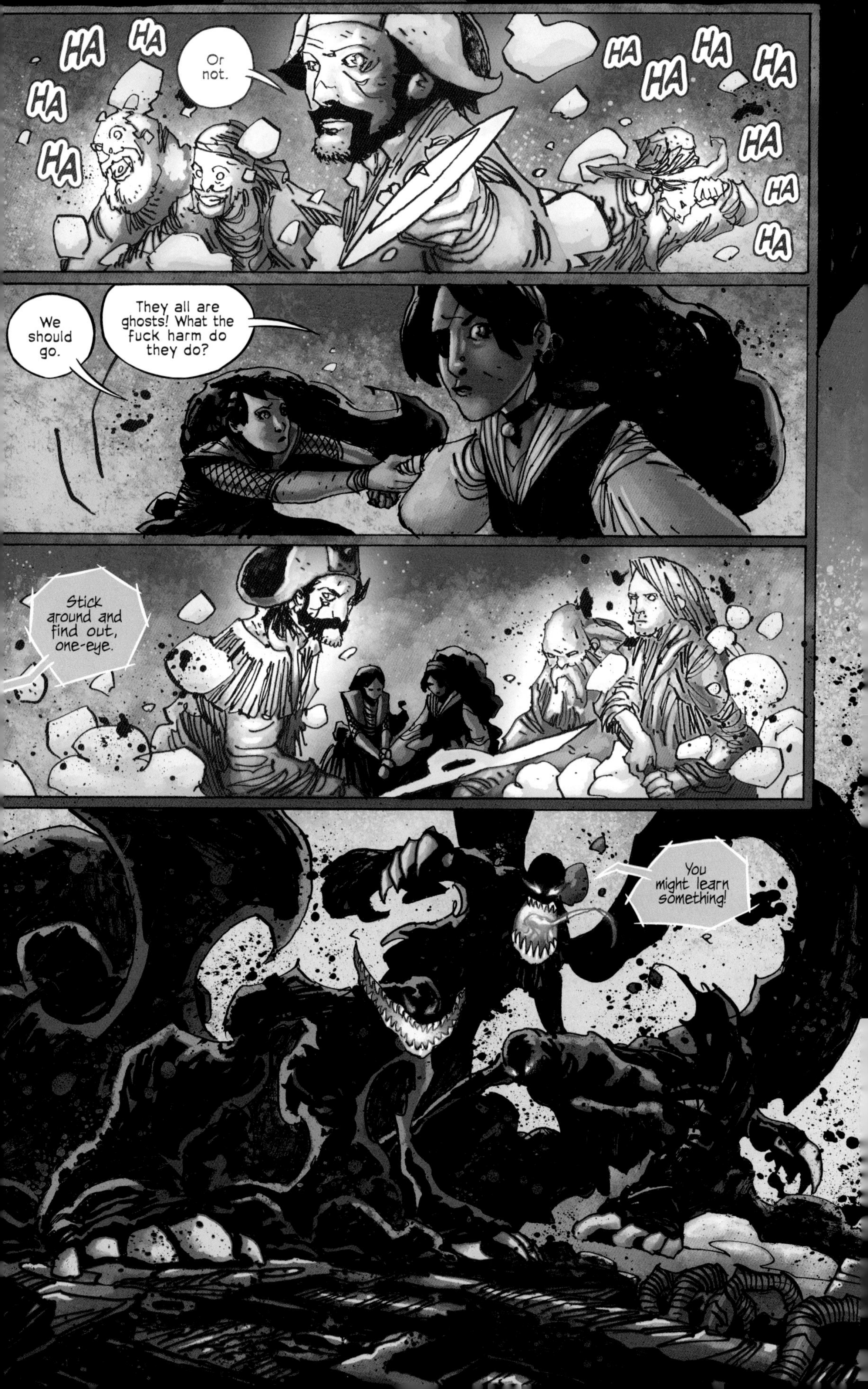
HA HA
HA
HA
Or not.
HA HA HA HA HA HA HA HA
We should go.
They all are ghosts! What the fuck harm do they do?
Stick around and find out, one-eye.
You might learn something!

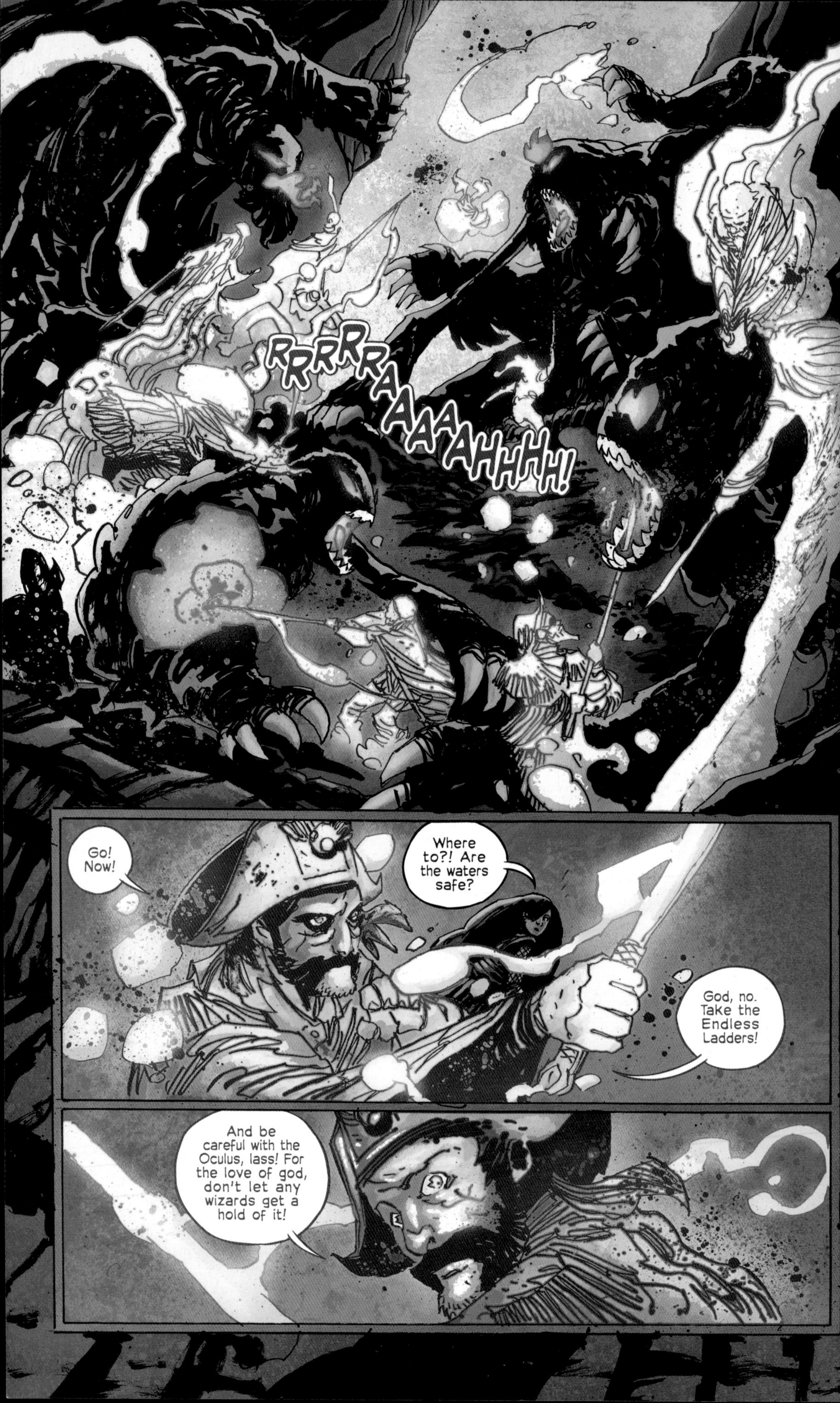
RRRRRAAAAAHHHH!
Go! Now!
Where to?! Are the waters safe?
God, no. Take the Endless Ladders!
And be careful with the Oculus, lass! For the love of god, don't let any wizards get a hold of it!

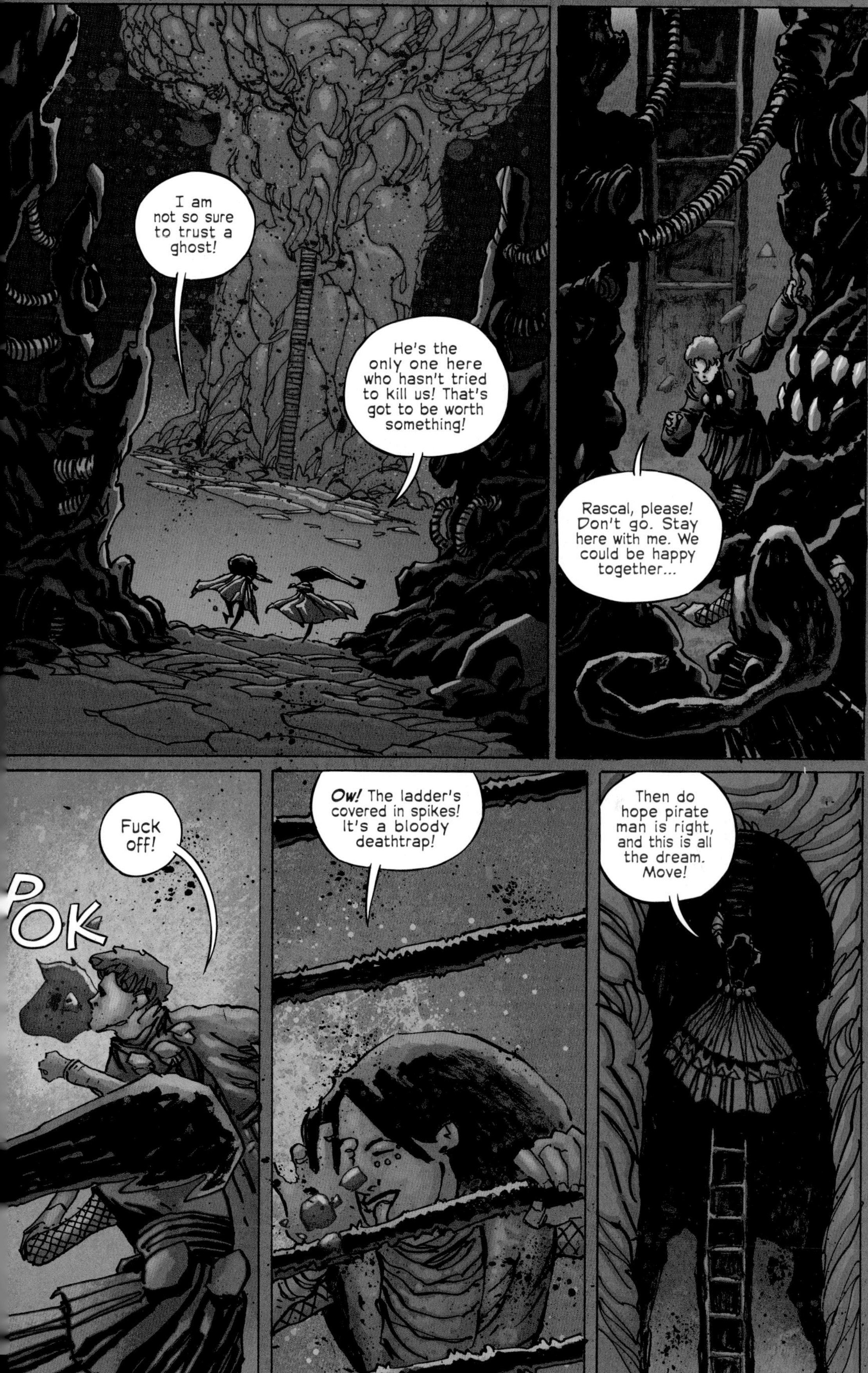
I am not so sure to trust a ghost!
He's the only one here who hasn't tried to kill us! That's got to be worth something!
Rascal, please! Don't go. Stay here with me. We could be happy together...
Fuck off!
POK
Ow! The ladder's covered in spikes! It's a bloody deathtrap!
Then do hope pirate man is right, and this is all the dream. Move!

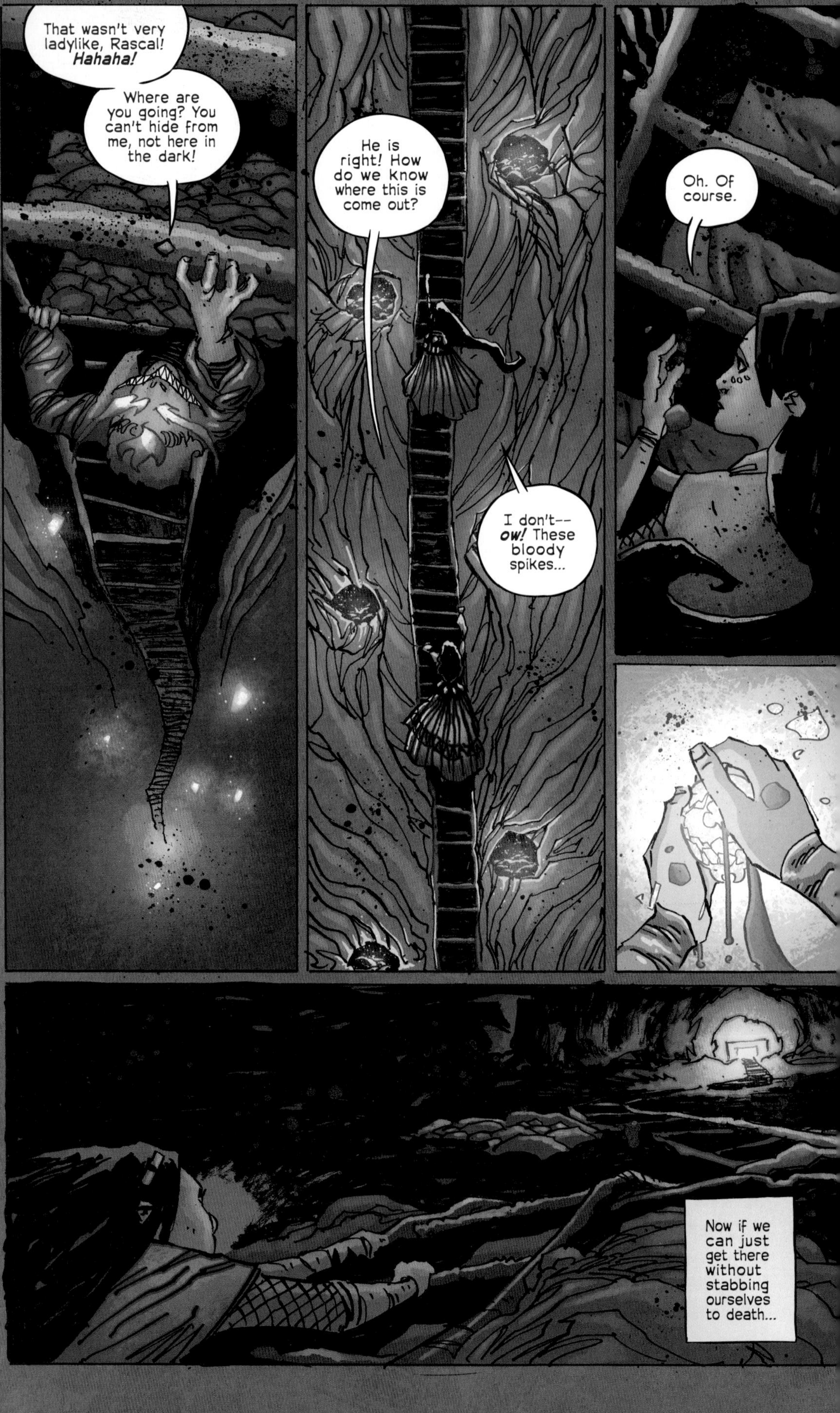

That wasn't very ladylike, Rascal! *Hahaha!*
Where are you going? You can't hide from me, not here in the dark!
He is right! How do we know where this is come out?
I don't-- *ow!* These bloody spikes...
Oh. Of course.
Now if we can just get there without stabbing ourselves to death...

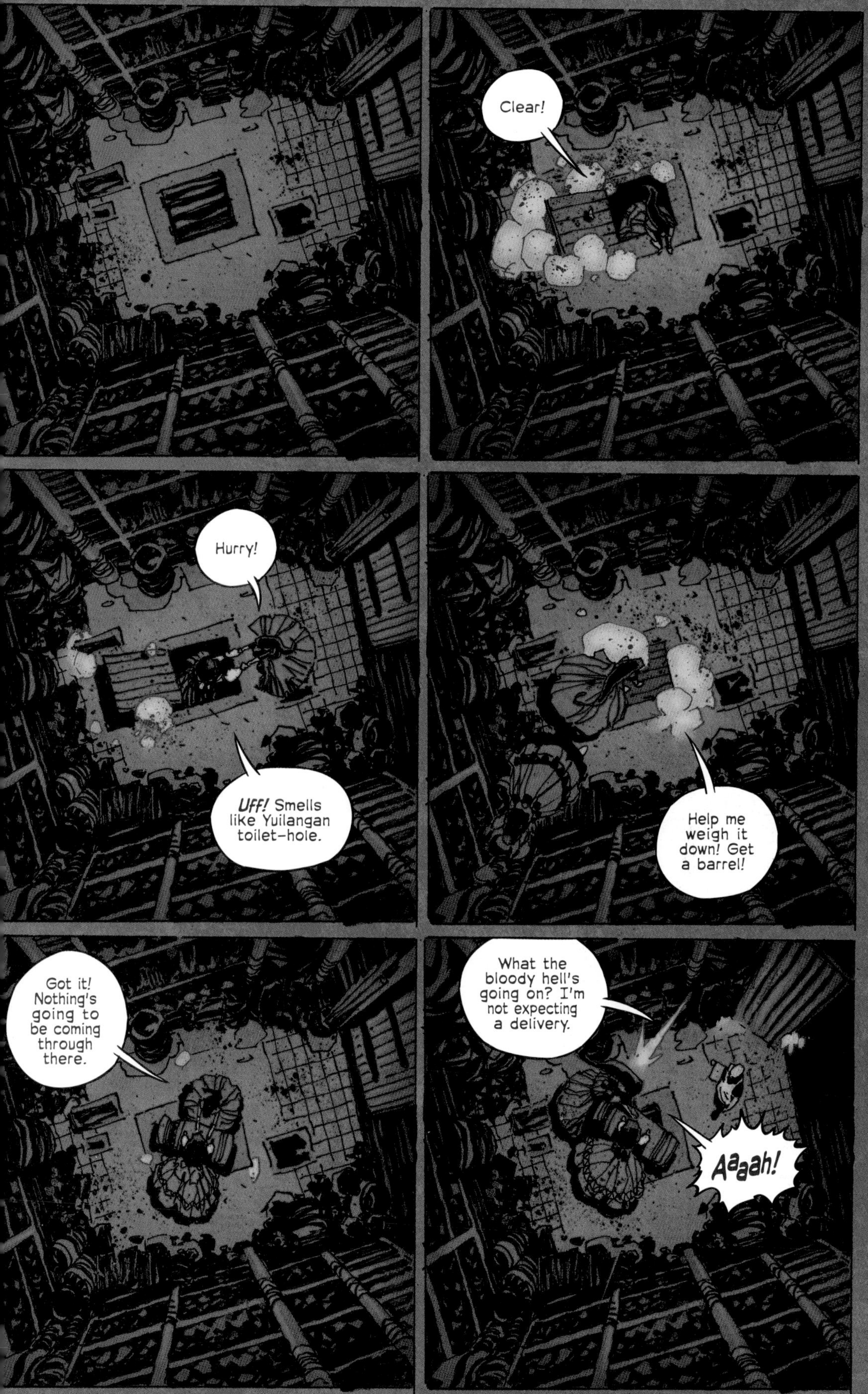
Clear!
Hurry!
Uff! Smells like Yuilangan toilet-hole.
Help me weigh it down! Get a barrel!
Got it! Nothing's going to be coming through there.
What the bloody hell's going on? I'm not expecting a delivery.
Aaaah!

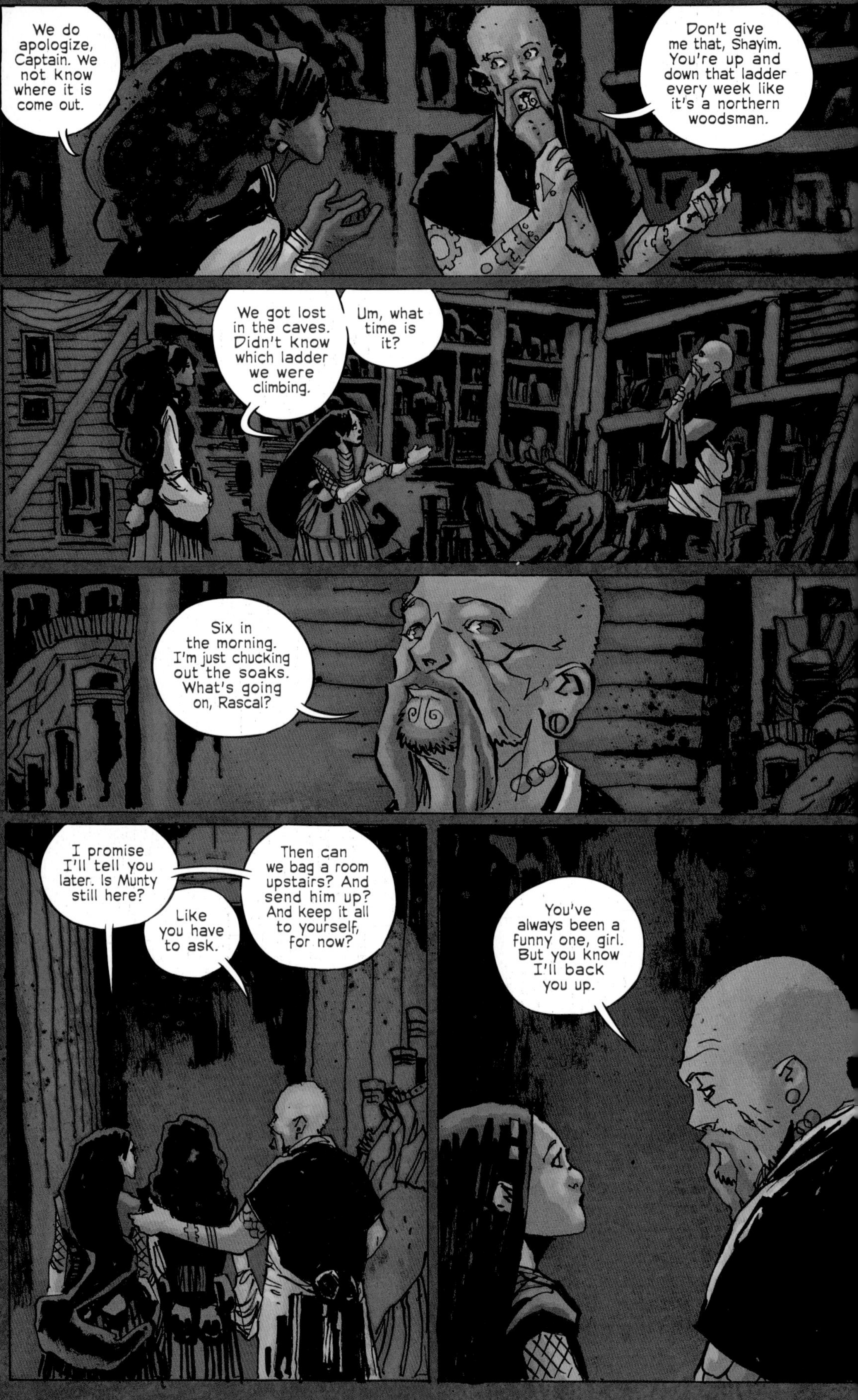
We do apologize, Captain. We not know where it is come out.
Don't give me that, Shayim. You're up and down that ladder every week like it's a northern woodsman.
We got lost in the caves. Didn't know which ladder we were climbing.
Um, what time is it?
Six in the morning. I'm just chucking out the soaks. What's going on, Rascal?
I promise I'll tell you later. Is Munty still here?
Like you have to ask.
Then can we bag a room upstairs? And send him up? And keep it all to yourself, for now?
You've always been a funny one, girl. But you know I'll back you up.

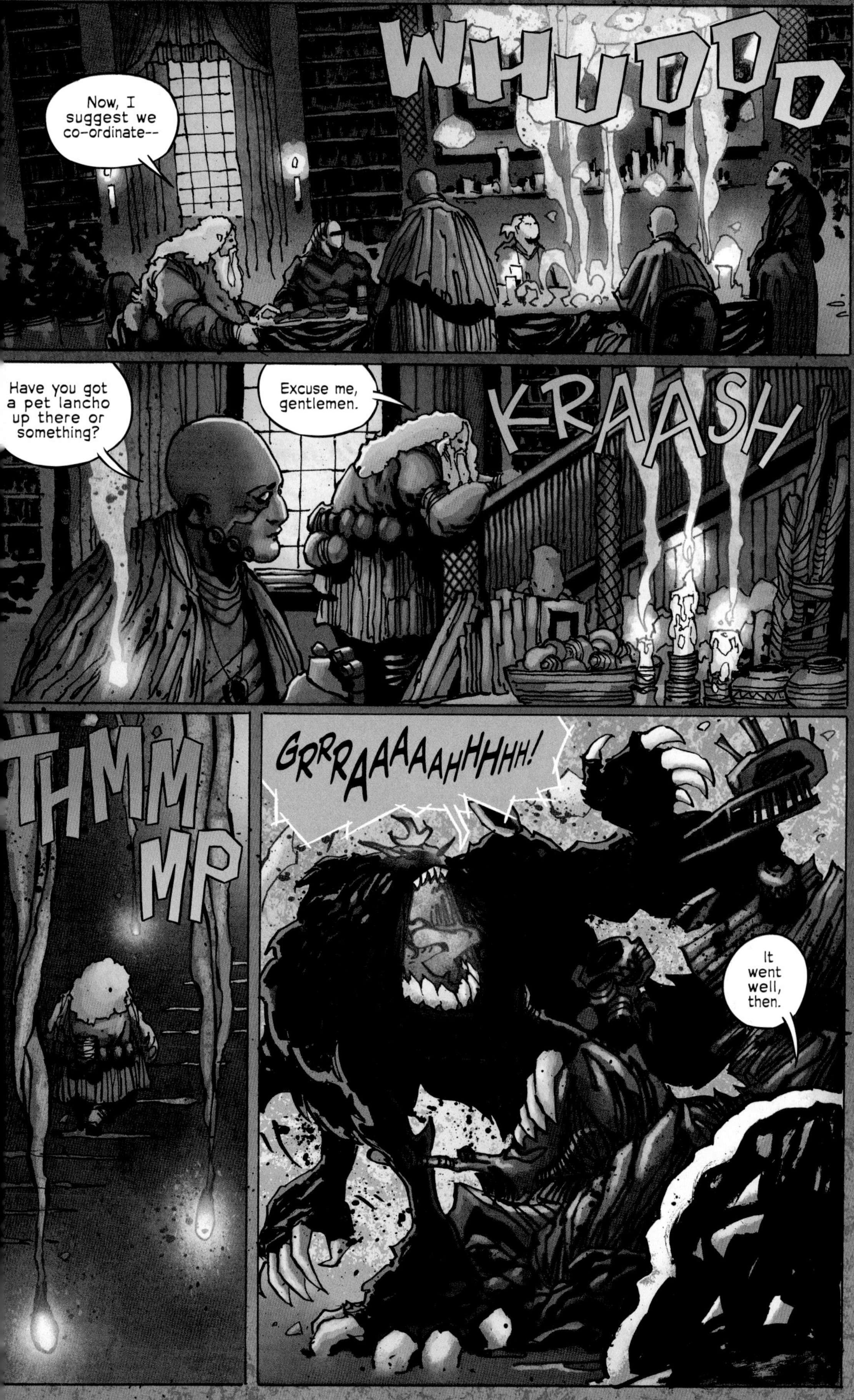
Now, I suggest we co-ordinate--
WHUDOOD
Have you got a pet lancho up there or something?
Excuse me, gentlemen.
KRAASH
THMMMP
GRRRAAAAAHHHHH!
It went well, then.

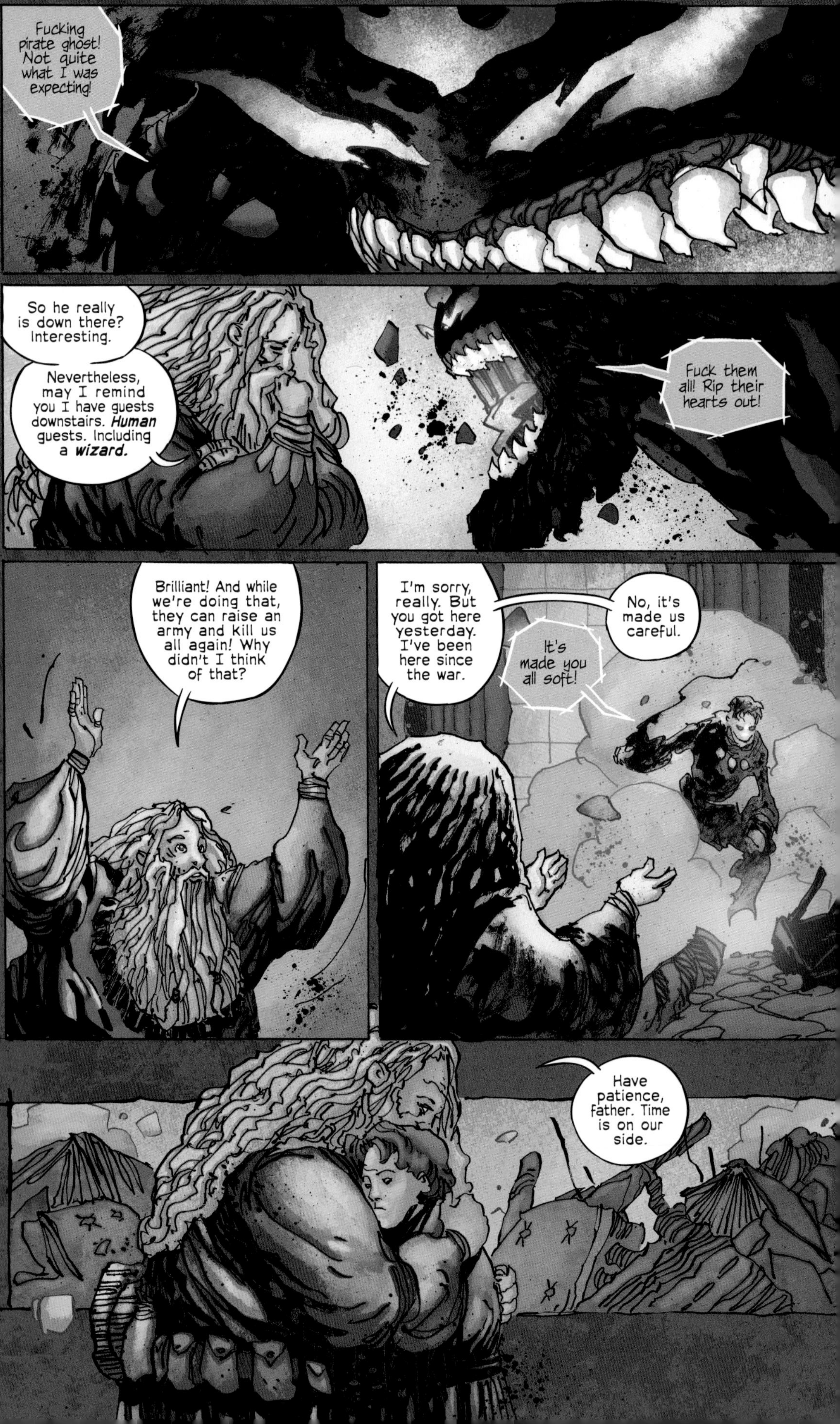
Fucking pirate ghost! Not quite what I was expecting!
So he really is down there? Interesting.
Nevertheless, may I remind you I have guests downstairs. Human guests. Including a wizard.
Fuck them all! Rip their hearts out!
Brilliant! And while we're doing that, they can raise an army and kill us all again! Why didn't I think of that?
I'm sorry, really. But you got here yesterday. I've been here since the war.
No, it's made us careful.
It's made you all soft!
Have patience, father. Time is on our side.

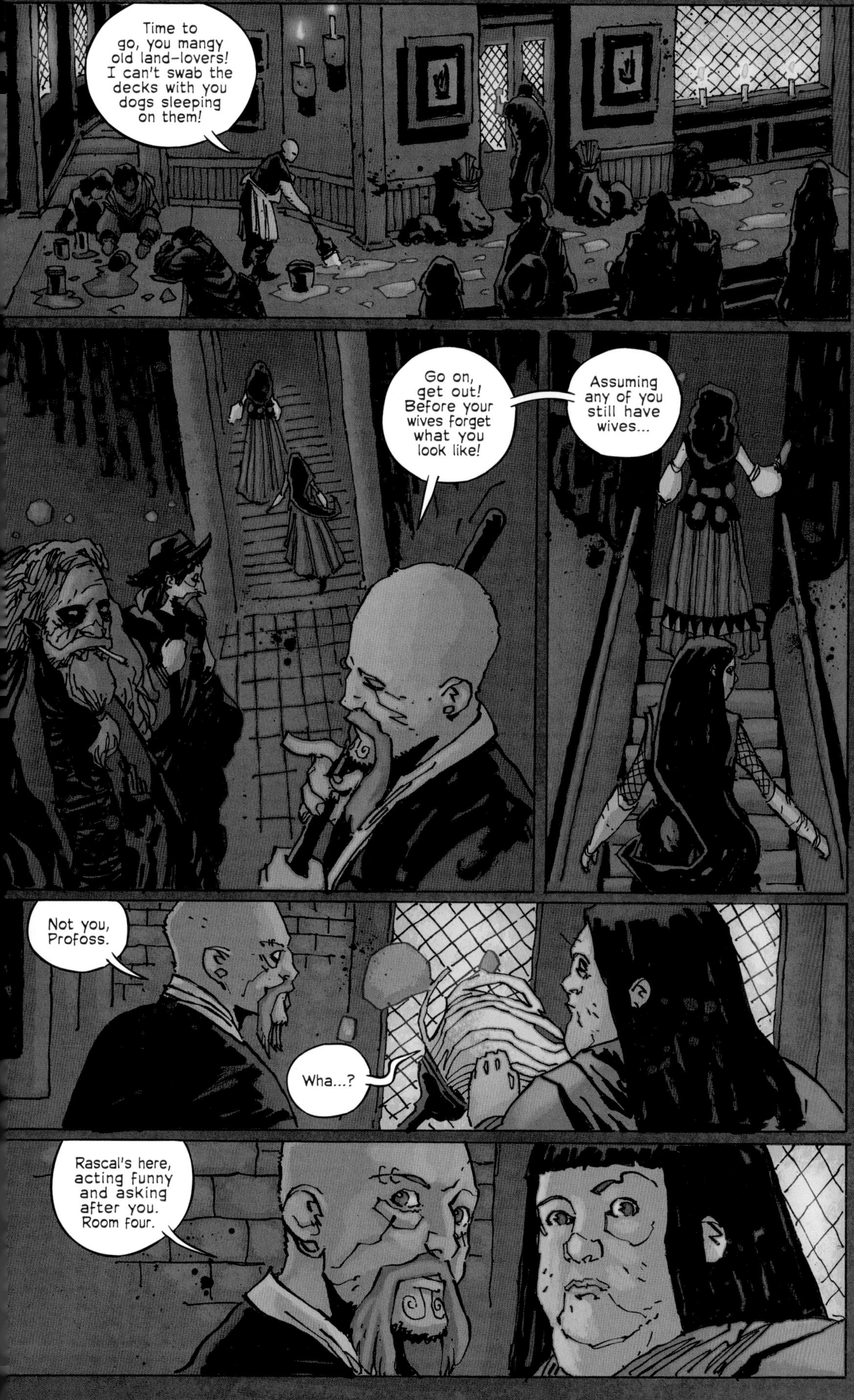
Time to go, you mangy old land-lovers! I can't swab the decks with you dogs sleeping on them!
Go on, get out! Before your wives forget what you look like!
Assuming any of you still have wives...
Not you, Profoss.
Wha...?
Rascal's here, acting funny and asking after you. Room four.

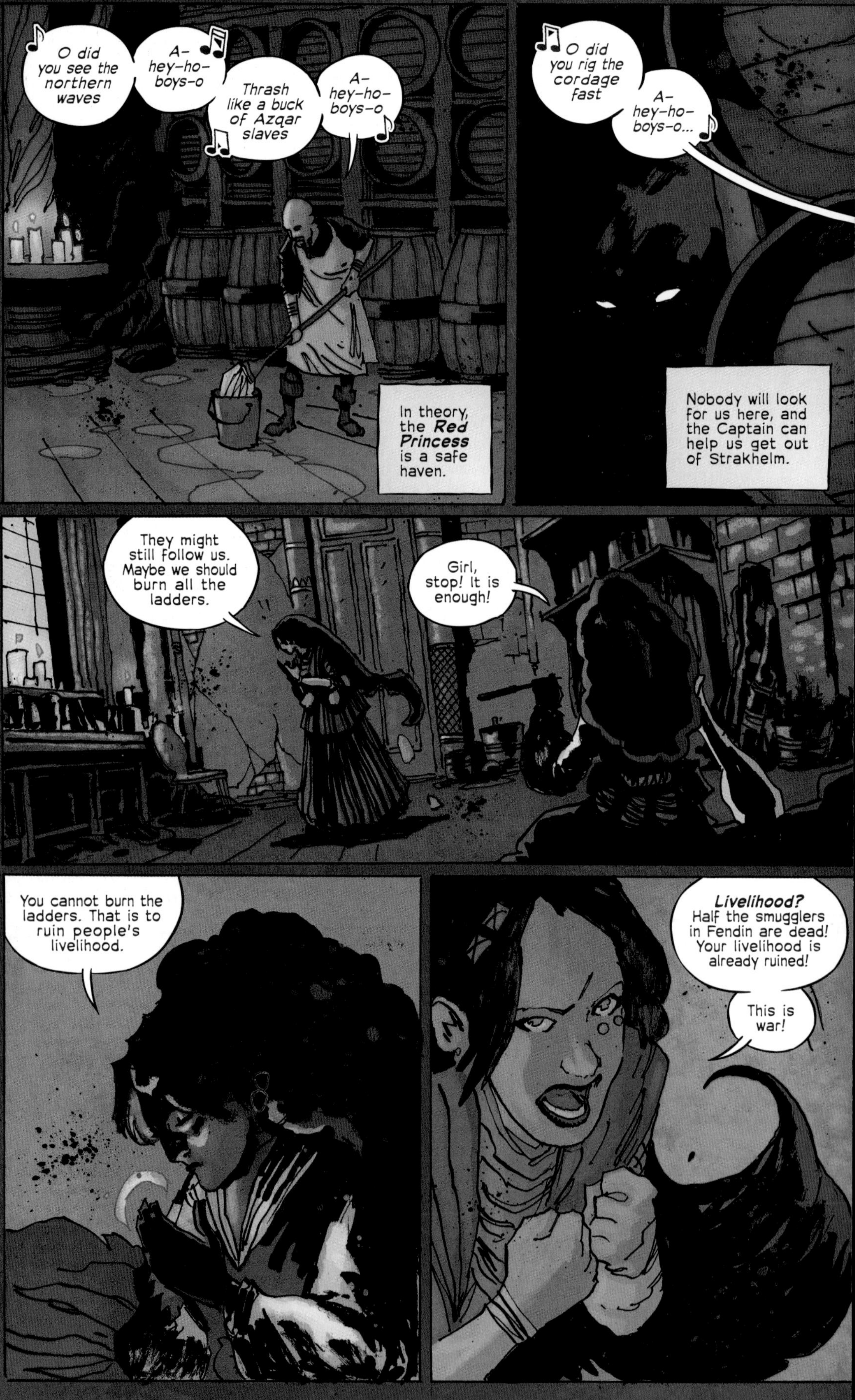
O did you see the northern waves
A-hey-ho-boys-o
Thrash like a buck of Azqar slaves
A-hey-ho-boys-o
In theory, the ***Red Princess*** is a safe haven.
O did you rig the cordage fast
A-hey-ho-boys-o...
Nobody will look for us here, and the Captain can help us get out of Strakhelm.
They might still follow us. Maybe we should burn all the ladders.
Girl, stop! It is enough!
You cannot burn the ladders. That is to ruin people's livelihood.
Livelihood? Half the smugglers in Fendin are dead! Your livelihood is already ruined!
This is war!

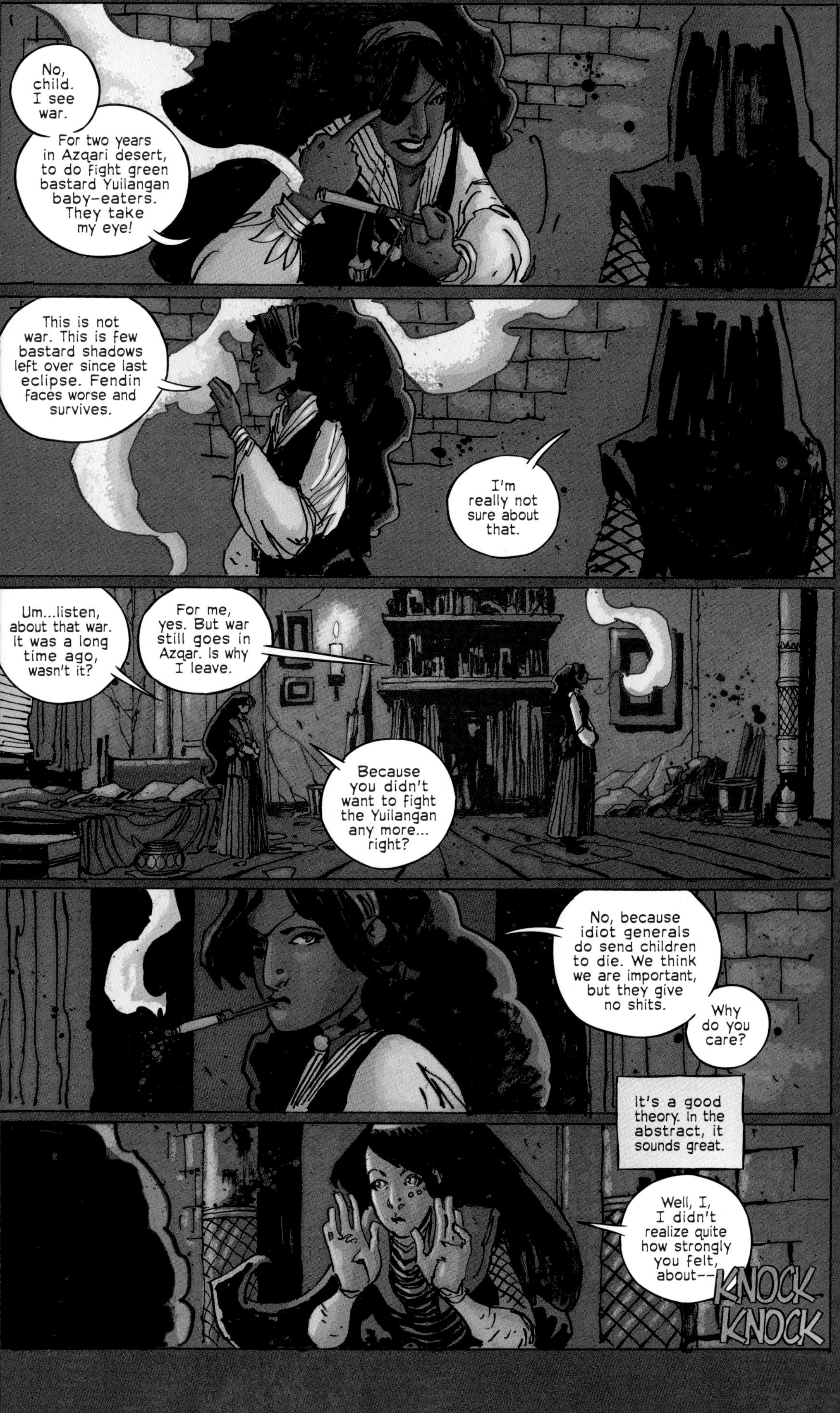
No, child. I see war.
For two years in Azqari desert, to do fight green bastard Yuilangan baby-eaters. They take my eye!
This is not war. This is few bastard shadows left over since last eclipse. Fendin faces worse and survives.
I'm really not sure about that.
Um...listen, about that war. It was a long time ago, wasn't it?
For me, yes. But war still goes in Azqar. Is why I leave.
Because you didn't want to fight the Yuilangan any more... right?
No, because idiot generals do send children to die. We think we are important, but they give no shits.
Why do you care?
It's a good theory. In the abstract, it sounds great.
Well, I, I didn't realize quite how strongly you felt, about--
KNOCK KNOCK

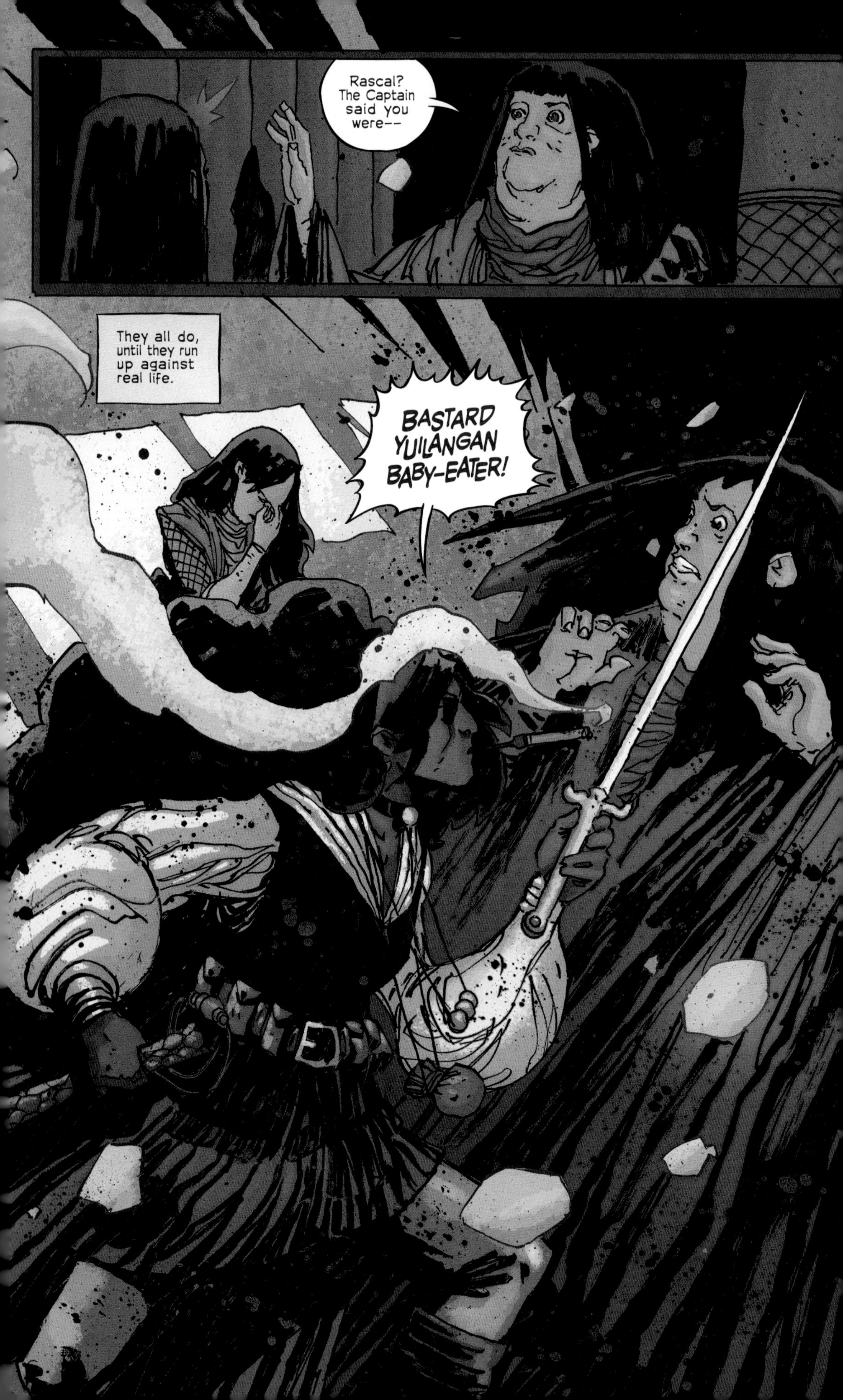

Rascal? The Captain said you were--
They all do, until they run up against real life.
BASTARD YUILANGAN BABY-EATER!

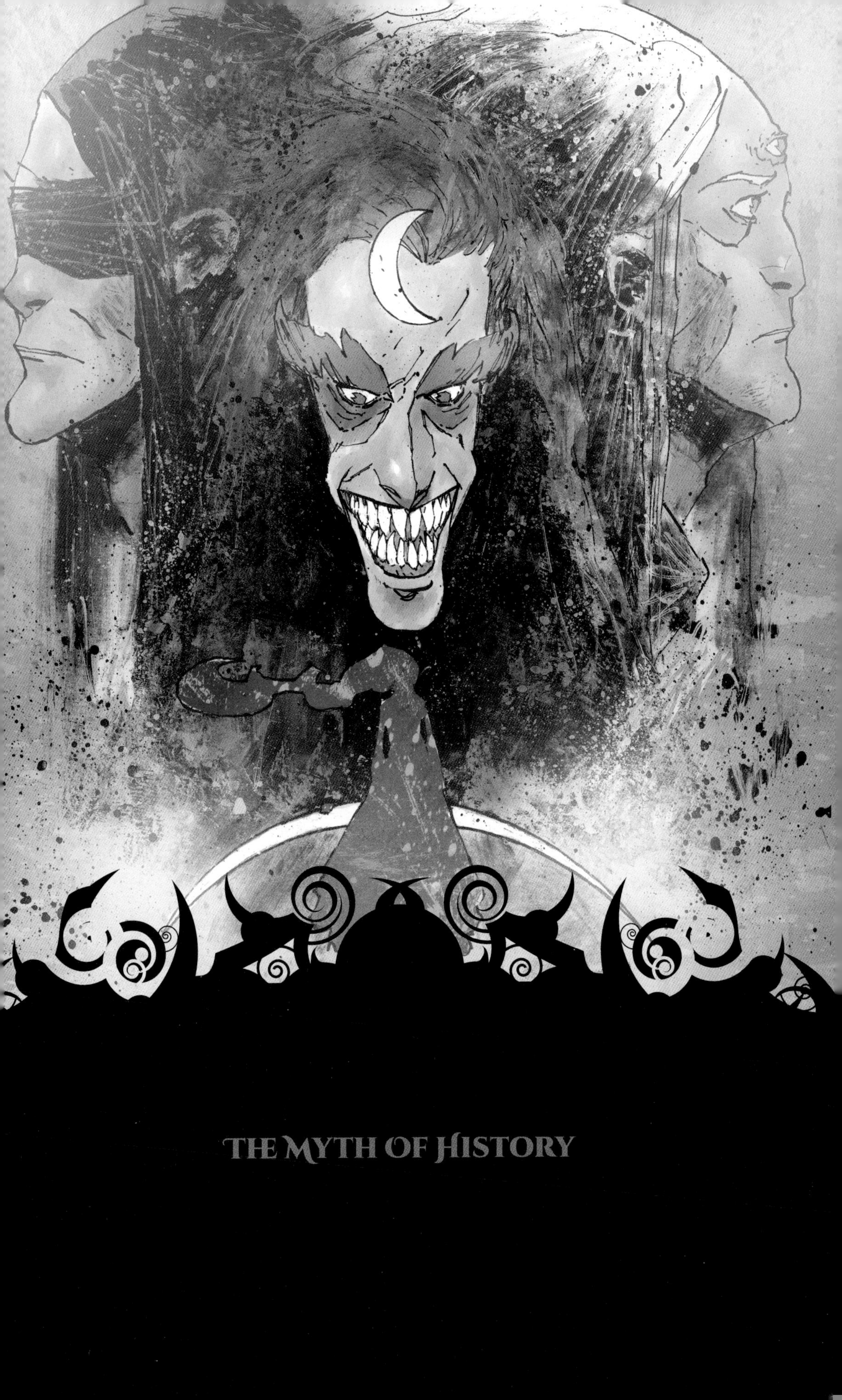

THE MYTH OF HISTORY

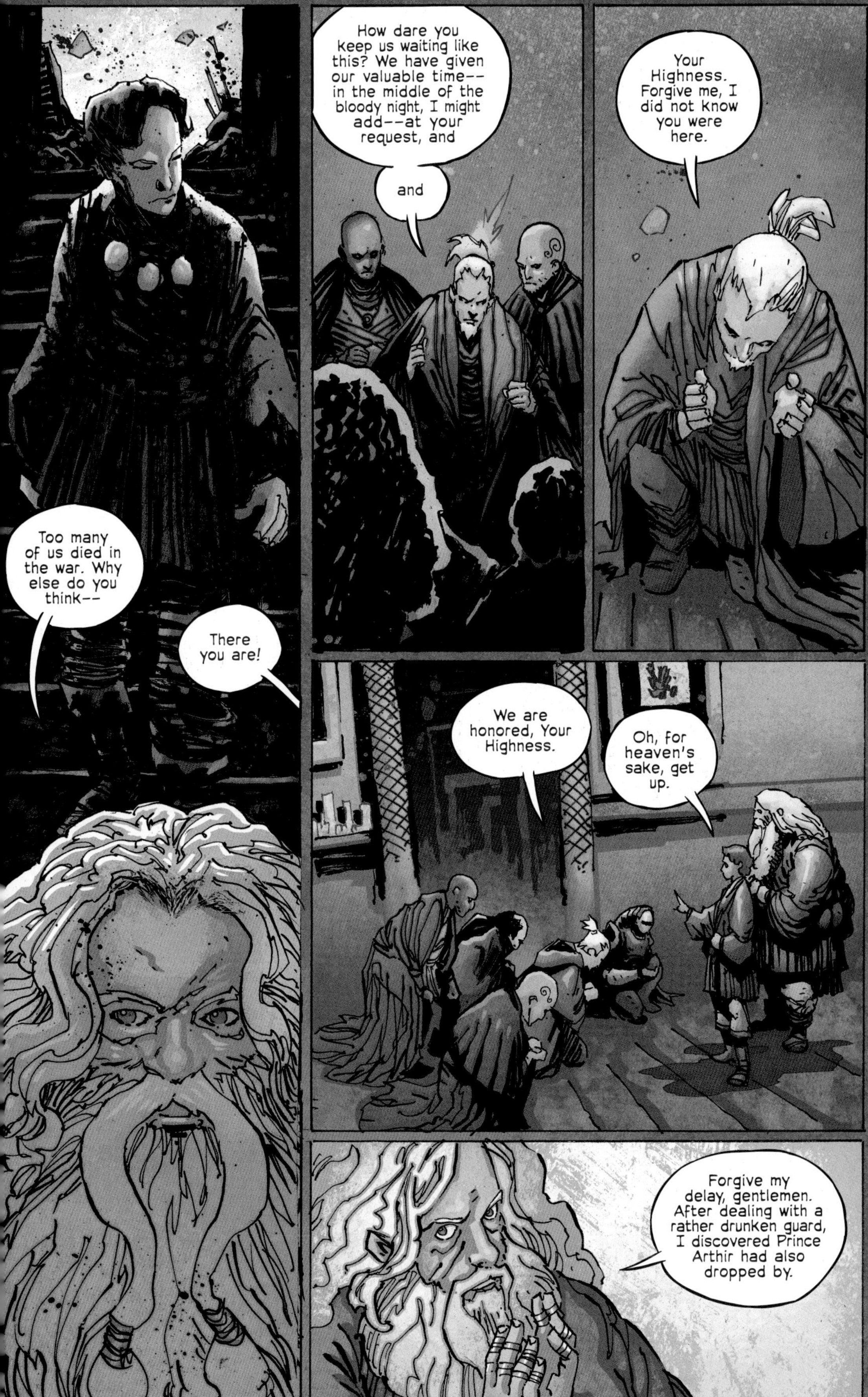
How dare you keep us waiting like this? We have given our valuable time-- in the middle of the bloody night, I might add--at your request, and
and
Your Highness. Forgive me, I did not know you were here.
Too many of us died in the war. Why else do you think--
There you are!
We are honored, Your Highness.
Oh, for heaven's sake, get up.
Forgive my delay, gentlemen. After dealing with a rather drunken guard, I discovered Prince Arthir had also dropped by.

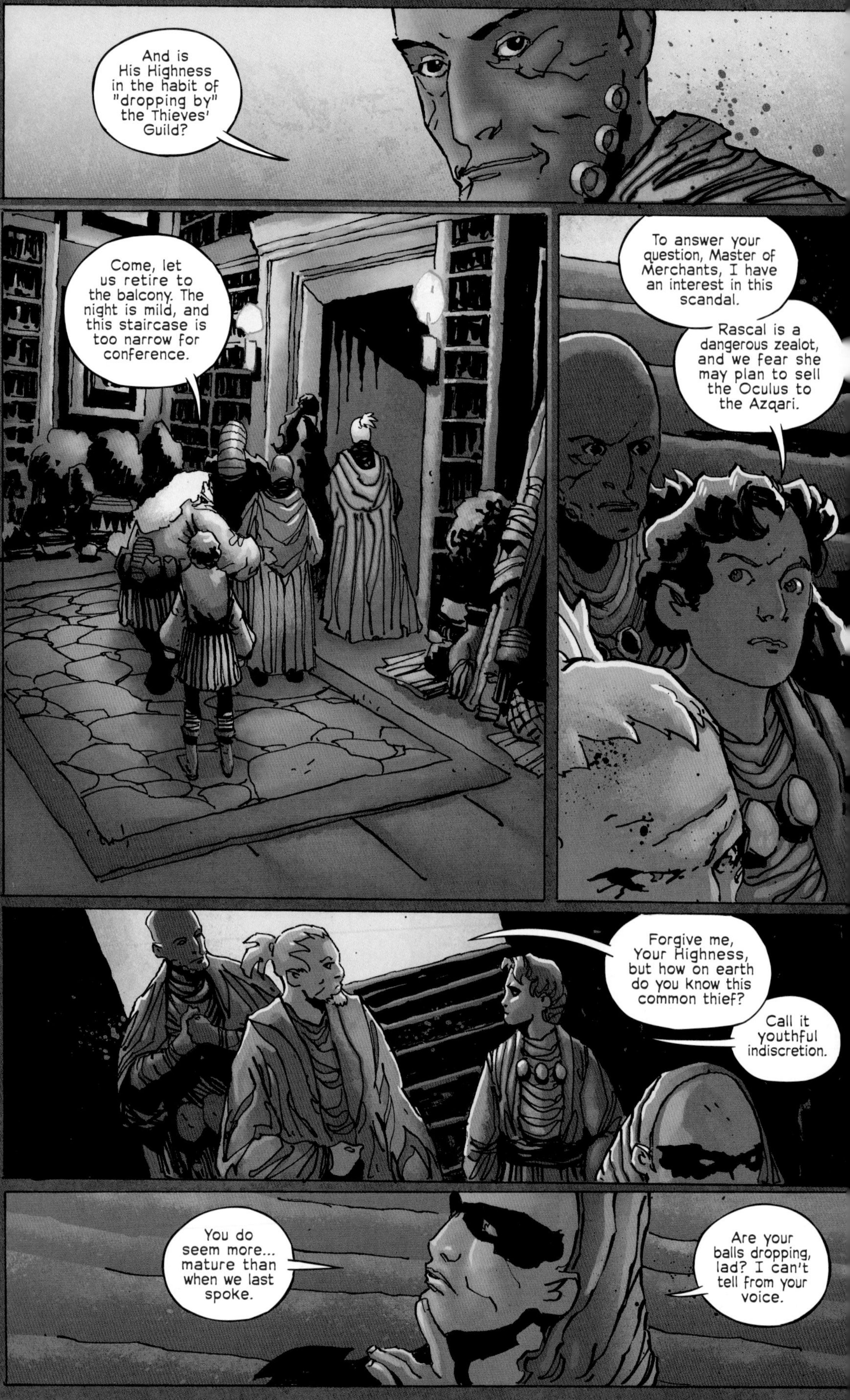
And is His Highness in the habit of "dropping by" the Thieves' Guild?
Come, let us retire to the balcony. The night is mild, and this staircase is too narrow for conference.
To answer your question, Master of Merchants, I have an interest in this scandal.
Rascal is a dangerous zealot, and we fear she may plan to sell the Oculus to the Azqari.
Forgive me, Your Highness, but how on earth do you know this common thief?
Call it youthful indiscretion.
You do seem more... mature than when we last spoke.
Are your balls dropping, lad? I can't tell from your voice.

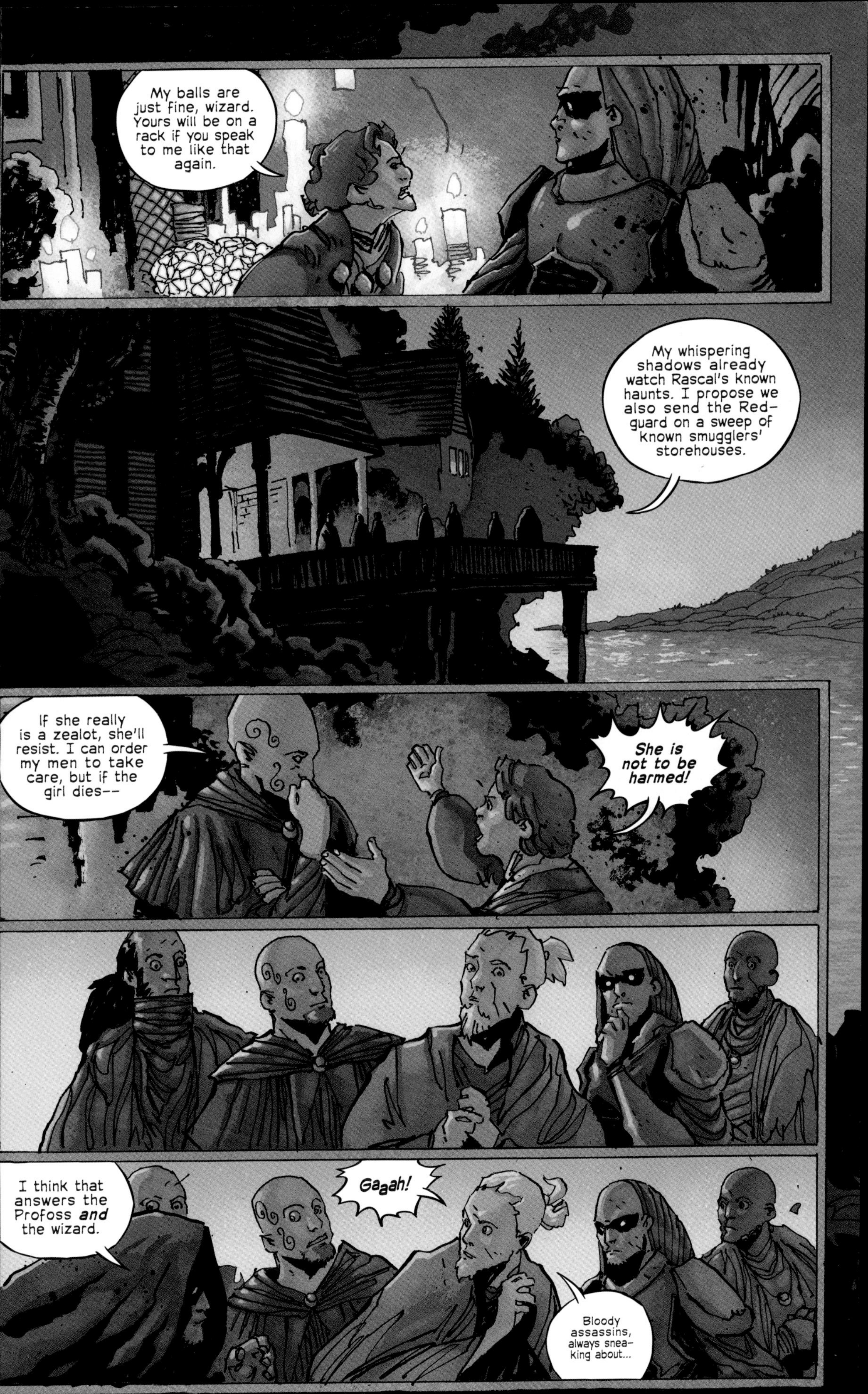
My balls are just fine, wizard. Yours will be on a rack if you speak to me like that again.
My whispering shadows already watch Rascal's known haunts. I propose we also send the Red-guard on a sweep of known smugglers' storehouses.
If she really is a zealot, she'll resist. I can order my men to take care, but if the girl dies--
She is not to be harmed!
I think that answers the Profoss *and* the wizard.
Gaaah!
Bloody assassins, always snea-king about...

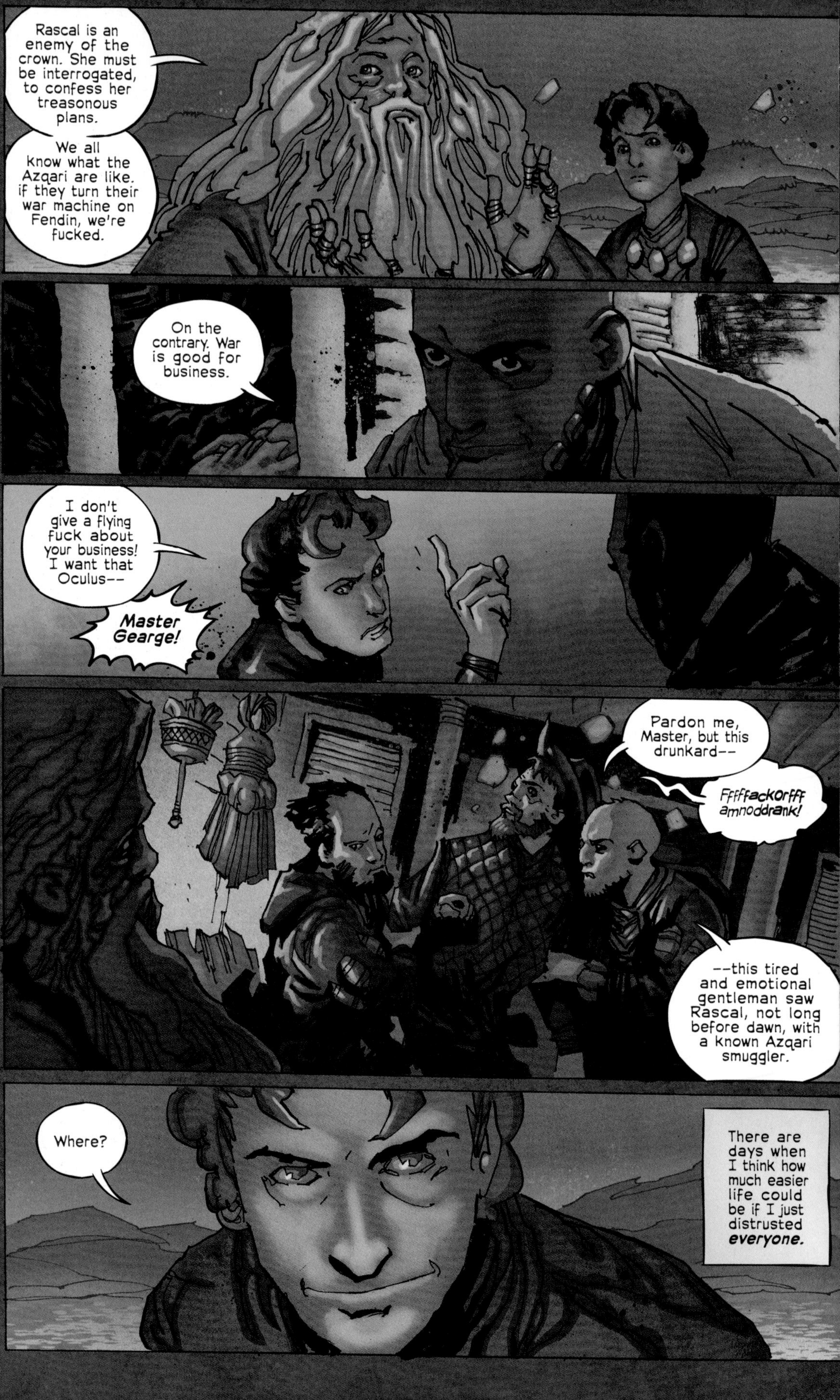
Rascal is an enemy of the crown. She must be interrogated, to confess her treasonous plans.
We all know what the Azqari are like. if they turn their war machine on Fendin, we're fucked.
On the contrary. War is good for business.
I don't give a flying fuck about your business! I want that Oculus--
Master Gearge!
Pardon me, Master, but this drunkard--
Fffffackorfff amnoddrank!
--this tired and emotional gentleman saw Rascal, not long before dawn, with a known Azqari smuggler.
Where?
There are days when I think how much easier life could be if I just distrusted everyone.

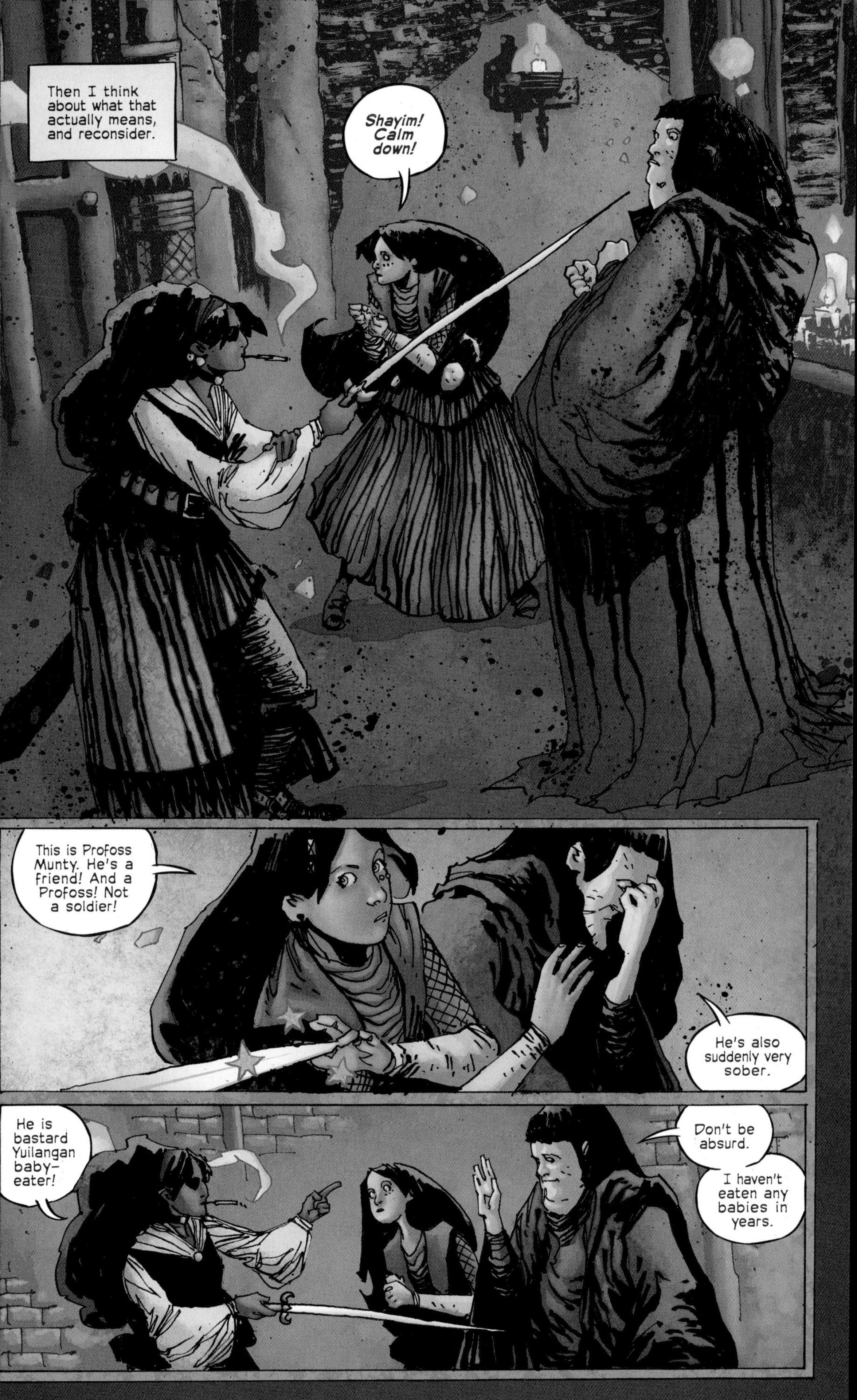
Then I think about what that actually means, and reconsider.
Shayim! Calm down!
This is Profoss Munty. He's a friend! And a Profoss! Not a soldier!
He's also suddenly very sober.
He is bastard Yuilangan baby-eater!
Don't be absurd.
I haven't eaten any babies in years.

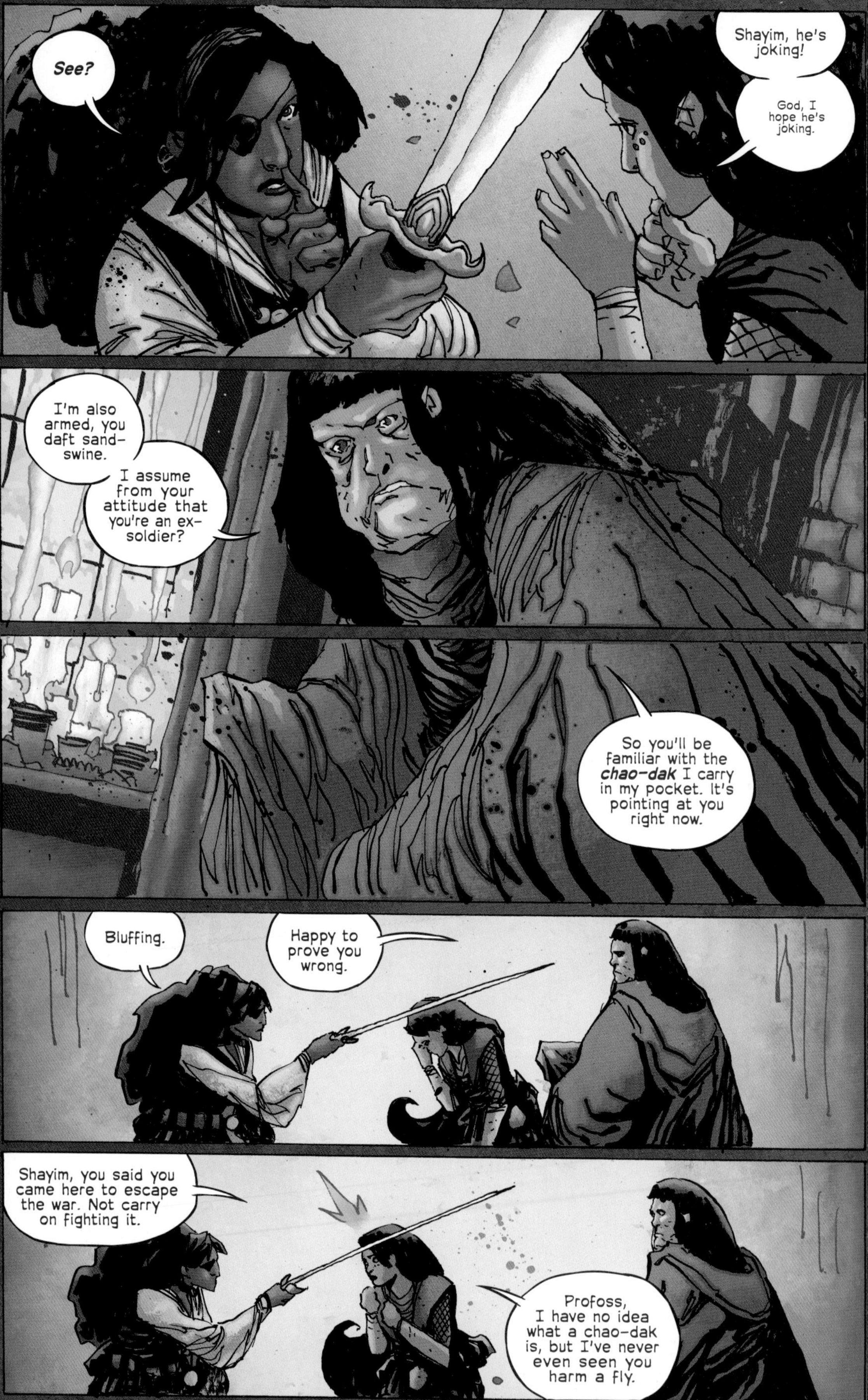
See?
Shayim, he's joking!
God, I hope he's joking.
I'm also armed, you daft sand-swine.
I assume from your attitude that you're an ex-soldier?
So you'll be familiar with the *chao-dak* I carry in my pocket. It's pointing at you right now.
Bluffing.
Happy to prove you wrong.
Shayim, you said you came here to escape the war. Not carry on fighting it.
Profoss, I have no idea what a chao-dak is, but I've never even seen you harm a fly.

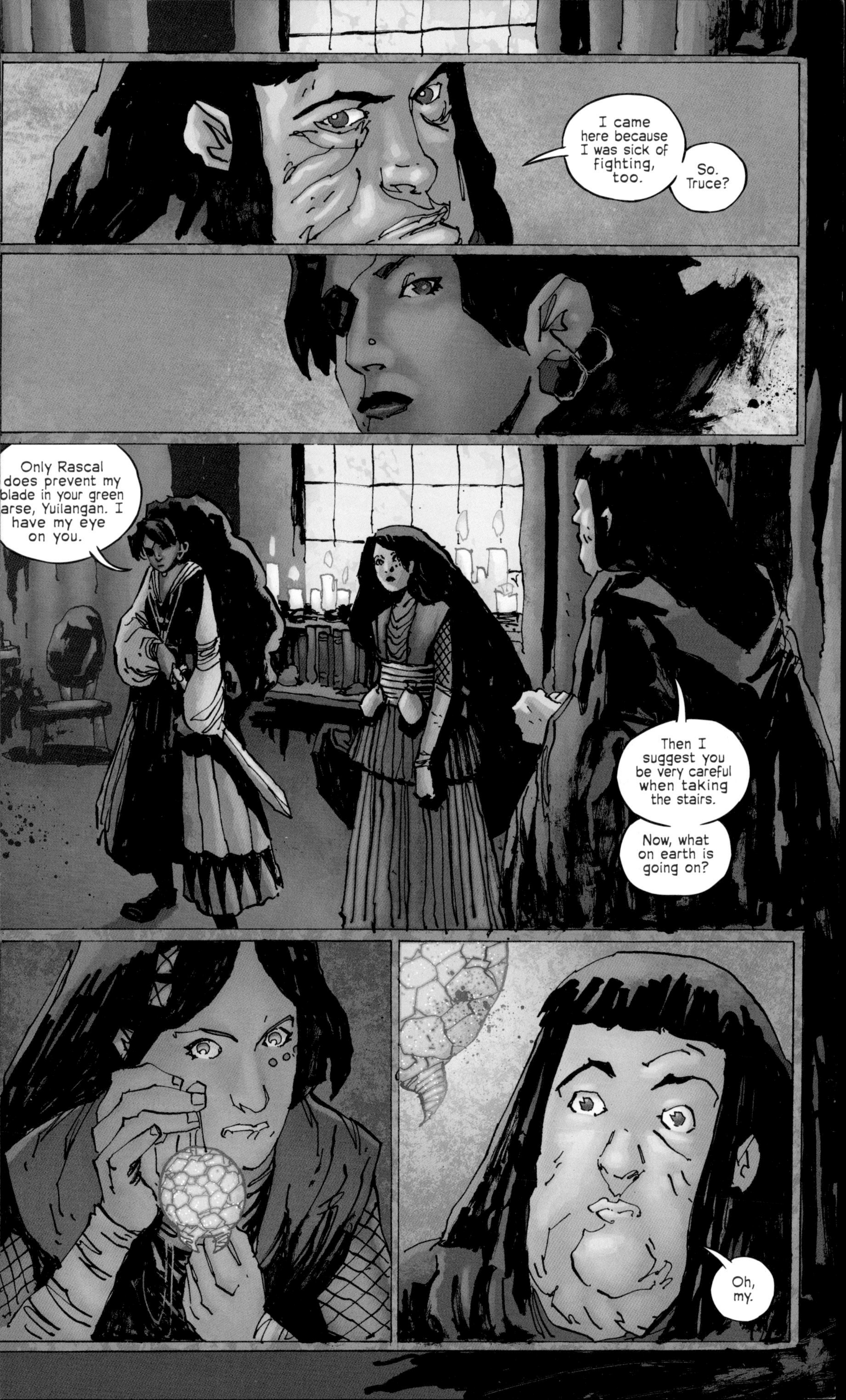
I came here because I was sick of fighting, too.
So. Truce?
Only Rascal does prevent my blade in your green arse, Yuilangan. I have my eye on you.
Then I suggest you be very careful when taking the stairs.
Now, what on earth is going on?
Oh, my.

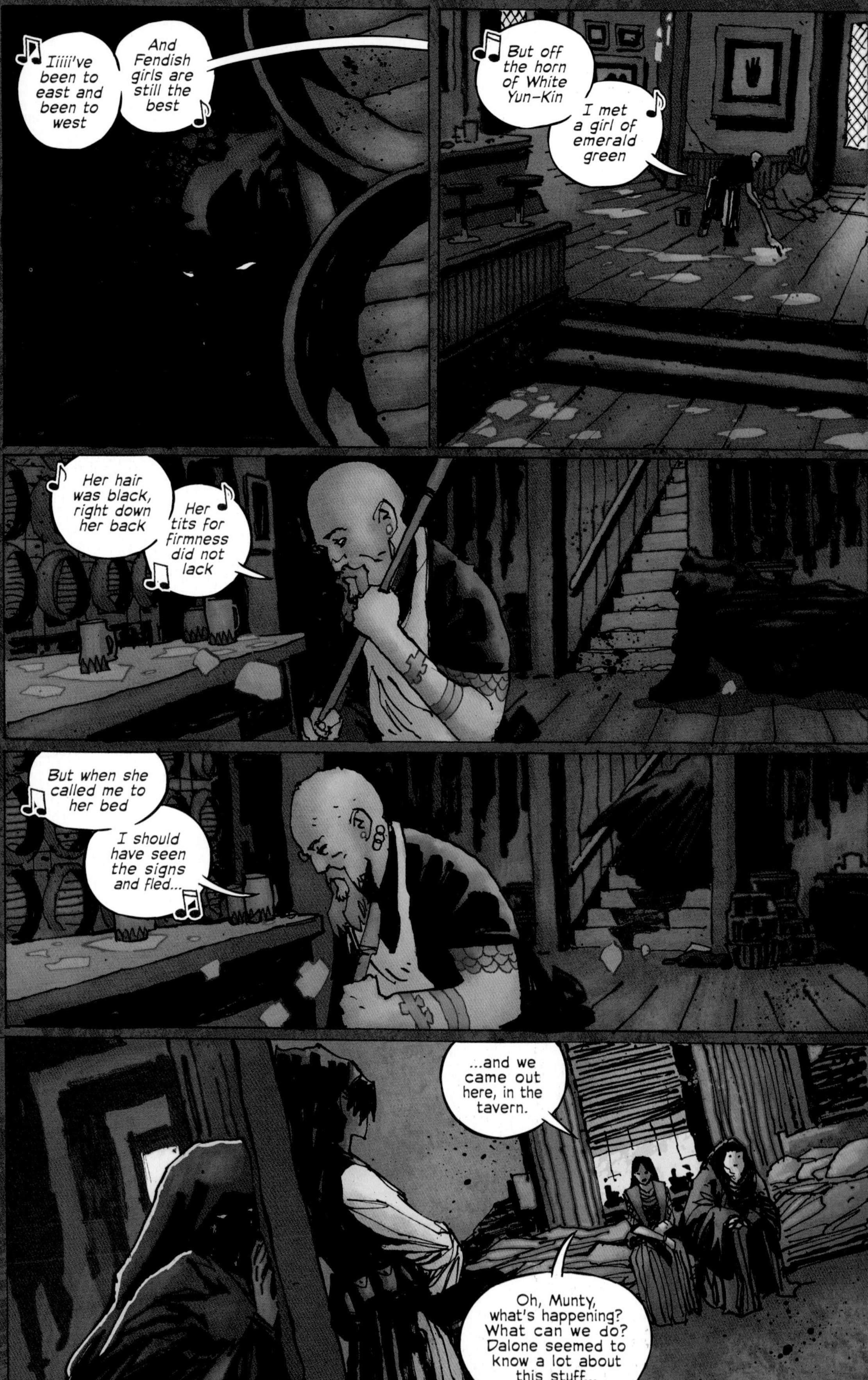
Iiiii've been to east and been to west
And Fendish girls are still the best
But off the horn of White Yun-Kin
I met a girl of emerald green
Her hair was black, right down her back
Her tits for firmness did not lack
But when she called me to her bed
I should have seen the signs and fled...
...and we came out here, in the tavern.
Oh, Munty, what's happening? What can we do? Dalone seemed to know a lot about this stuff...

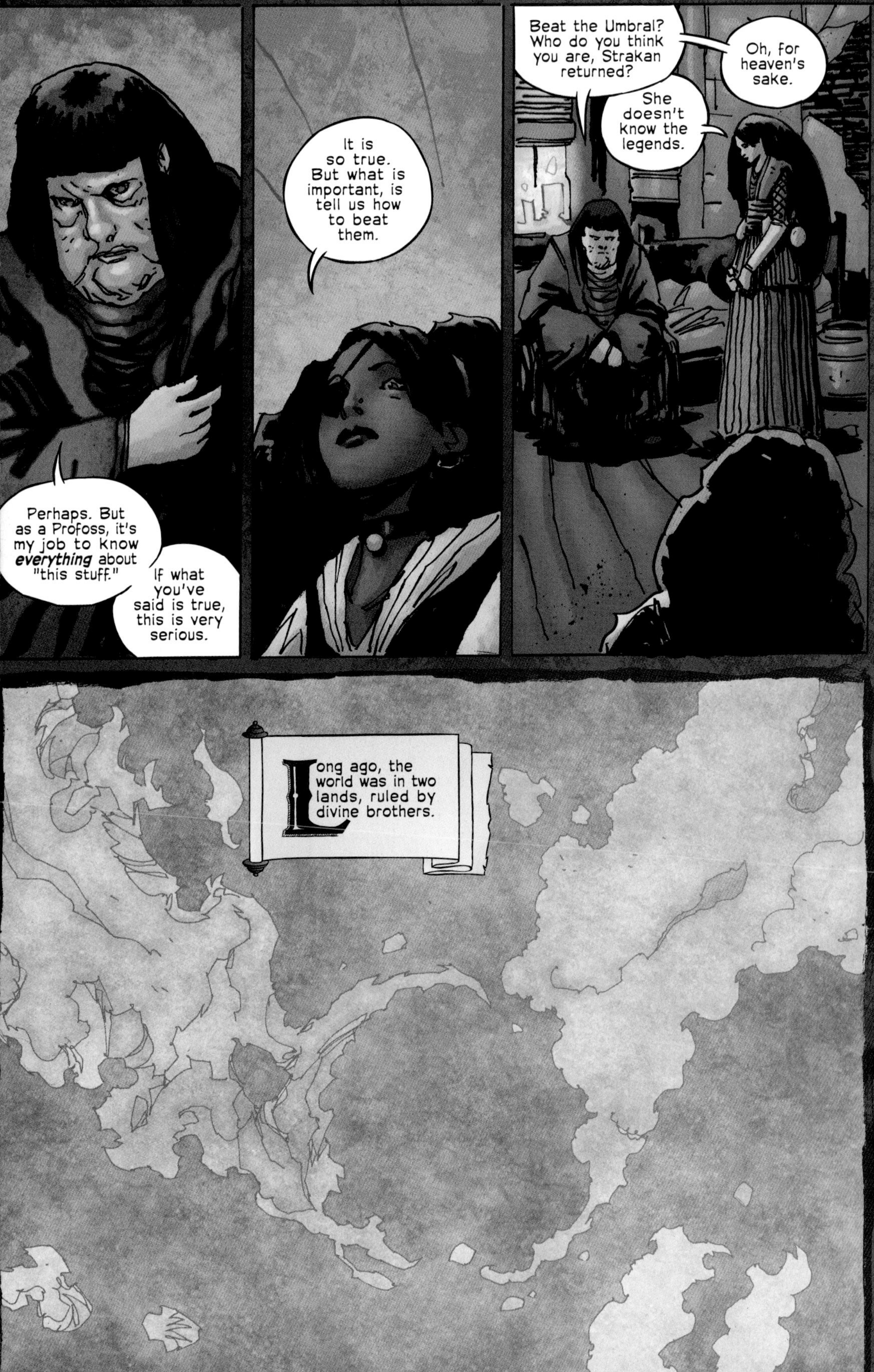
Perhaps. But as a Profoss, it's my job to know *everything* about "this stuff."
If what you've said is true, this is very serious.
It is so true. But what is important, is tell us how to beat them.
Beat the Umbral? Who do you think you are, Strakan returned?
Oh, for heaven's sake.
She doesn't know the legends.
Long ago, the world was in two lands, ruled by divine brothers.

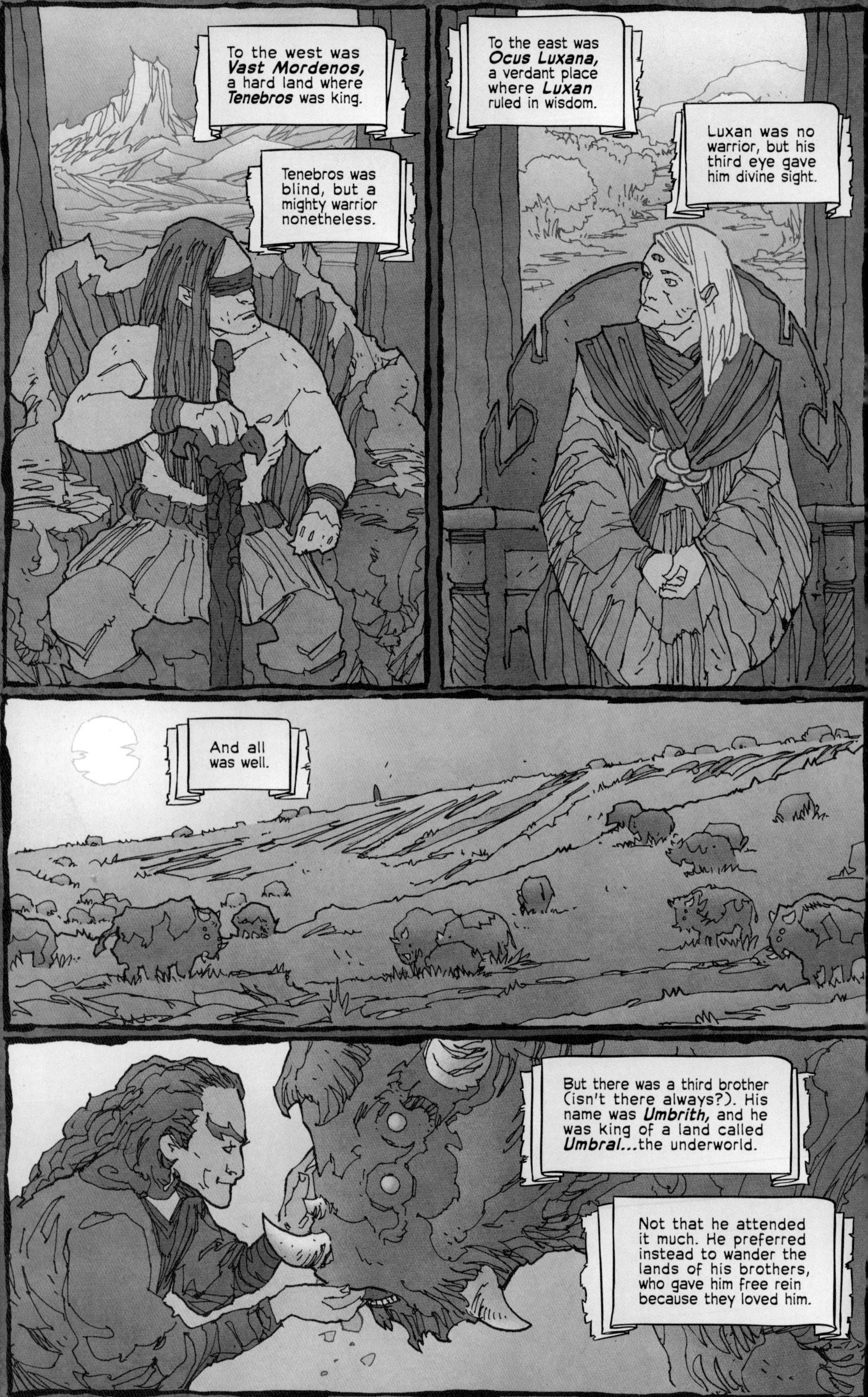
To the west was Vast Mordenos, a hard land where Tenebros was King.
Tenebros was blind, but a mighty warrior nonetheless.
To the east was Ocus Luxana, a verdant place where Luxan ruled in wisdom.
Luxan was no warrior, but his third eye gave him divine sight.
And all was well.
But there was a third brother (isn't there always?). His name was Umbrith, and he was king of a land called Umbral...the underworld.
Not that he attended it much. He preferred instead to wander the lands of his brothers, who gave him free rein because they loved him.

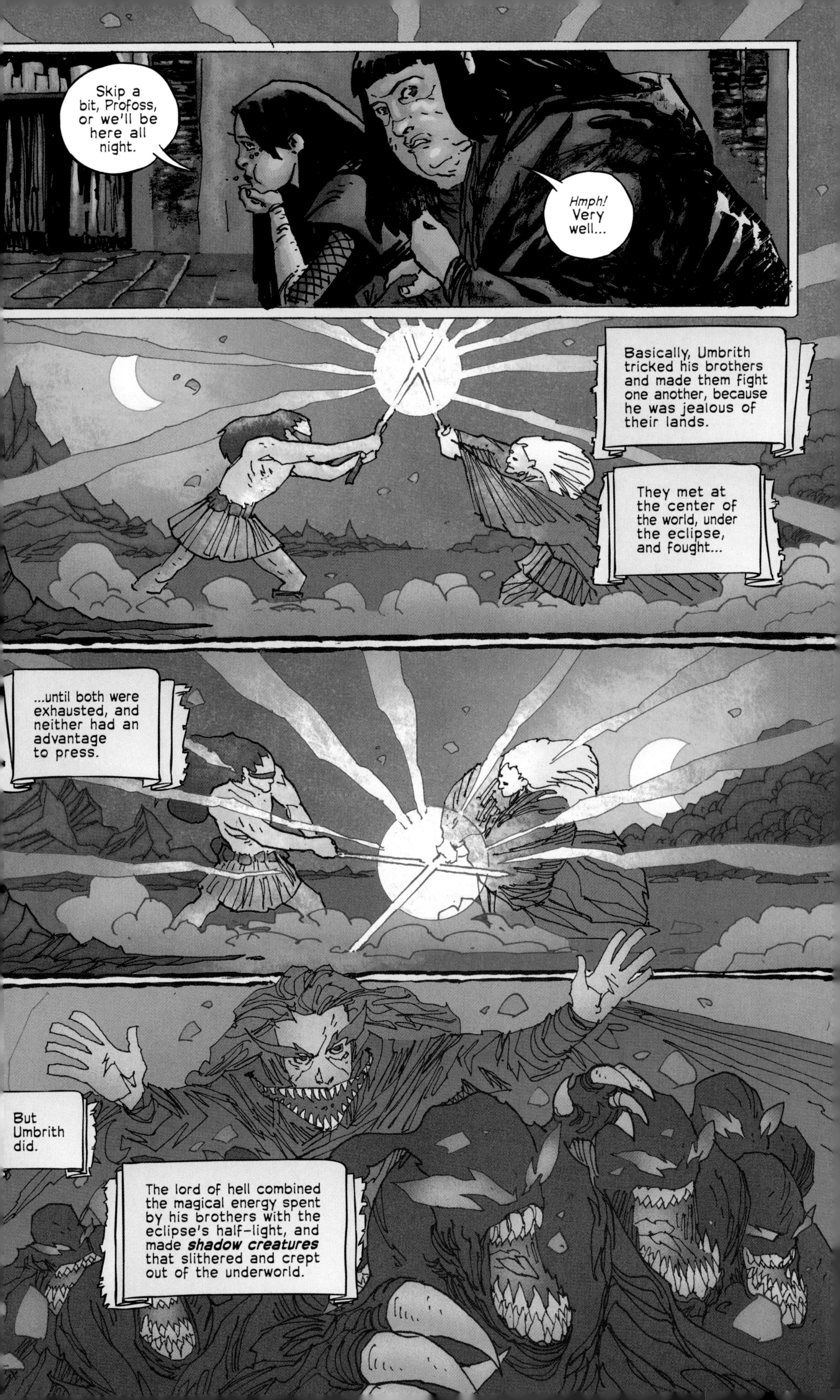

Skip a bit, Profoss, or we'll be here all night.
Hmph! Very well...
Basically, Umbrith tricked his brothers and made them fight one another, because he was jealous of their lands.
They met at the center of the world, under the eclipse, and fought...
...until both were exhausted, and neither had an advantage to press.
But Umbrith did.
The lord of hell combined the magical energy spent by his brothers with the eclipse's half-light, and made ***shadow creatures*** that slithered and crept out of the underworld.

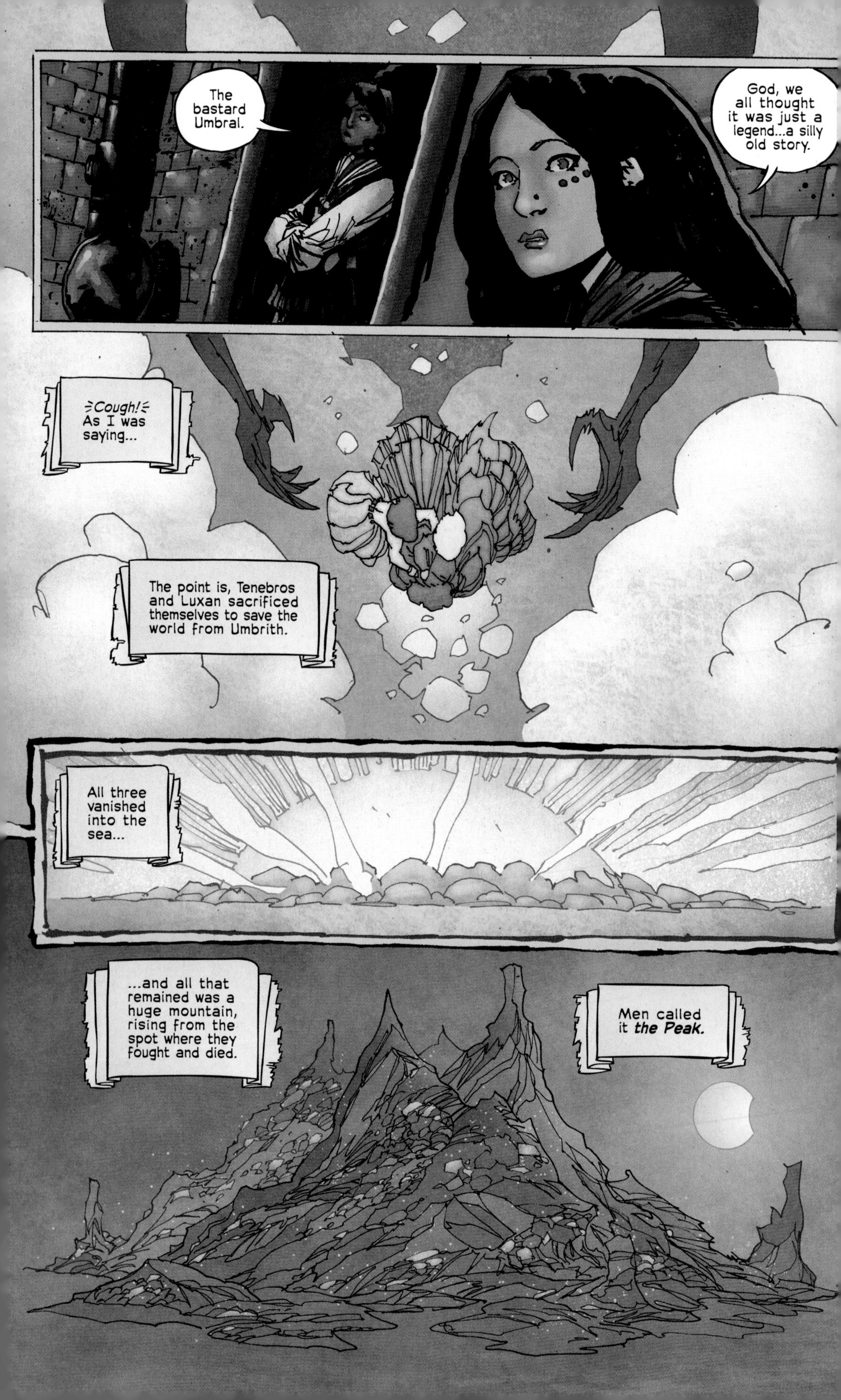

The bastard Umbral.
God, we all thought it was just a legend...a silly old story.
≡Cough!≡ As I was saying...
The point is, Tenebros and Luxan sacrificed themselves to save the world from Umbrith.
All three vanished into the sea...
...and all that remained was a huge mountain, rising from the spot where they fought and died.
Men called it *the Peak.*

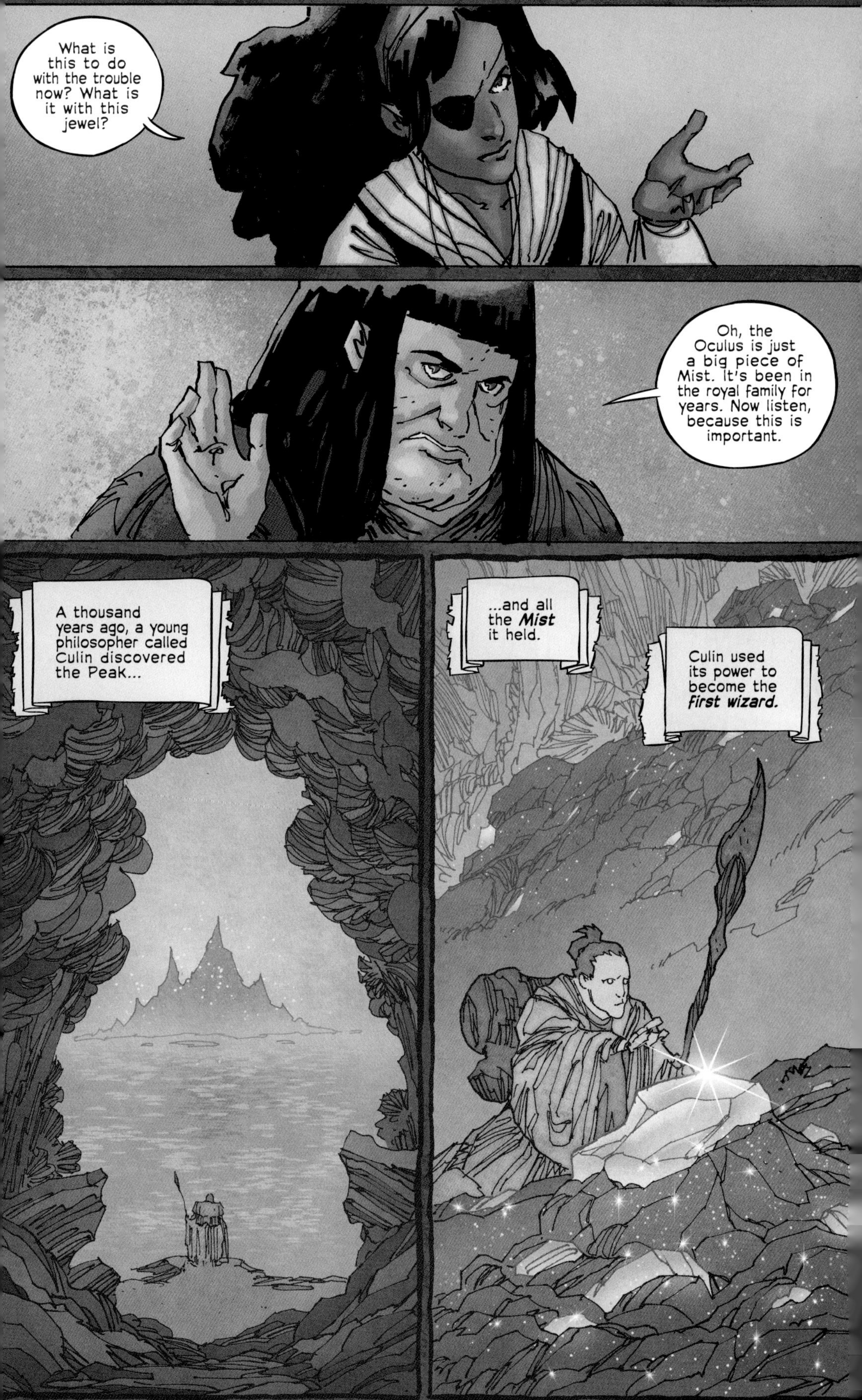
What is this to do with the trouble now? What is it with this jewel?
Oh, the Oculus is just a big piece of Mist. It's been in the royal family for years. Now listen, because this is important.
A thousand years ago, a young philosopher called Culin discovered the Peak...
...and all the *Mist* it held.
Culin used its power to become the *first wizard.*

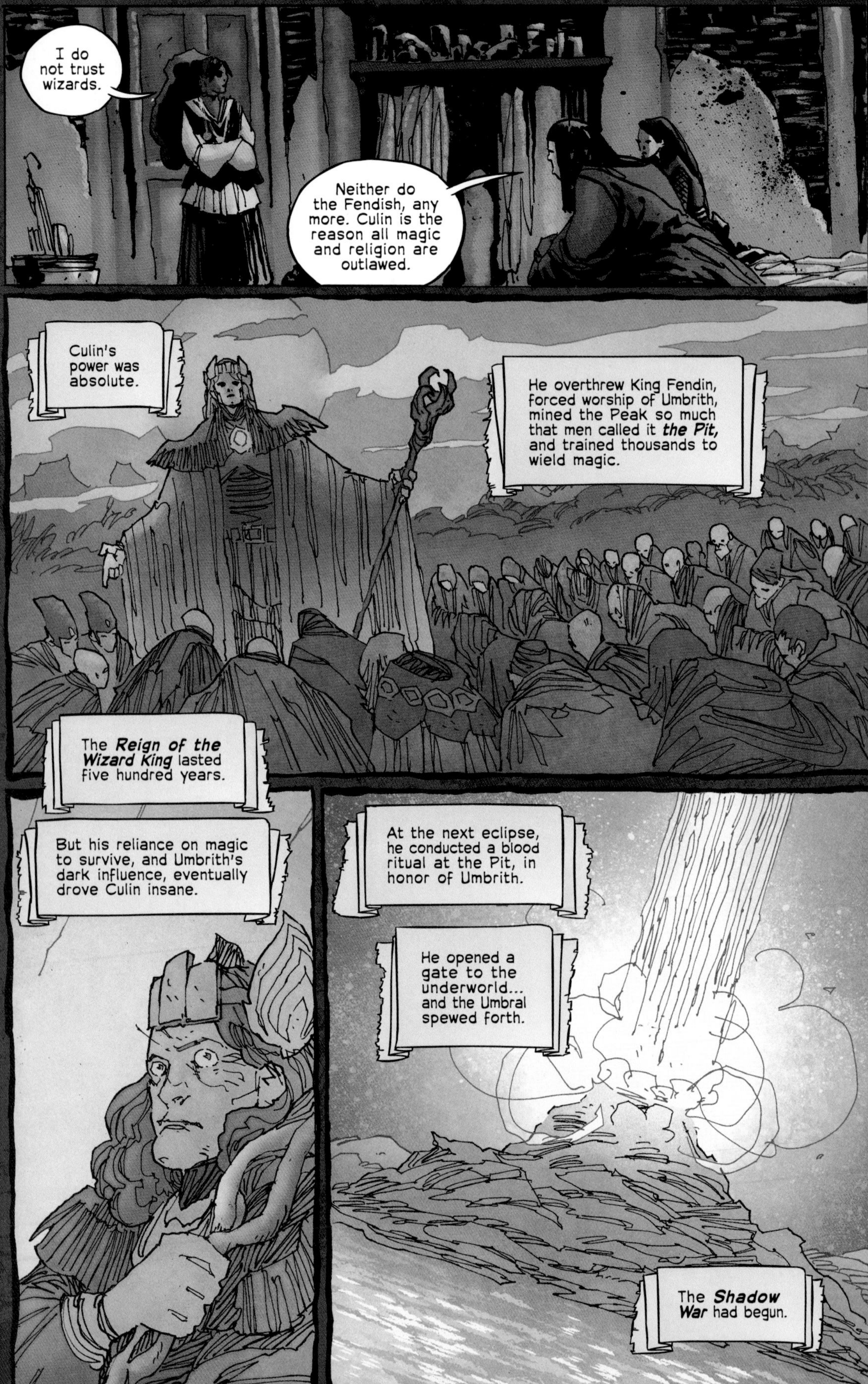
I do not trust wizards.
Neither do the Fendish, any more. Culin is the reason all magic and religion are outlawed.
Culin's power was absolute.
He overthrew King Fendin, forced worship of Umbrith, mined the Peak so much that men called it the Pit, and trained thousands to wield magic.
The Reign of the Wizard King lasted five hundred years.
But his reliance on magic to survive, and Umbrith's dark influence, eventually drove Culin insane.
At the next eclipse, he conducted a blood ritual at the Pit, in honor of Umbrith.
He opened a gate to the underworld... and the Umbral spewed forth.
The Shadow War had begun.

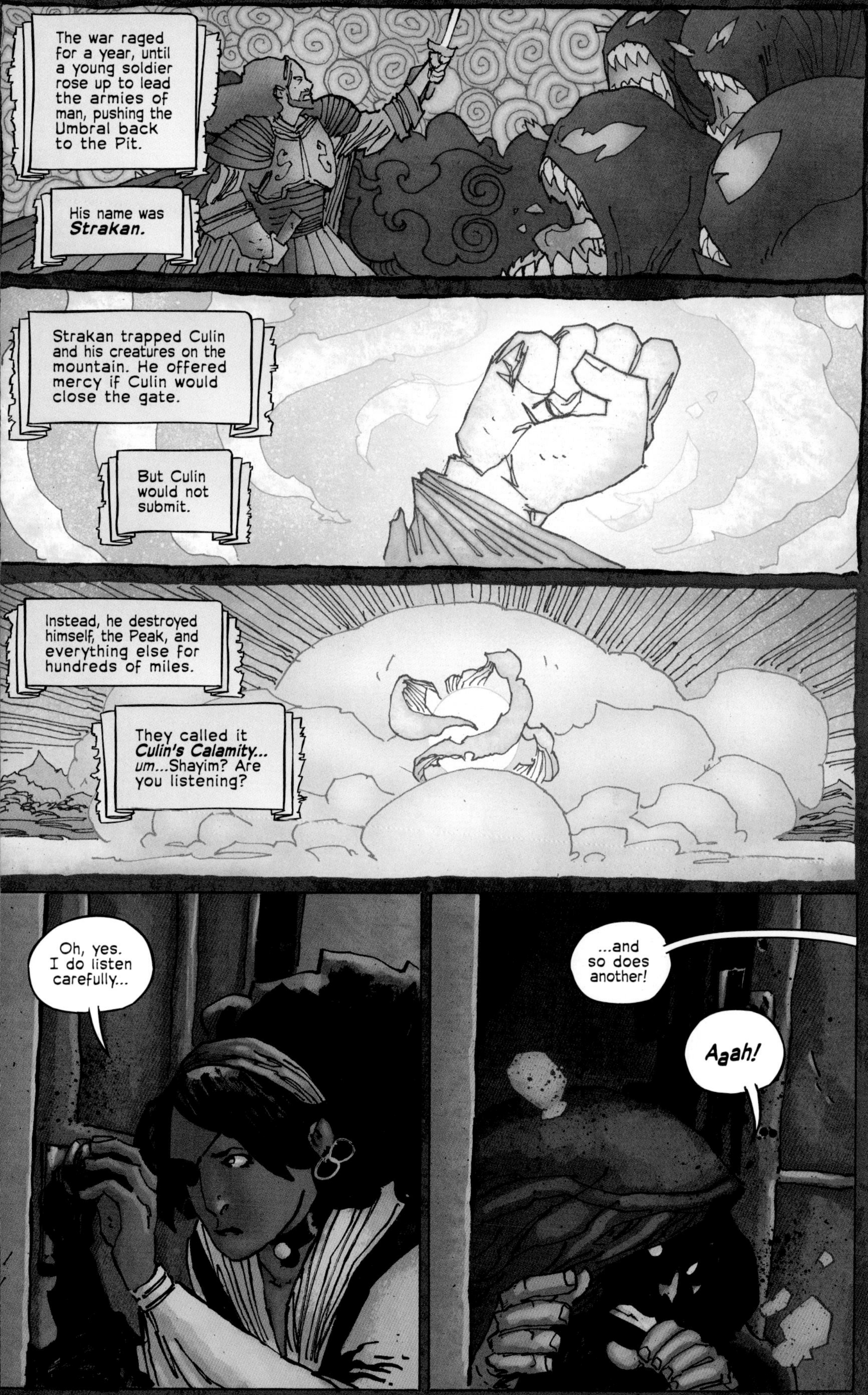

The war raged for a year, until a young soldier rose up to lead the armies of man, pushing the Umbral back to the Pit.
His name was ***Strakan.***
Strakan trapped Culin and his creatures on the mountain. He offered mercy if Culin would close the gate.
But Culin would not submit.
Instead, he destroyed himself, the Peak, and everything else for hundreds of miles.
They called it ***Culin's Calamity...*** *um...*Shayim? Are you listening?
Oh, yes. I do listen carefully...
...and so does another!
Aaah!

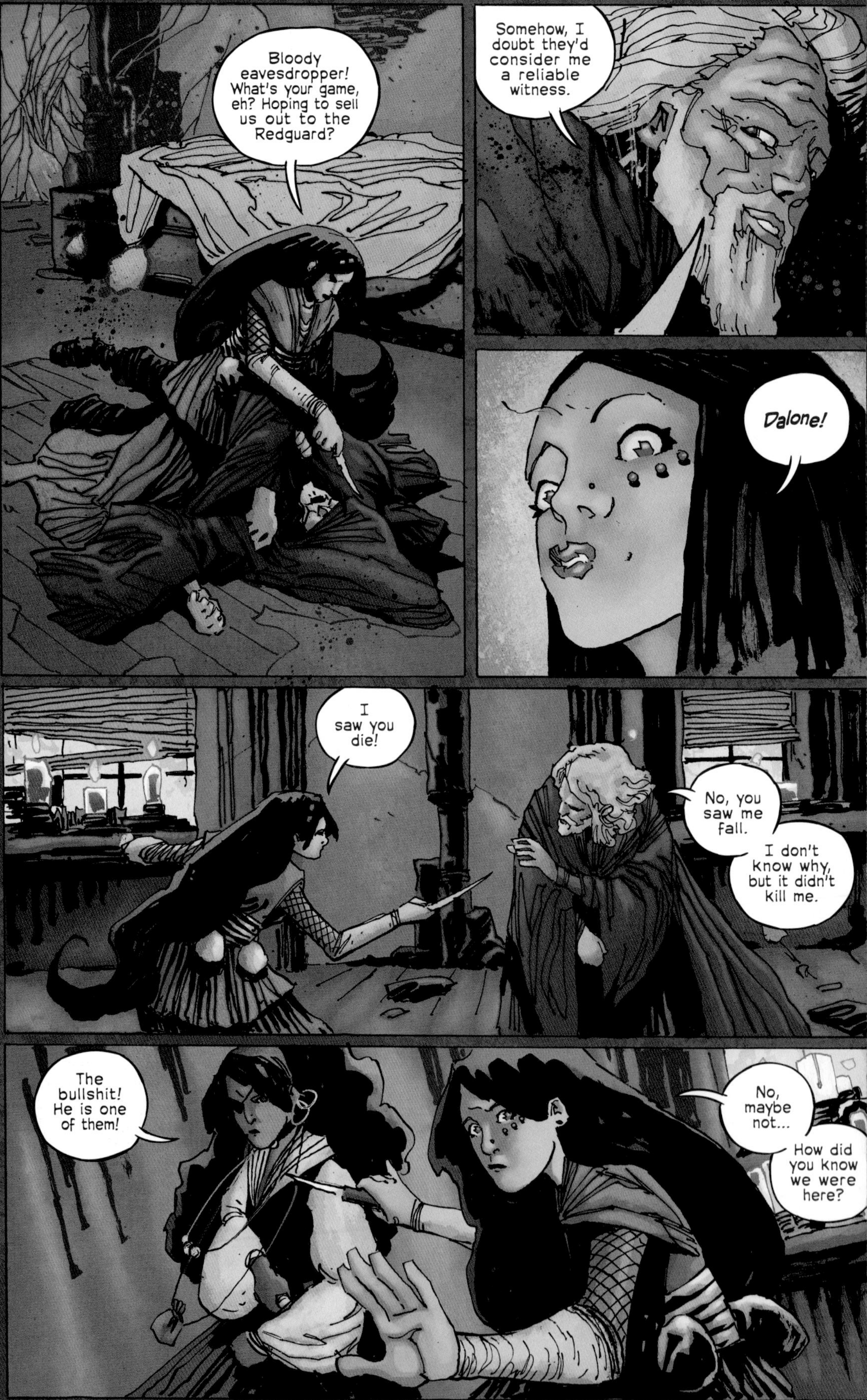
Bloody eavesdropper! What's your game, eh? Hoping to sell us out to the Redguard?
Somehow, I doubt they'd consider me a reliable witness.
Dalone!
I saw you die!
No, you saw me fall.
I don't know why, but it didn't kill me.
The bullshit! He is one of them!
No, maybe not...
How did you know we were here?

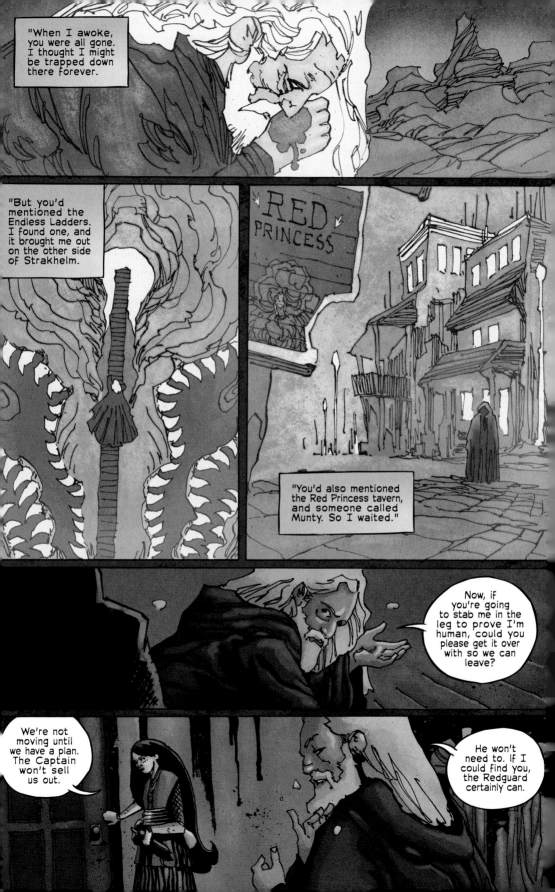

"When I awoke, you were all gone. I thought I might be trapped down there forever."

"But you'd mentioned the Endless Ladders. I found one, and it brought me out on the other side of Strakhelm.

RED PRINCESS

"You'd also mentioned the Red Princess tavern, and someone called Munty. So I waited."

Now, if you're going to stab me in the leg to prove I'm human, could you please get it over with so we can leave?

We're not moving until we have a plan. The Captain won't sell us out.

He won't need to. If I could find you, the Redguard certainly can.

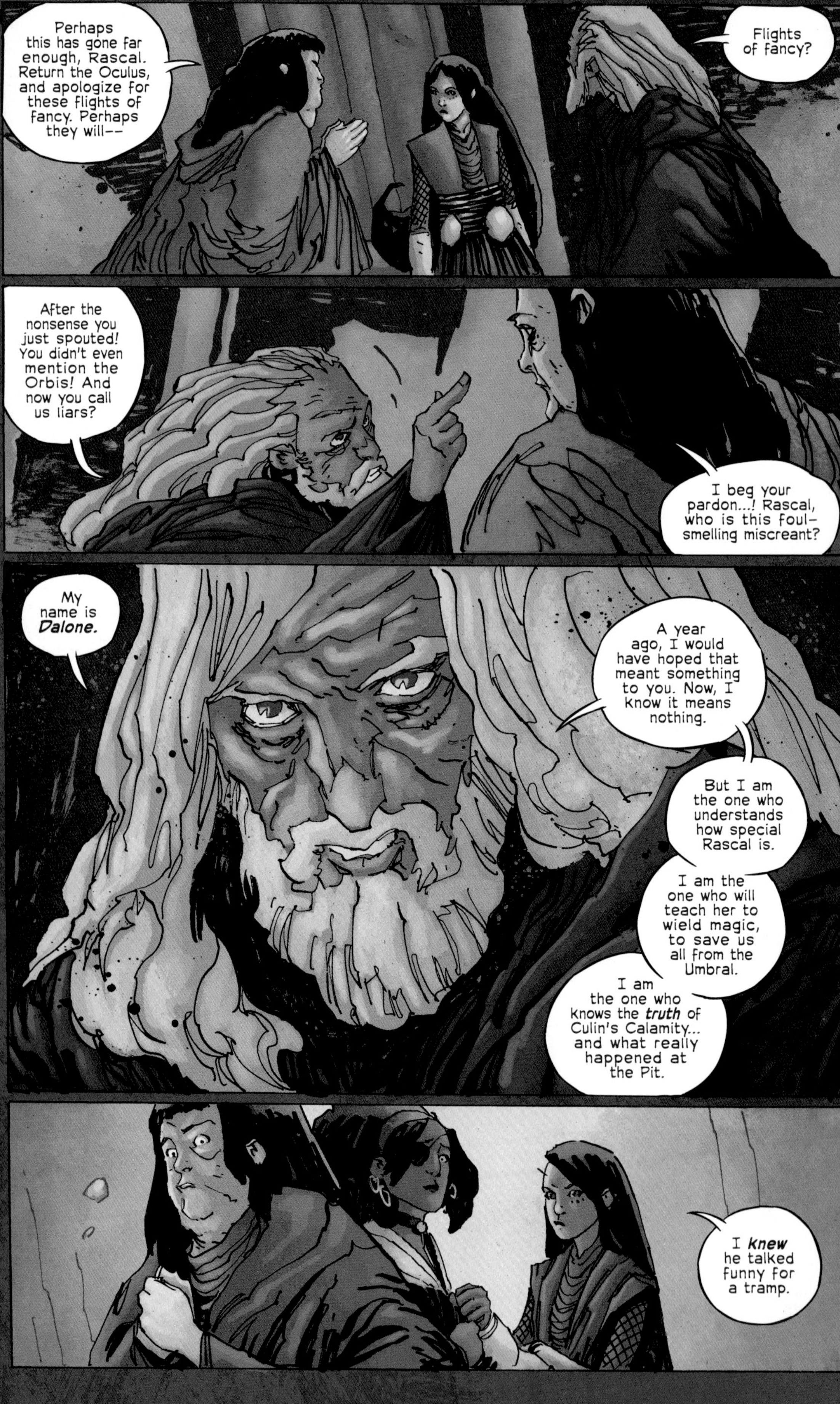
Perhaps this has gone far enough, Rascal. Return the Oculus, and apologize for these flights of fancy. Perhaps they will--
Flights of fancy?
After the nonsense you just spouted! You didn't even mention the Orbis! And now you call us liars?
I beg your pardon...! Rascal, who is this foul-smelling miscreant?
My name is *Dalone.*
A year ago, I would have hoped that meant something to you. Now, I know it means nothing.
But I am the one who understands how special Rascal is.
I am the one who will teach her to wield magic, to save us all from the Umbral.
I am the one who knows the *truth* of Culin's Calamity... and what really happened at the Pit.
I *knew* he talked funny for a tramp.

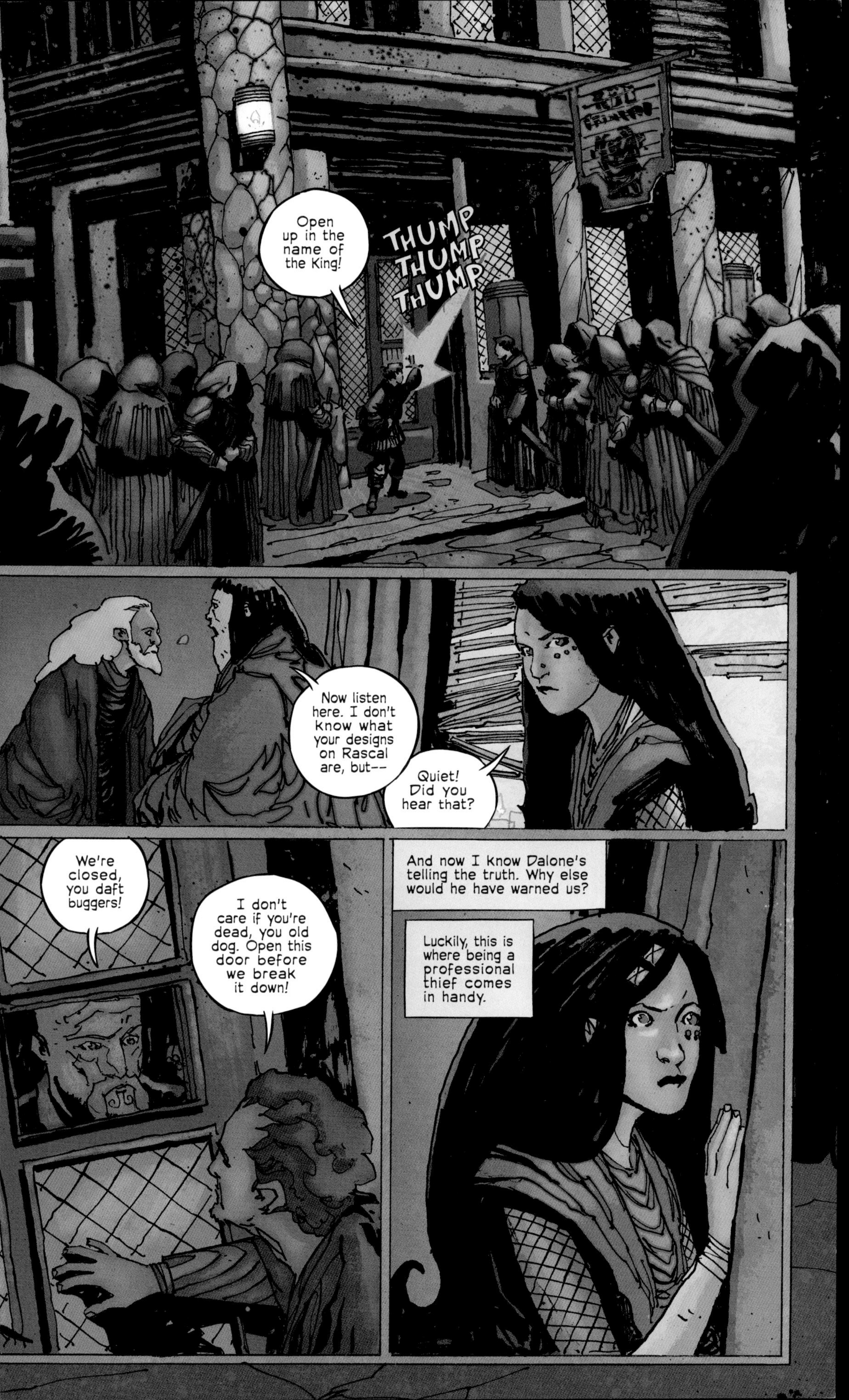

Open up in the name of the King!
THUMP THUMP THUMP
Now listen here. I don't know what your designs on Rascal are, but--
Quiet! Did you hear that?
We're closed, you daft buggers!
I don't care if you're dead, you old dog. Open this door before we break it down!
And now I know Dalone's telling the truth. Why else would he have warned us?
Luckily, this is where being a professional thief comes in handy.

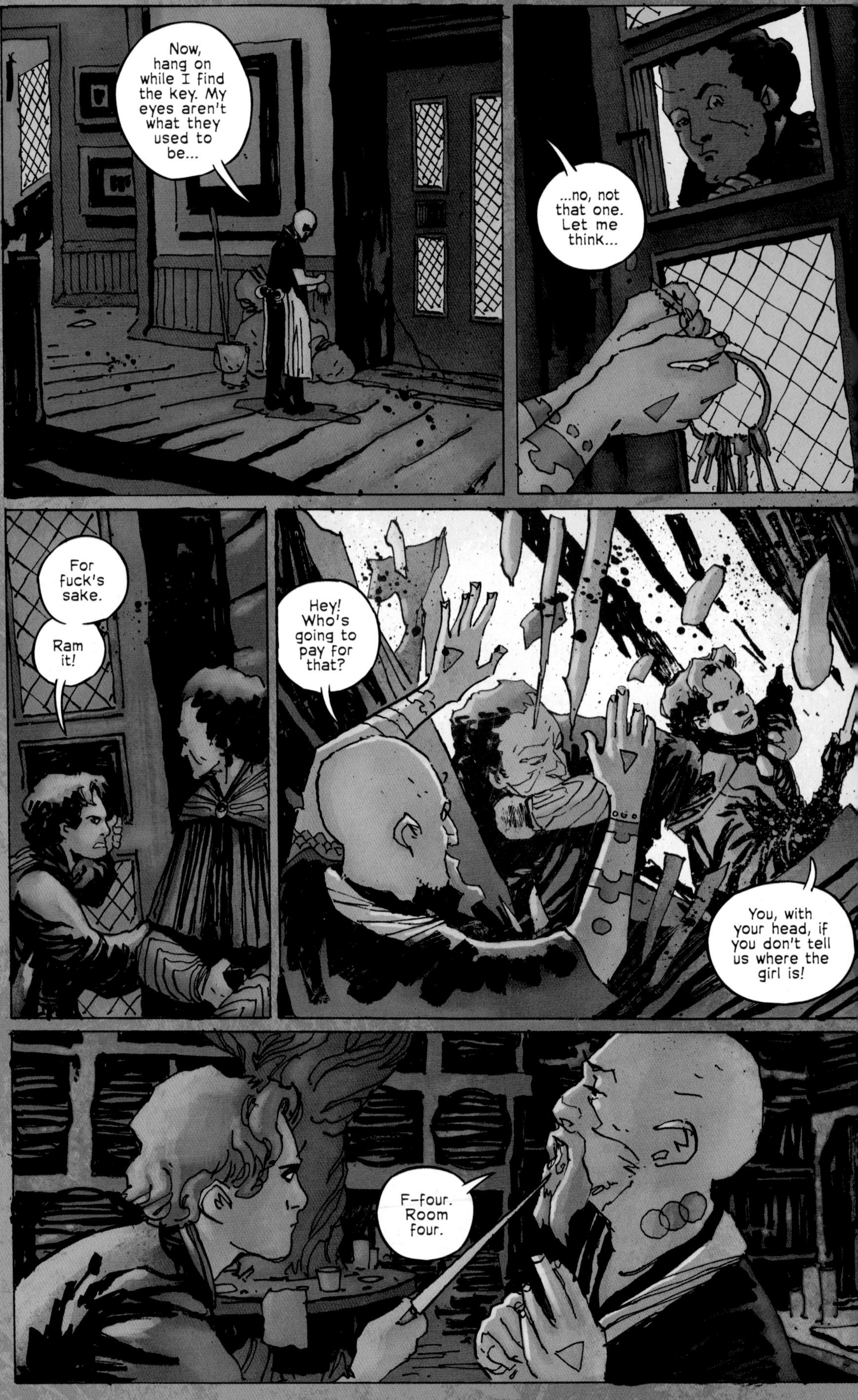
Now, hang on while I find the key. My eyes aren't what they used to be...
...no, not that one. Let me think...
For fuck's sake.
Ram it!
Hey! Who's going to pay for that?
You, with your head, if you don't tell us where the girl is!
F-four. Room four.

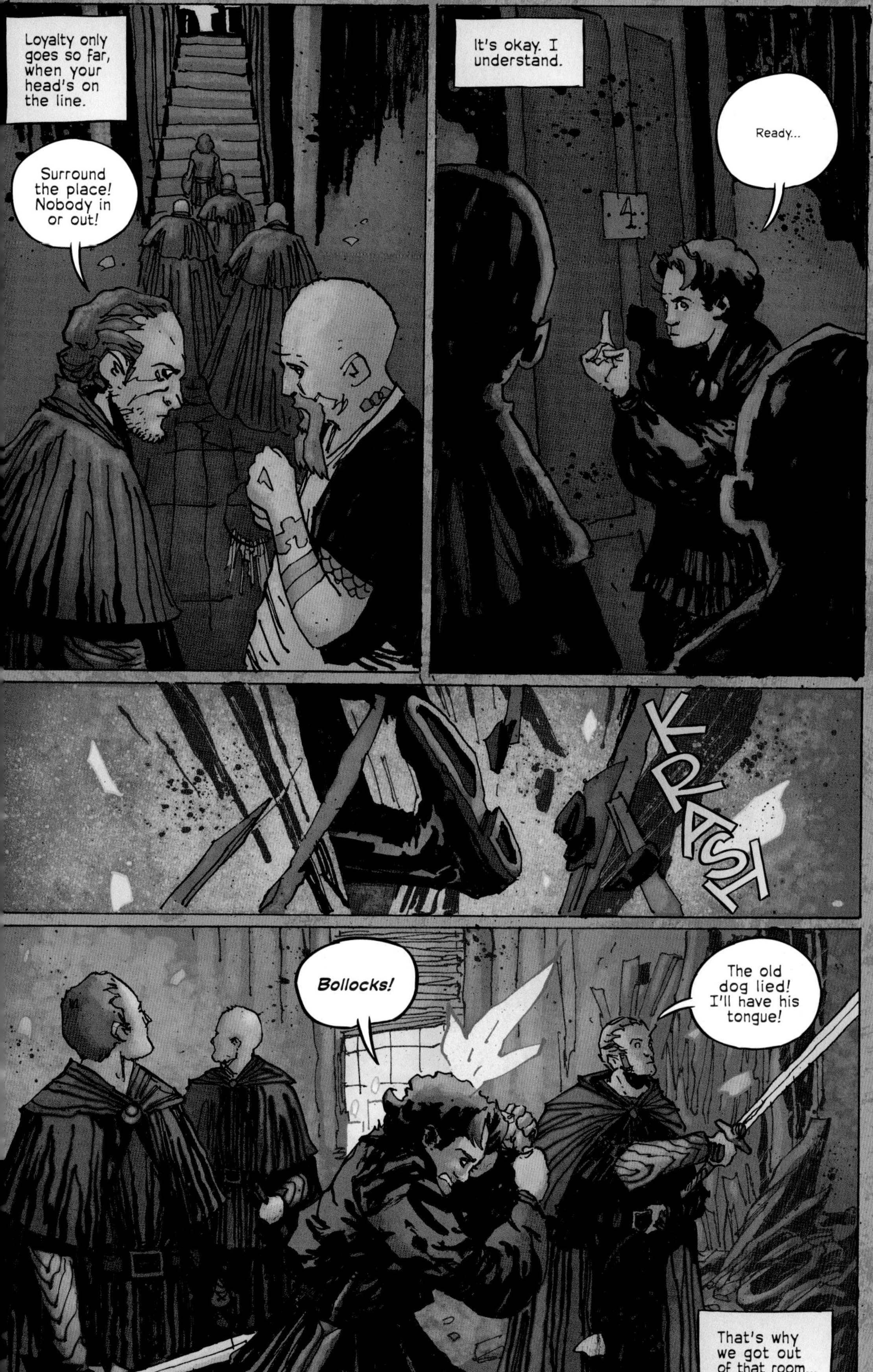
Loyalty only goes so far, when your head's on the line.
Surround the place! Nobody in or out!
It's okay. I understand.
Ready...
KRASH
Bollocks!
The old dog lied! I'll have his tongue!
That's why we got out of that room...

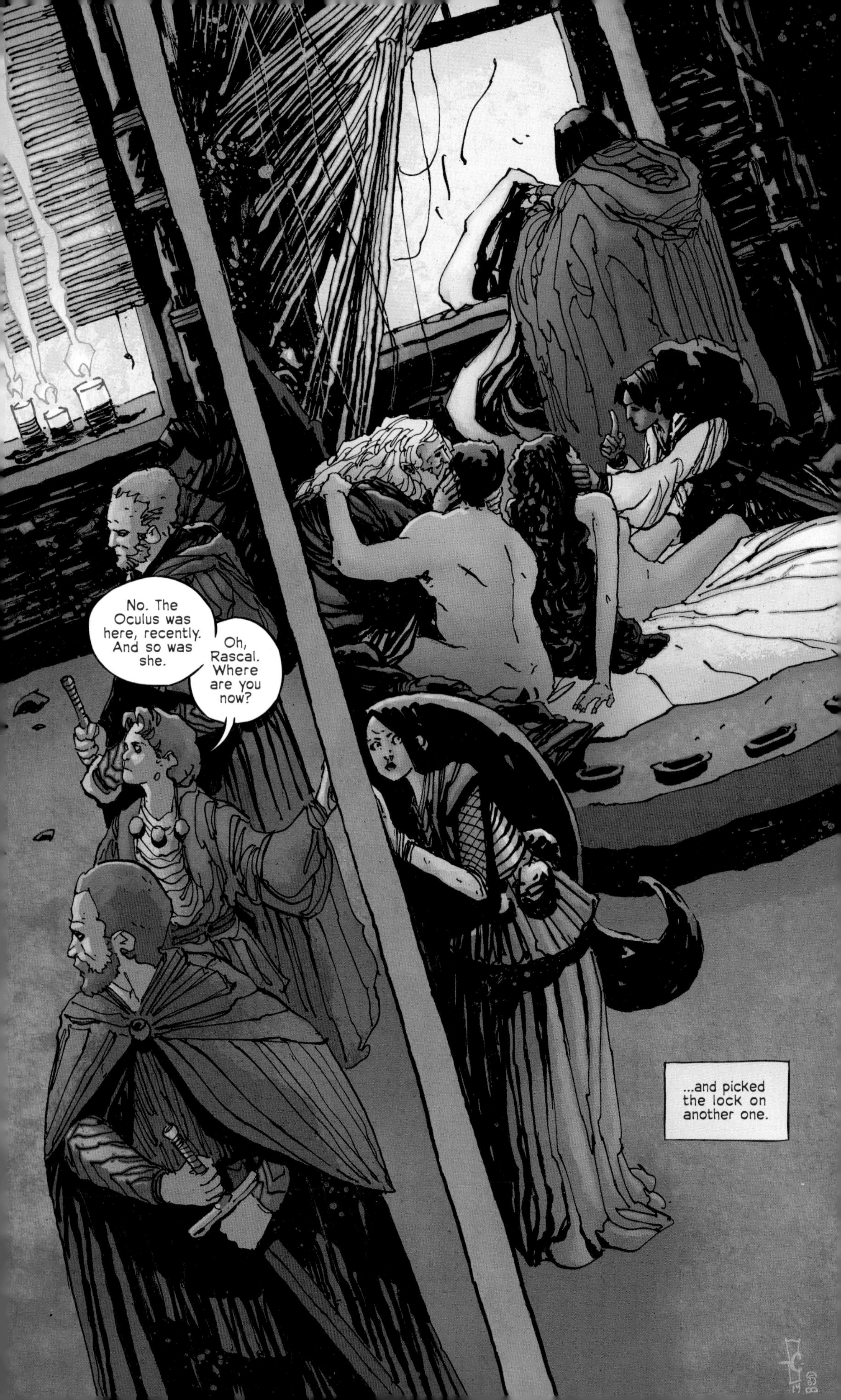
No. The Oculus was here, recently. And so was she.
Oh, Rascal. Where are you now?
...and picked the lock on another one.

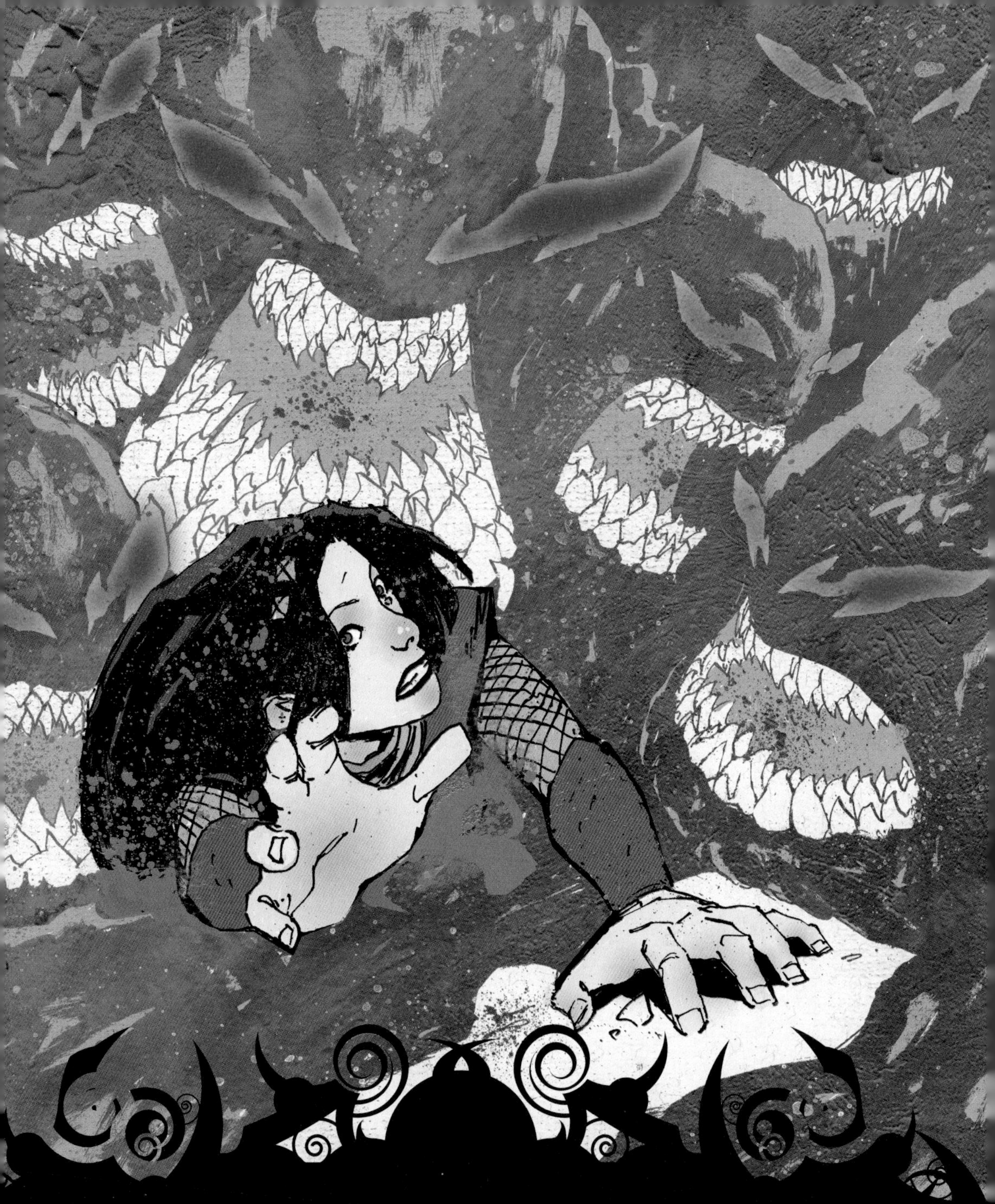

CHASING SHADOWS

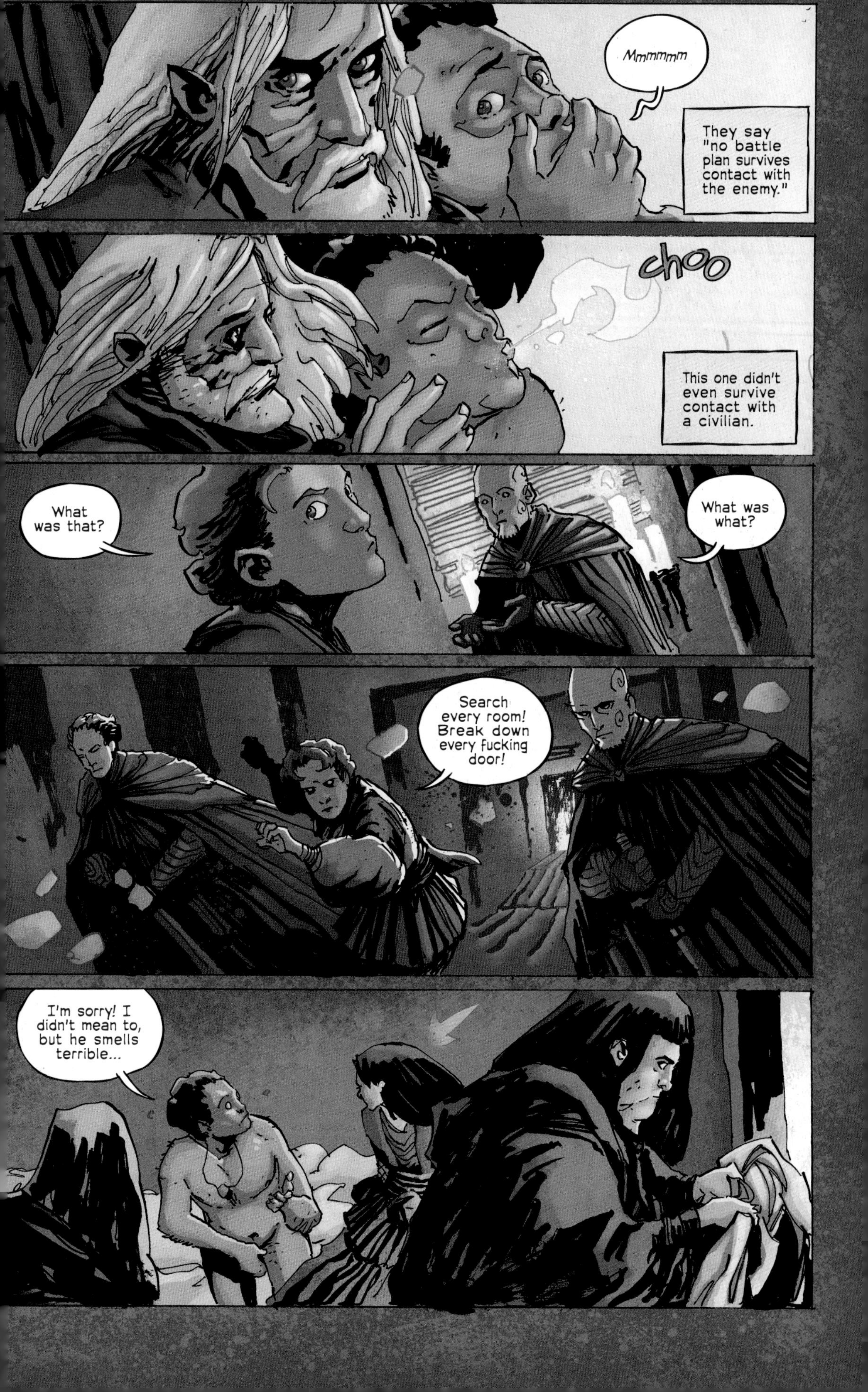
Mmmmmm
They say "no battle plan survives contact with the enemy."
choo
This one didn't even survive contact with a civilian.
What was that?
What was what?
Search every room! Break down every fucking door!
I'm sorry! I didn't mean to, but he smells terrible...

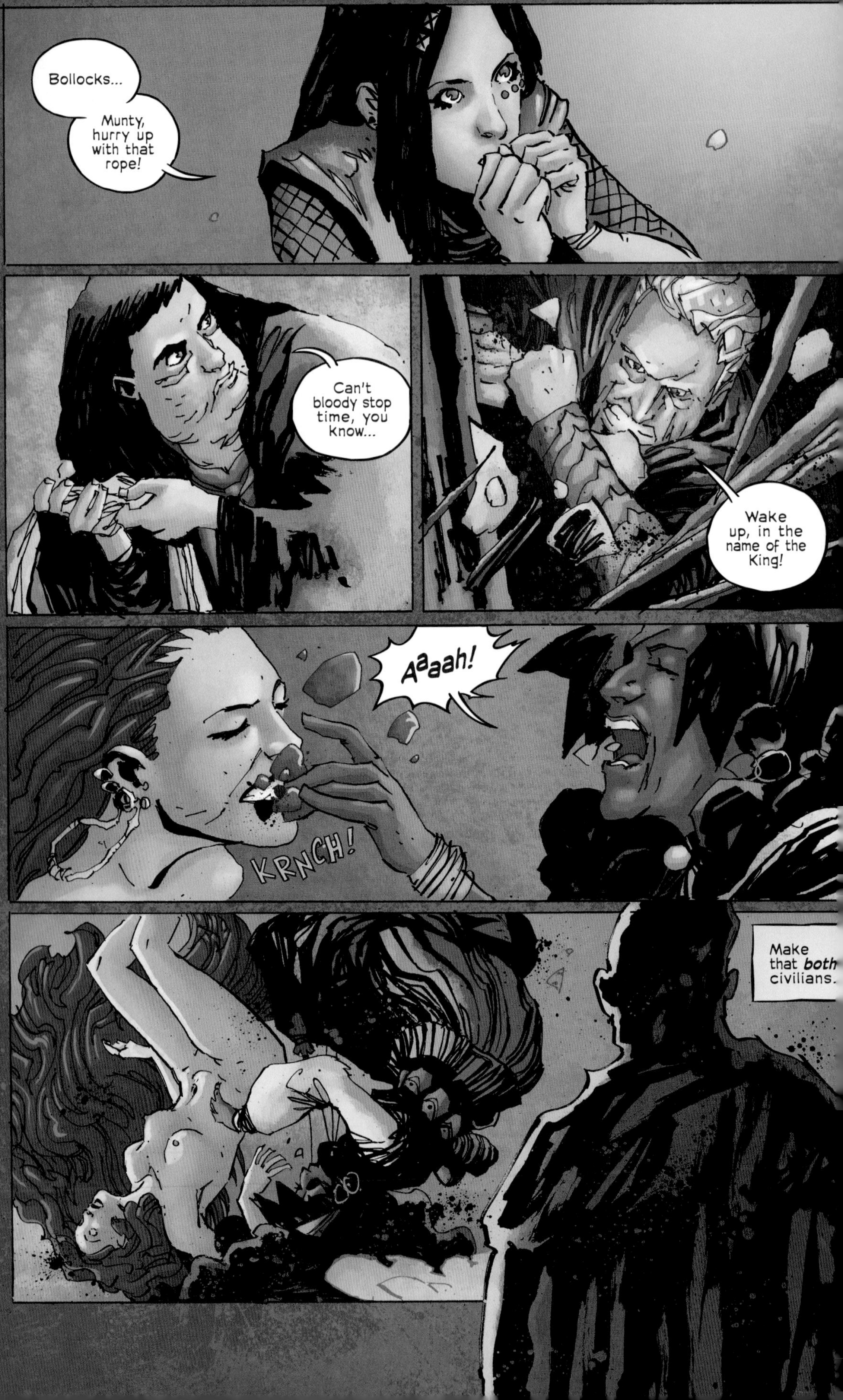
Bollocks...
Munty, hurry up with that rope!
Can't bloody stop time, you know...
Wake up, in the name of the King!
Aaaah!
KRNCH!
Make that *both* civilians.

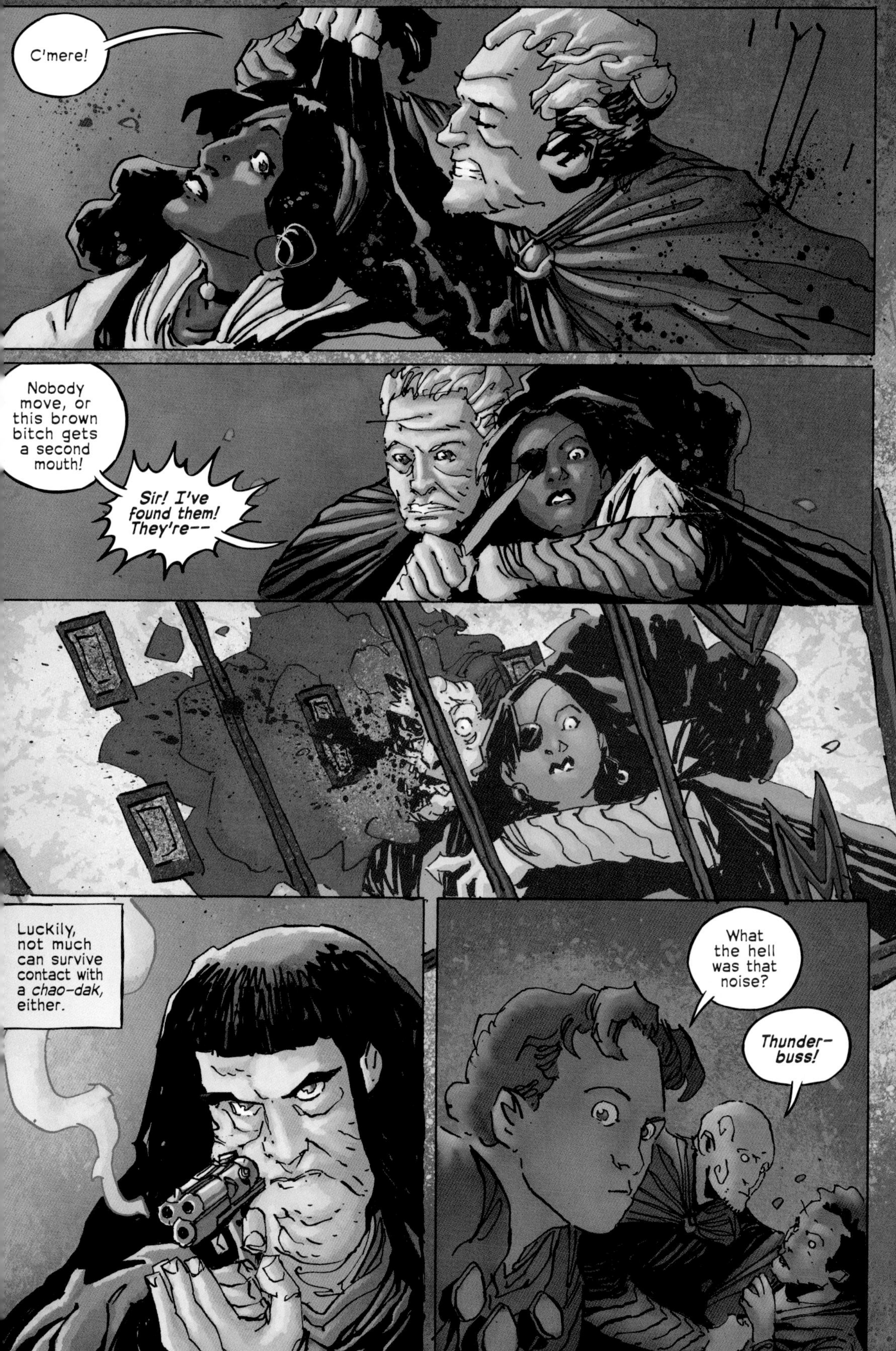
C'mere!
Nobody move, or this brown bitch gets a second mouth!
Sir! I've found them! They're--
Luckily, not much can survive contact with a *chao-dak,* either.
What the hell was that noise?
Thunder-buss!

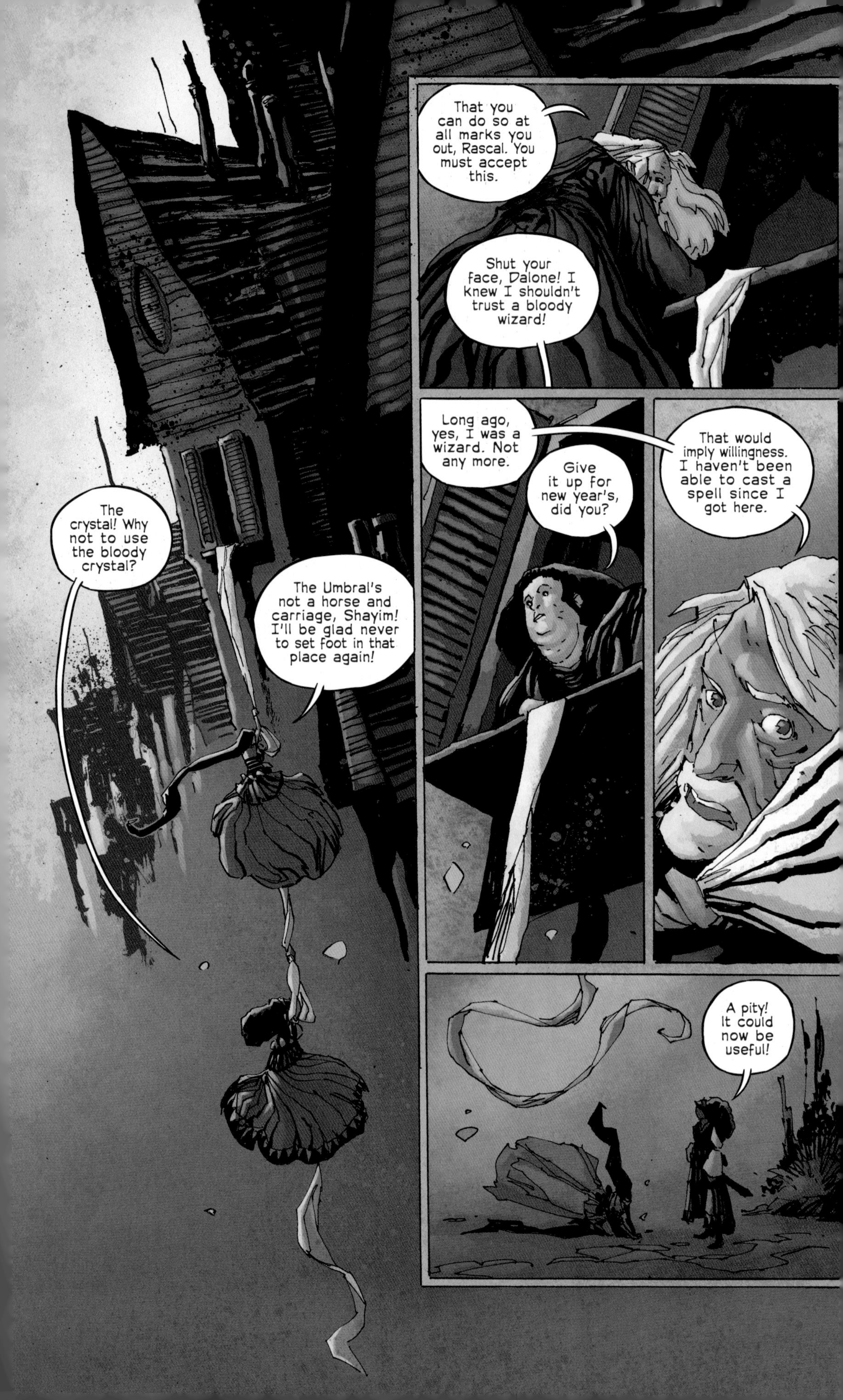
The crystal! Why not to use the bloody crystal?
The Umbral's not a horse and carriage, Shayim! I'll be glad never to set foot in that place again!
That you can do so at all marks you out, Rascal. You must accept this.
Shut your face, Dalone! I knew I shouldn't trust a bloody wizard!
Long ago, yes, I was a wizard. Not any more.
Give it up for new year's, did you?
That would imply willingness. I haven't been able to cast a spell since I got here.
A pity! It could now be useful!

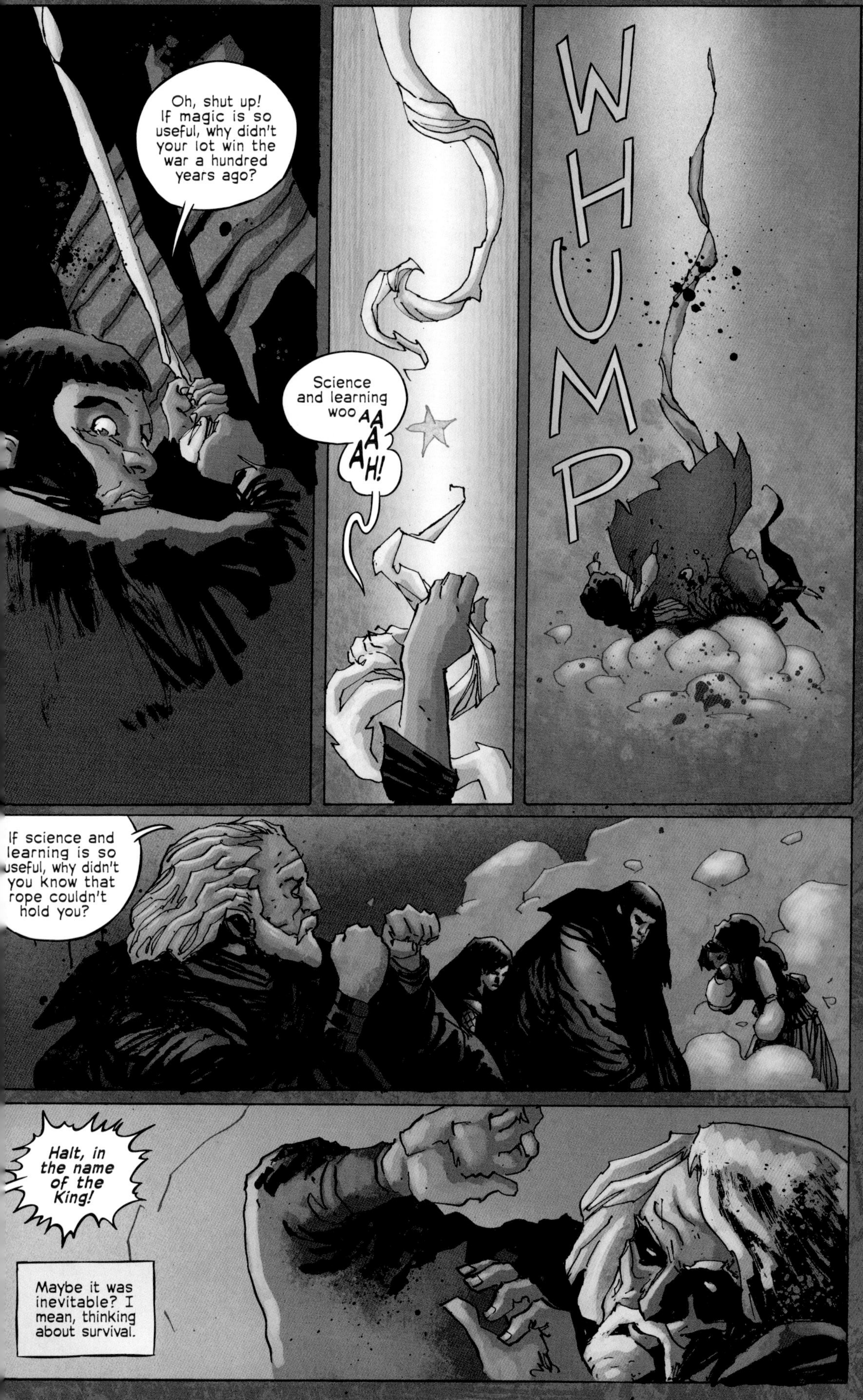

Oh, shut up! If magic is so useful, why didn't your lot win the war a hundred years ago?
Science and learning wooAAAAH!
WHUMP
If science and learning is so useful, why didn't you know that rope couldn't hold you?
Halt, in the name of the King!
Maybe it was inevitable? I mean, thinking about survival.

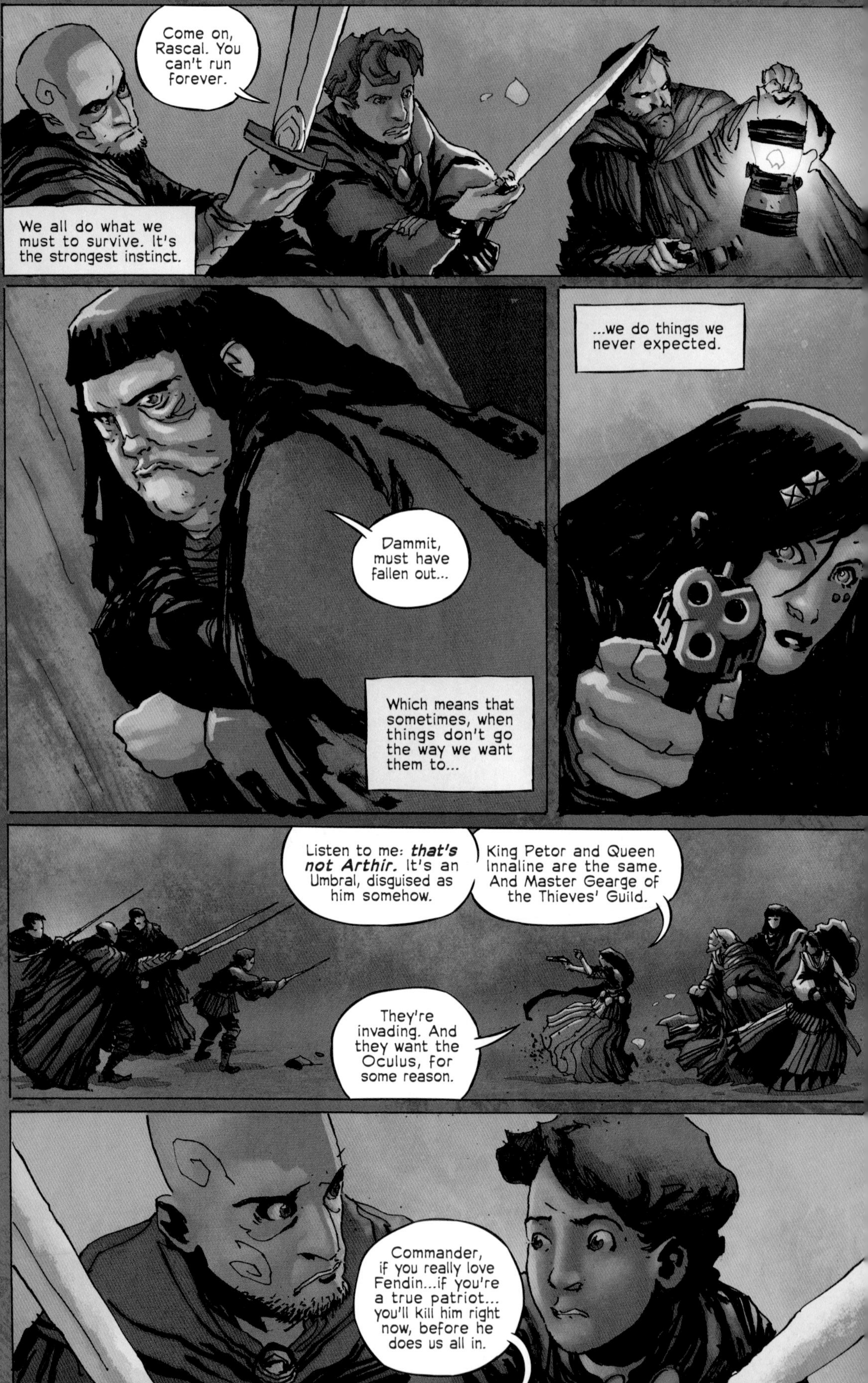
Come on, Rascal. You can't run forever.
We all do what we must to survive. It's the strongest instinct.
Dammit, must have fallen out...
Which means that sometimes, when things don't go the way we want them to...
...we do things we never expected.
Listen to me: ***that's not Arthir.*** It's an Umbral, disguised as him somehow.
King Petor and Queen Innaline are the same. And Master Gearge of the Thieves' Guild.
They're invading. And they want the Oculus, for some reason.
Commander, if you really love Fendin...if you're a true patriot... you'll kill him right now, before he does us all in.

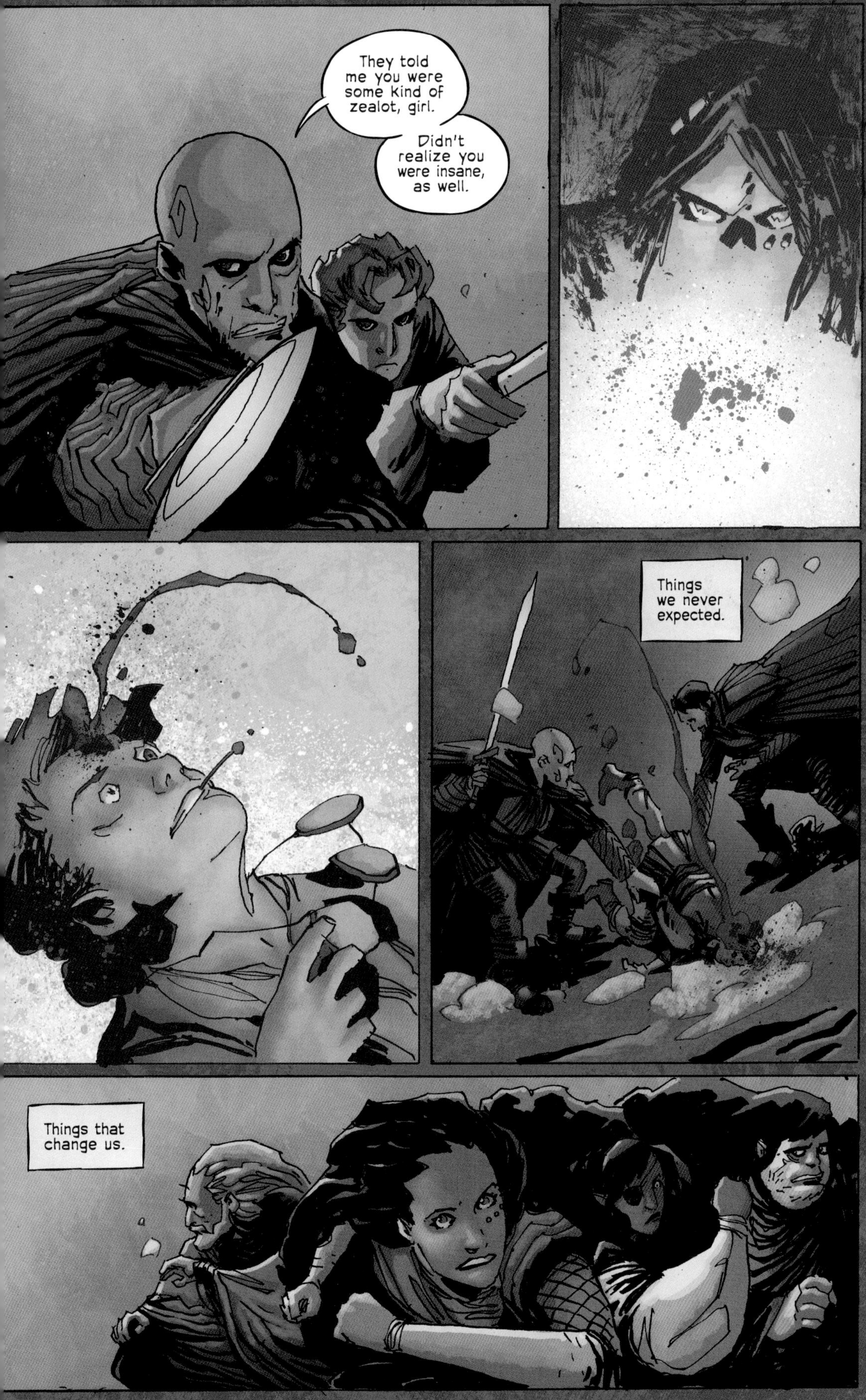
They told me you were some kind of zealot, girl.
Didn't realize you were insane, as well.
Things we never expected.
Things that change us.

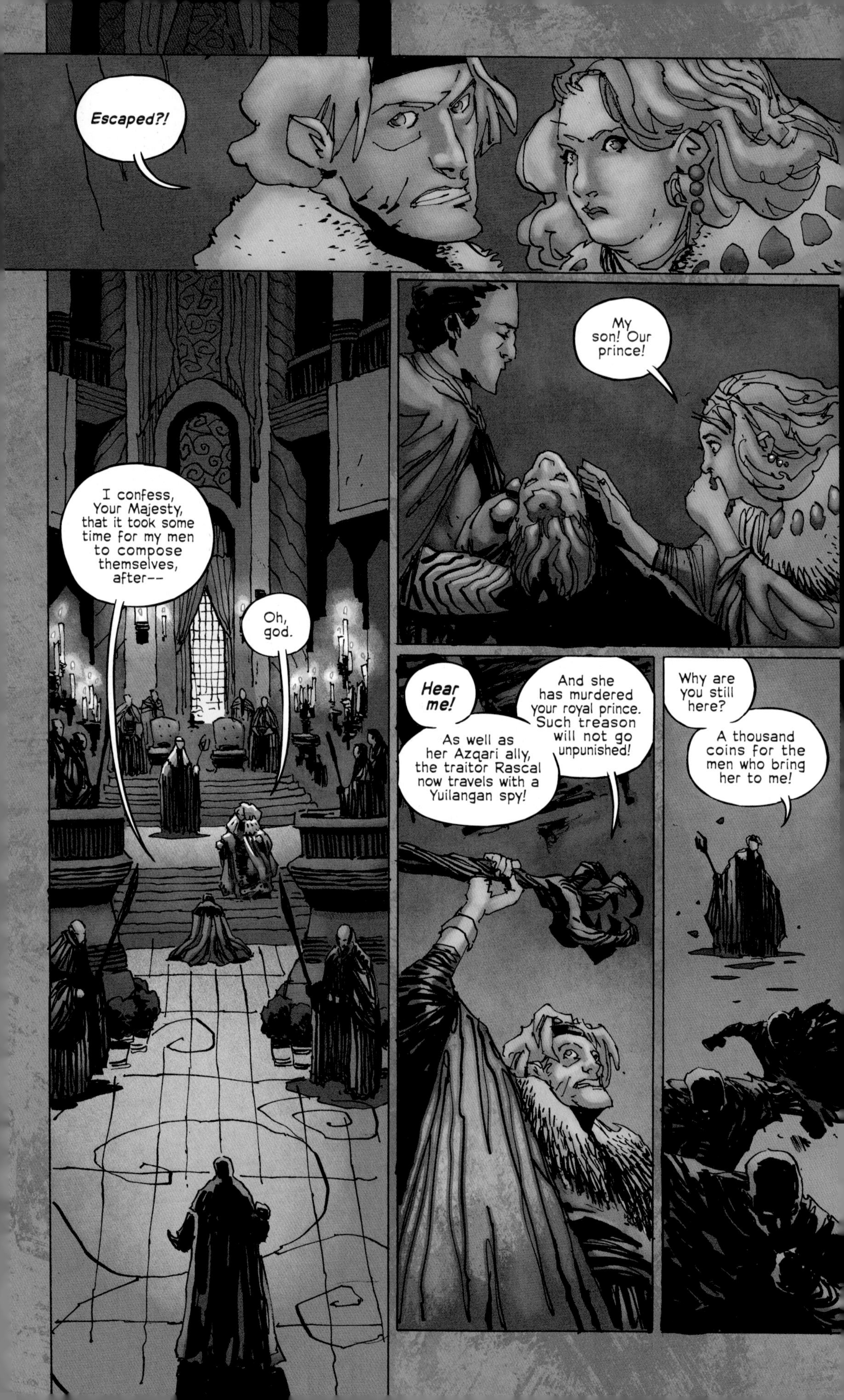

Escaped?!
I confess, Your Majesty, that it took some time for my men to compose themselves, after--
Oh, god.
My son! Our prince!
Hear me!
As well as her Azqari ally, the traitor Rascal now travels with a Yuilangan spy!
And she has murdered your royal prince. Such treason will not go unpunished!
Why are you still here?
A thousand coins for the men who bring her to me!

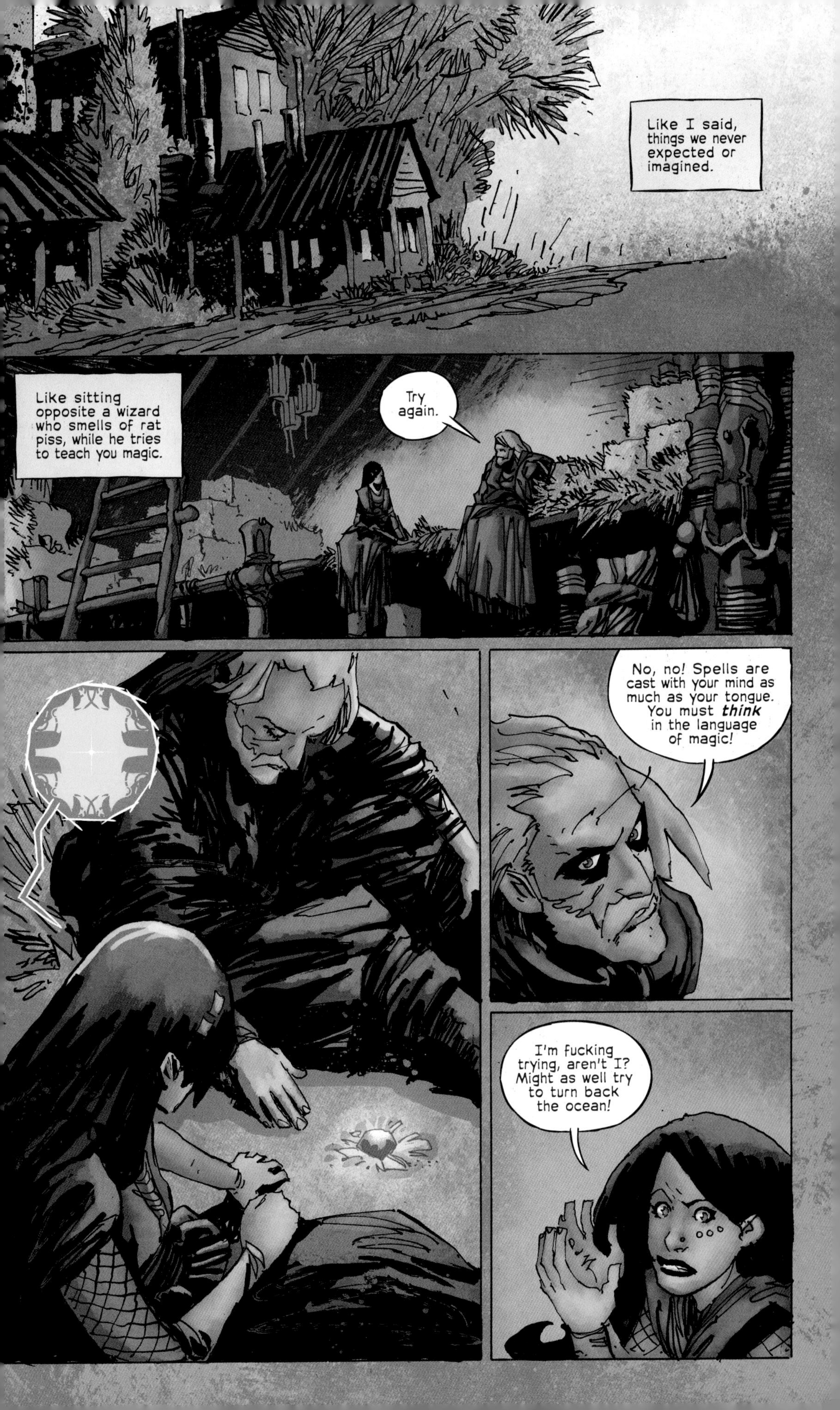
Like I said, things we never expected or imagined.
Like sitting opposite a wizard who smells of rat piss, while he tries to teach you magic.
Try again.
No, no! Spells are cast with your mind as much as your tongue. You must ***think*** in the language of magic!
I'm fucking trying, aren't I? Might as well try to turn back the ocean!

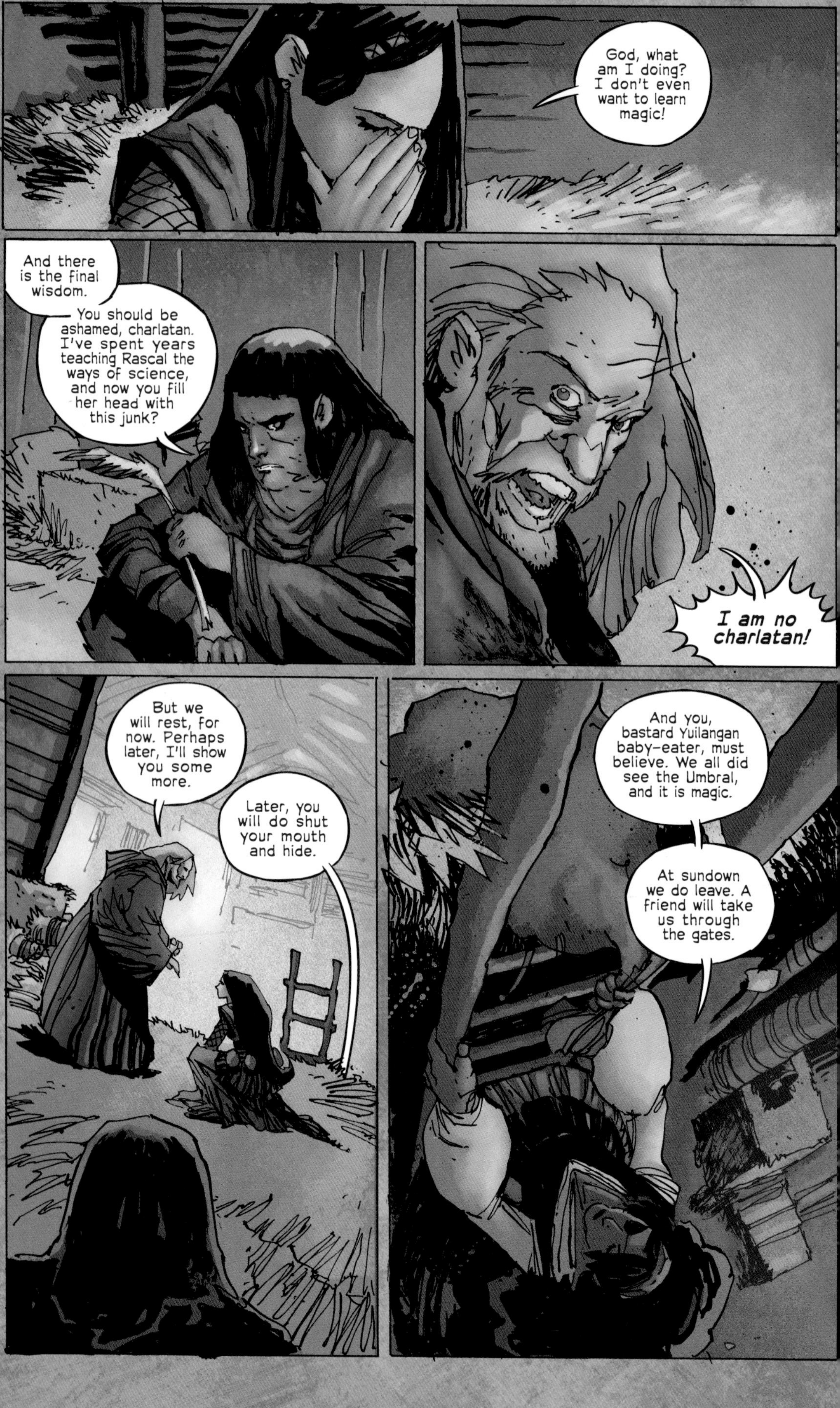
God, what am I doing? I don't even want to learn magic!
And there is the final wisdom.
You should be ashamed, charlatan. I've spent years teaching Rascal the ways of science, and now you fill her head with this junk?
I am no charlatan!
But we will rest, for now. Perhaps later, I'll show you some more.
Later, you will do shut your mouth and hide.
And you, bastard Yuilangan baby-eater, must believe. We all did see the Umbral, and it is magic.
At sundown we do leave. A friend will take us through the gates.

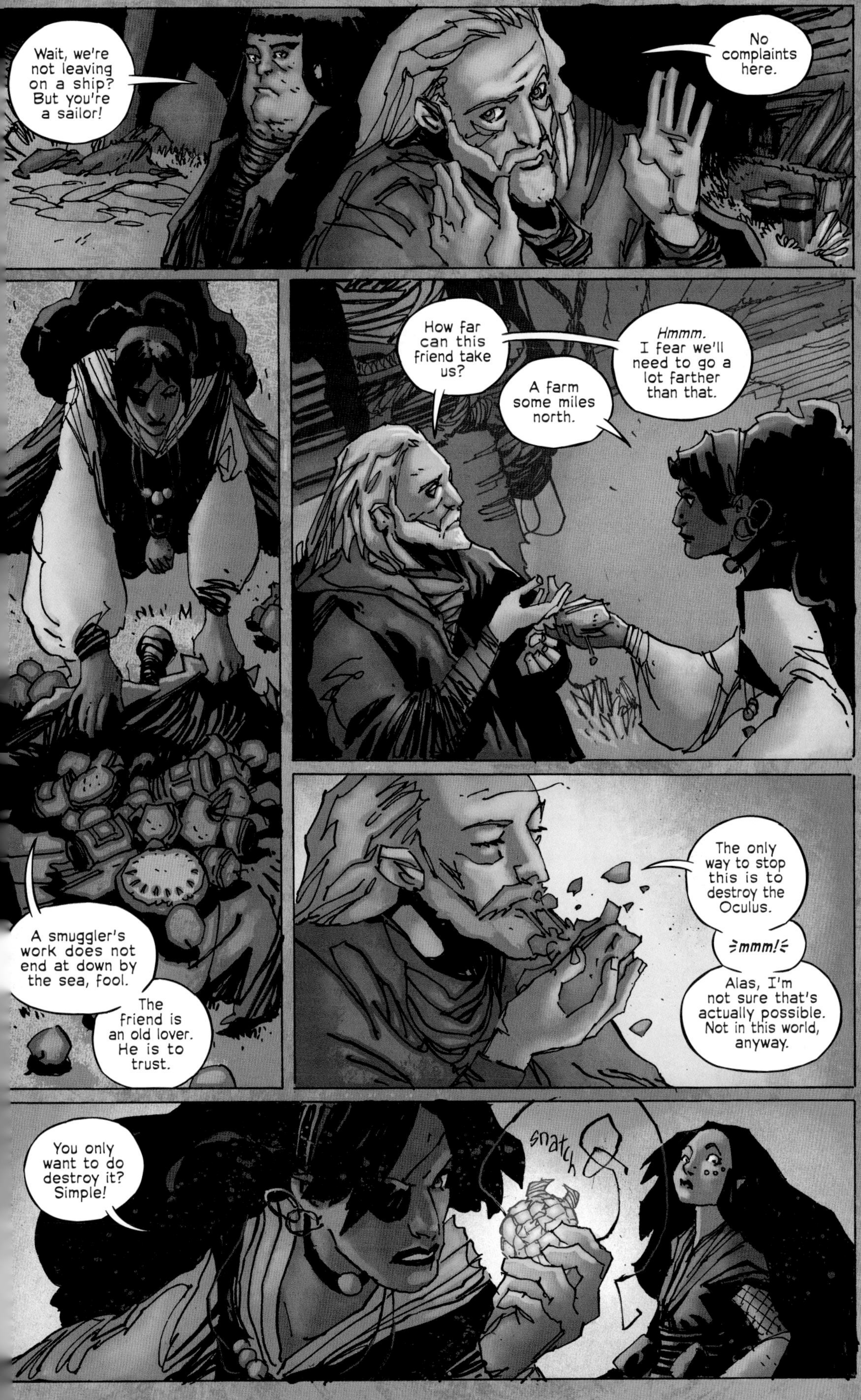
Wait, we're not leaving on a ship? But you're a sailor!
No complaints here.
How far can this friend take us?
A farm some miles north.
Hmmm. I fear we'll need to go a lot farther than that.
A smuggler's work does not end at down by the sea, fool.
The friend is an old lover. He is to trust.
The only way to stop this is to destroy the Oculus.
mmm!
Alas, I'm not sure that's actually possible. Not in this world, anyway.
You only want to do destroy it? Simple!
snatch

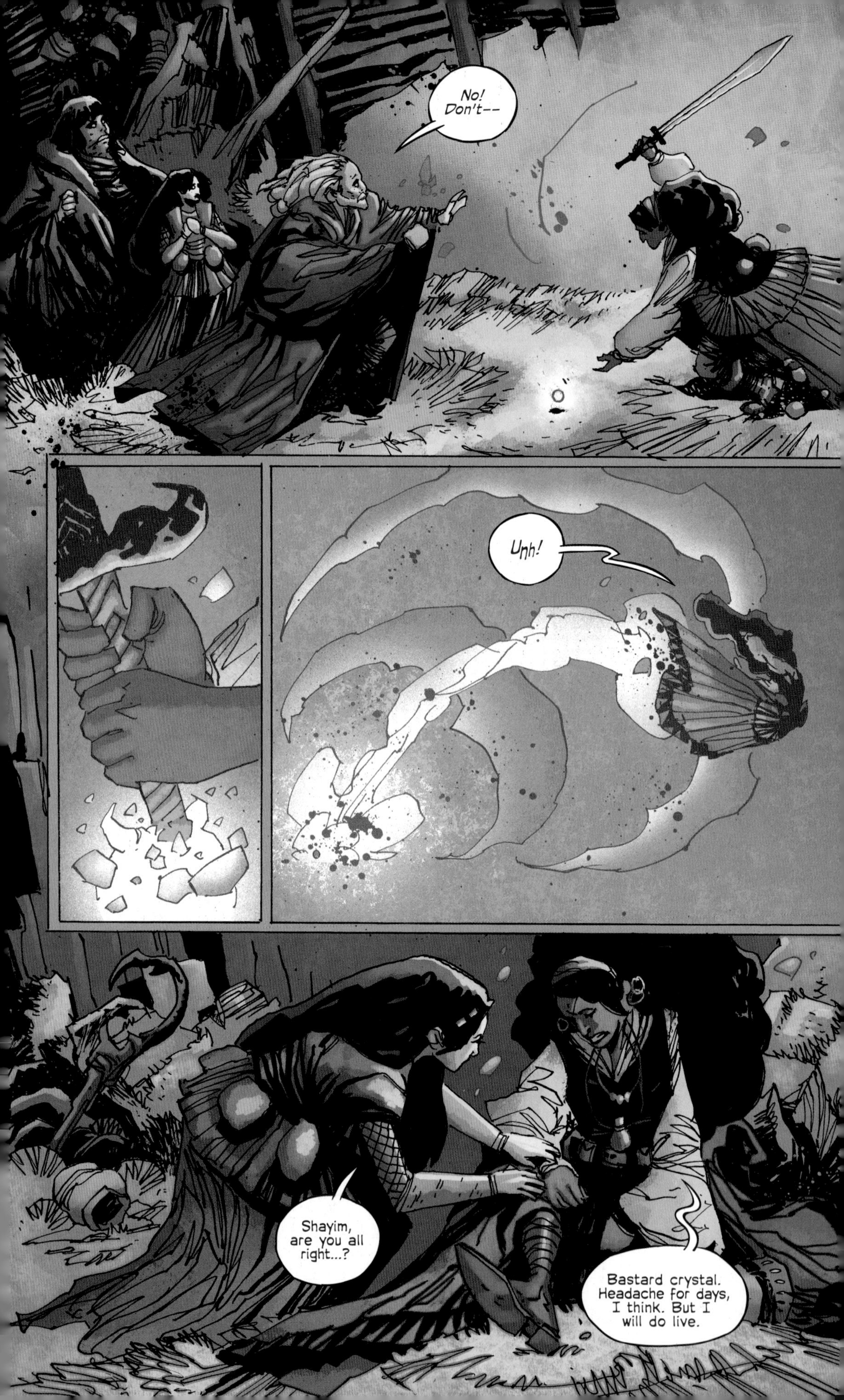
No! Don't--
Unh!
Shayim, are you all right...?
Bastard crystal. Headache for days, I think. But I will do live.

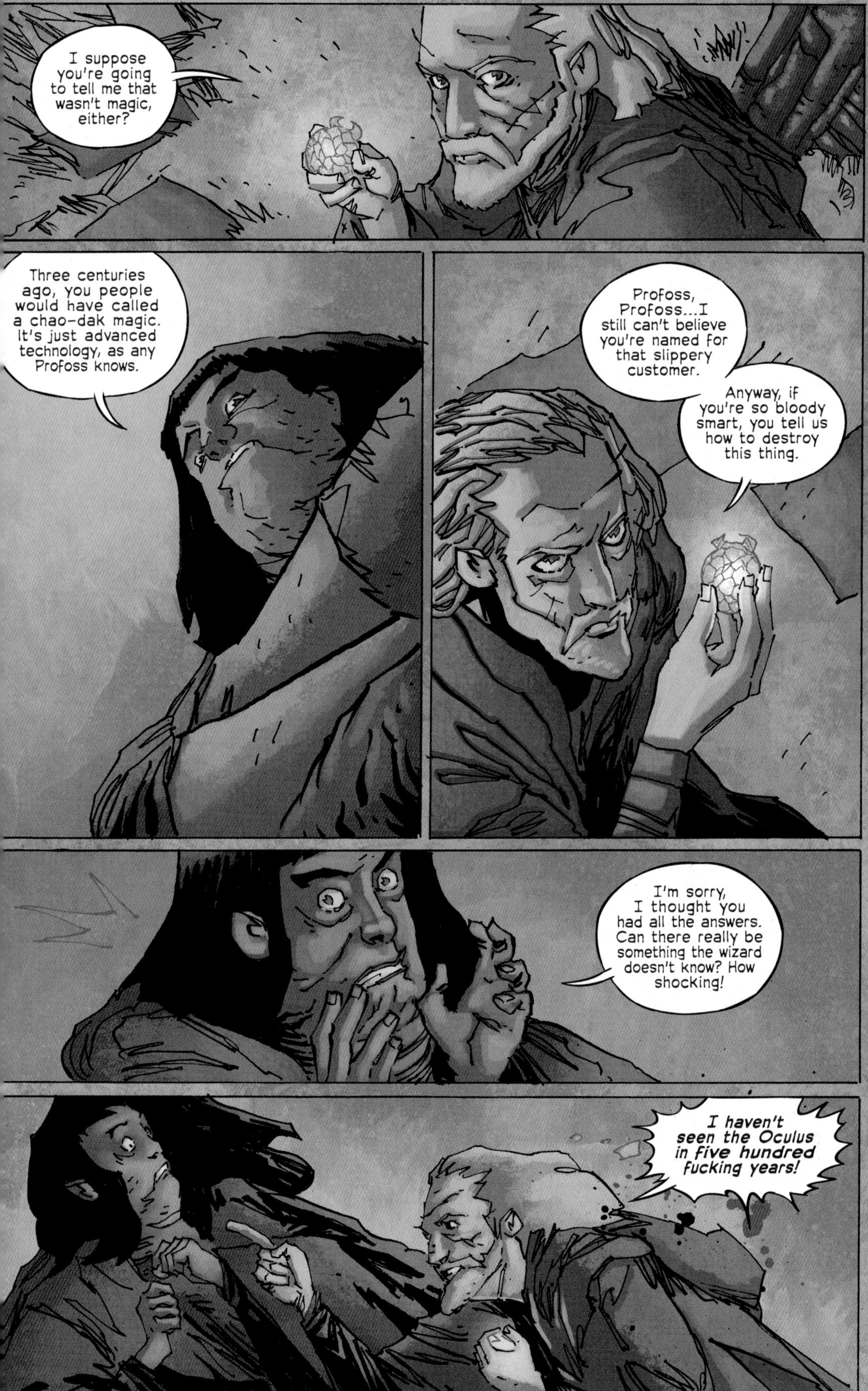
I suppose you're going to tell me that wasn't magic, either?
Three centuries ago, you people would have called a chao-dak magic. It's just advanced technology, as any Profoss knows.
Profoss, Profoss...I still can't believe you're named for that slippery customer.
Anyway, if you're so bloody smart, you tell us how to destroy this thing.
I'm sorry, I thought you had all the answers. Can there really be something the wizard doesn't know? How shocking!
I haven't seen the Oculus in five hundred fucking years!

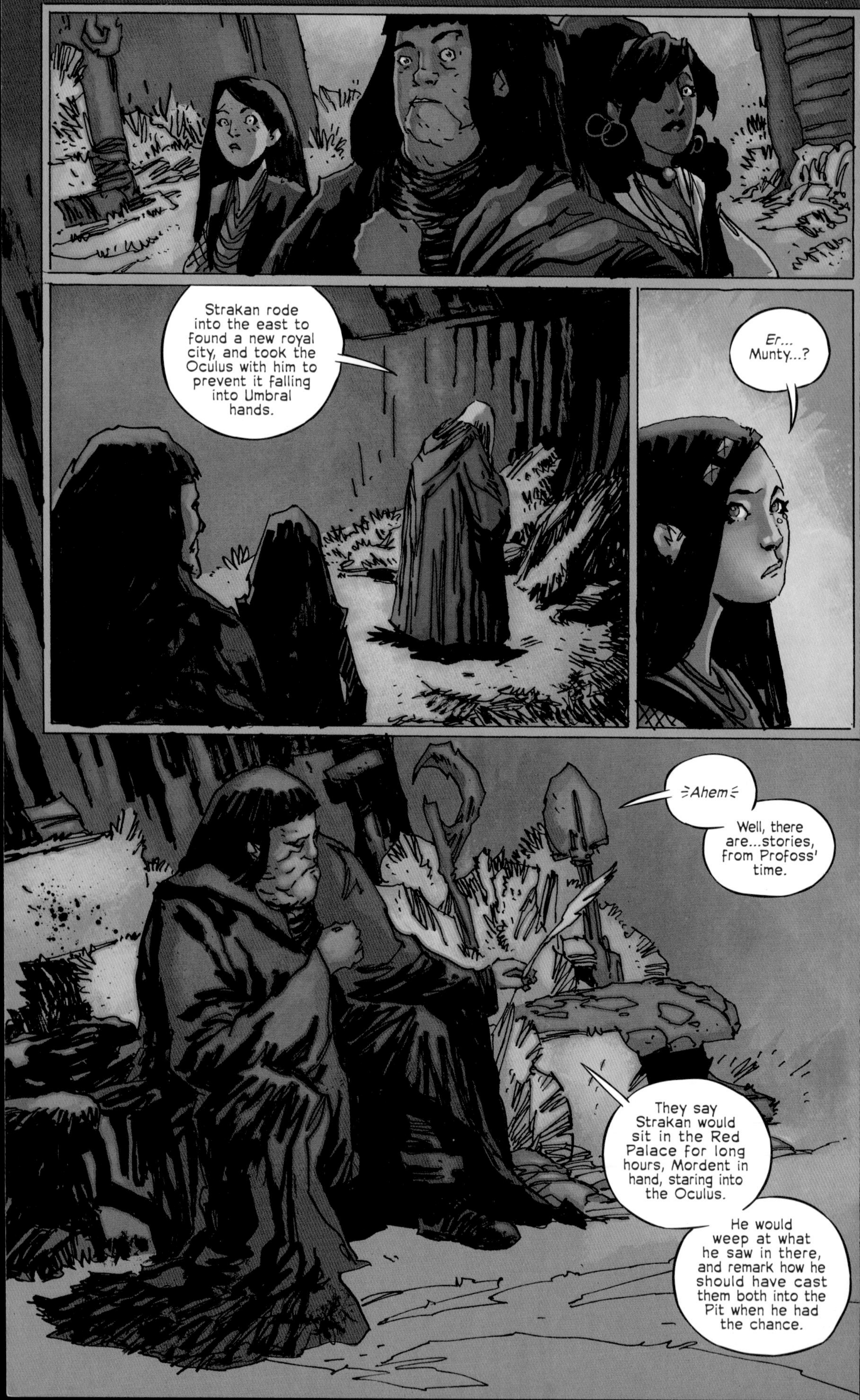
Strakan rode into the east to found a new royal city, and took the Oculus with him to prevent it falling into Umbral hands.
Er... Munty...?
Ahem
Well, there are...stories, from Profoss' time.
They say Strakan would sit in the Red Palace for long hours, Mordent in hand, staring into the Oculus.
He would weep at what he saw in there, and remark how he should have cast them both into the Pit when he had the chance.

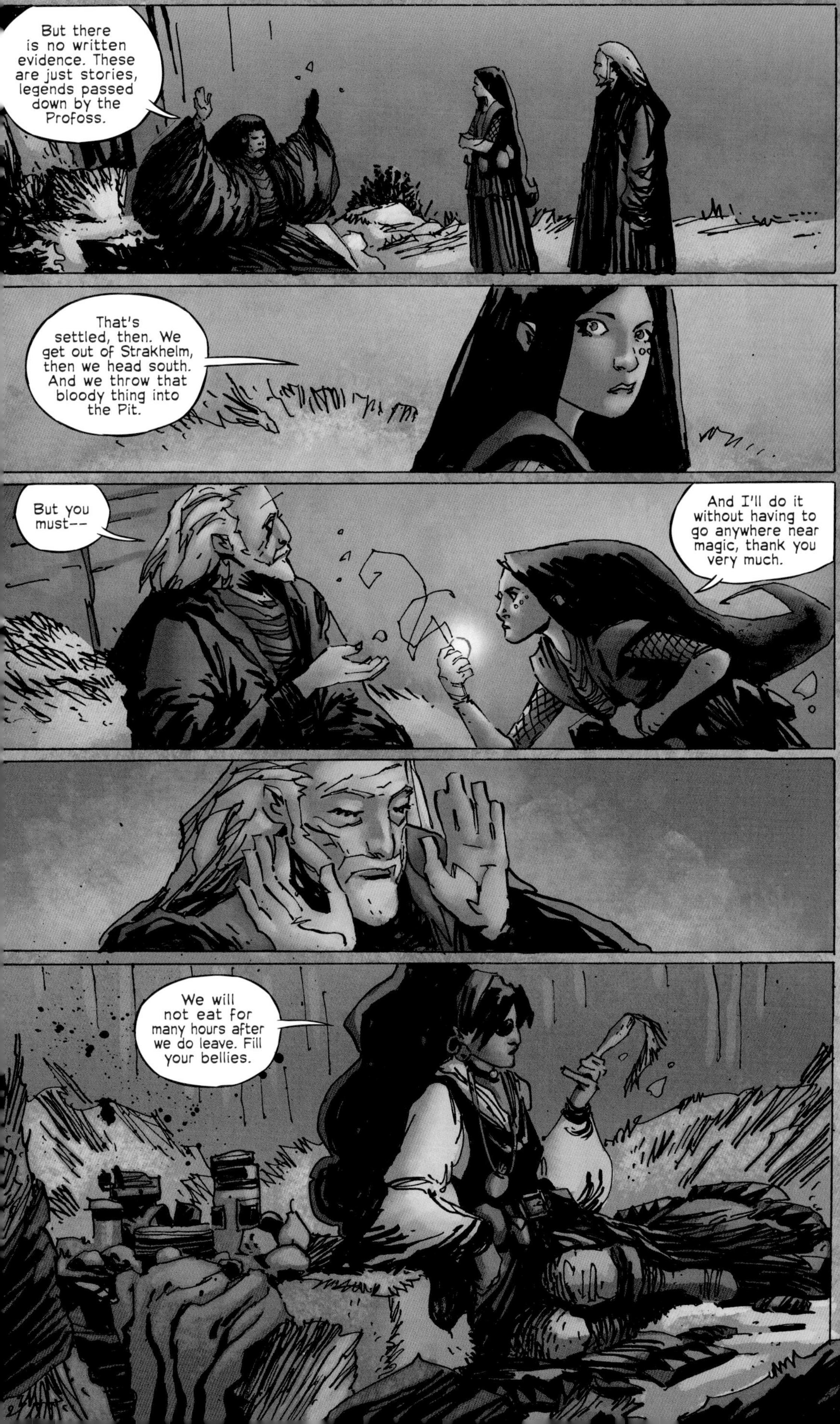
But there is no written evidence. These are just stories, legends passed down by the Profoss.
That's settled, then. We get out of Strakhelm, then we head south. And we throw that bloody thing into the Pit.
But you must--
And I'll do it without having to go anywhere near magic, thank you very much.
We will not eat for many hours after we do leave. Fill your bellies.

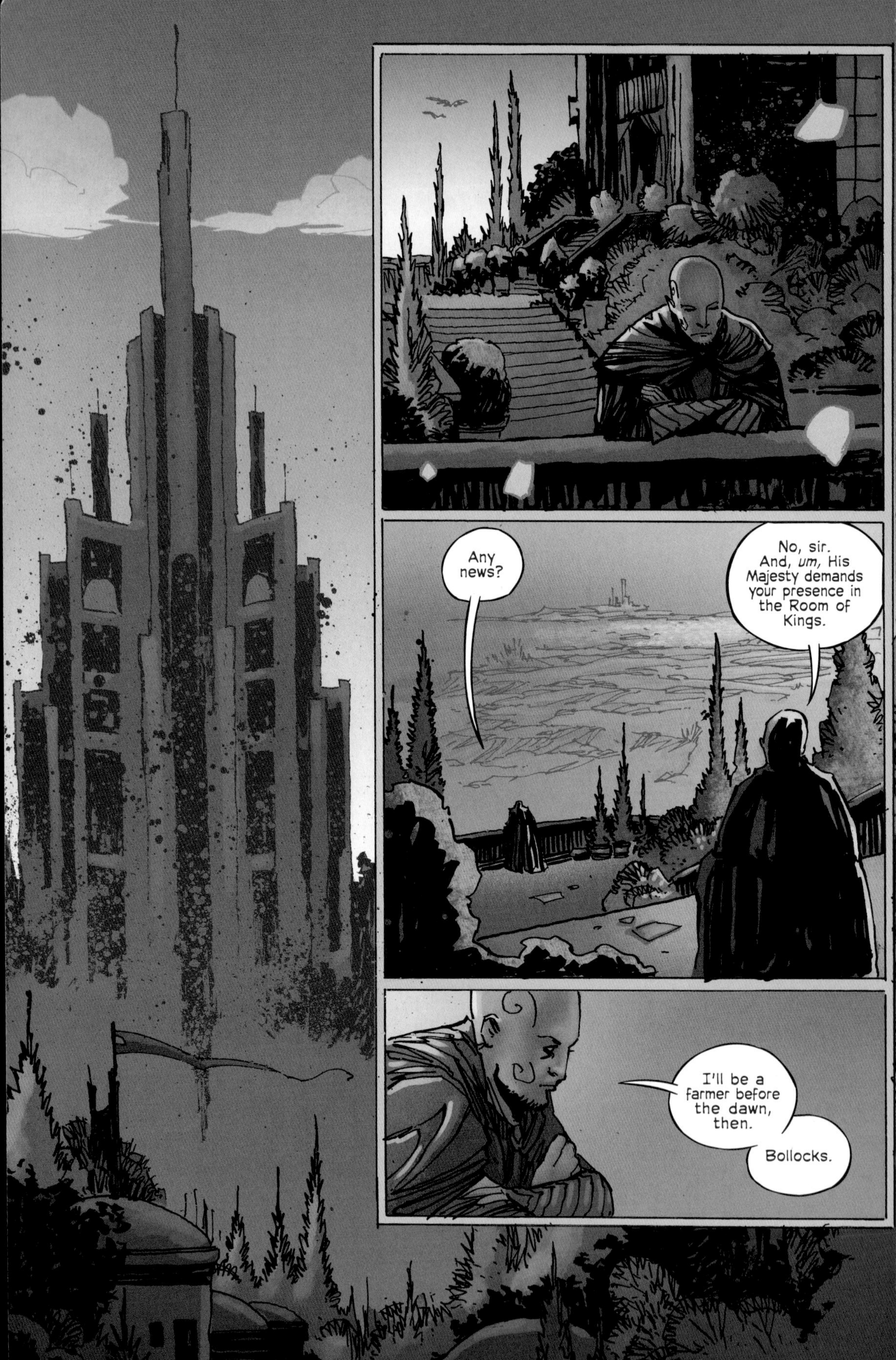
Any news?
No, sir. And, *um,* His Majesty demands your presence in the Room of Kings.
I'll be a farmer before the dawn, then.
Bollocks.

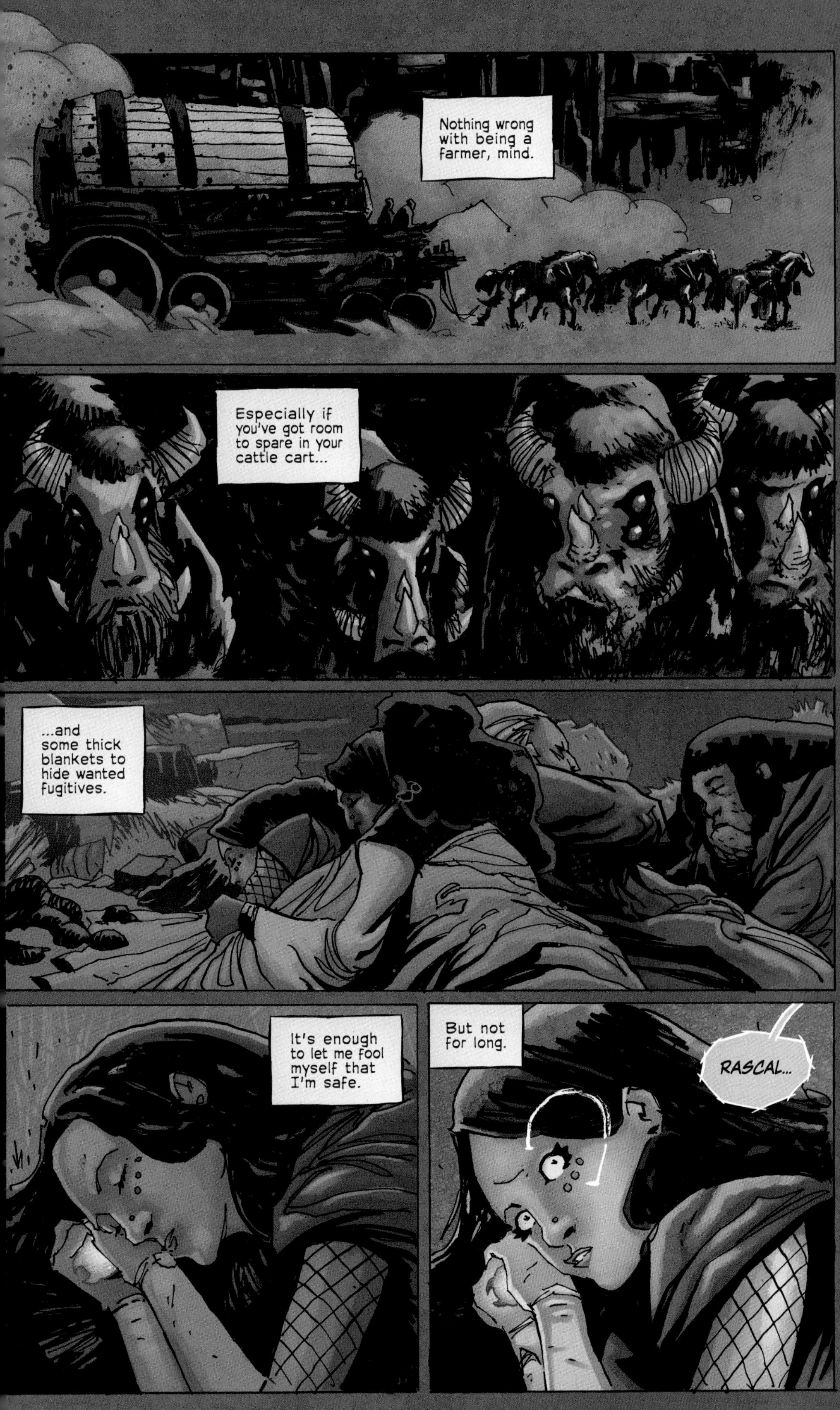
Nothing wrong with being a farmer, mind.
Especially if you've got room to spare in your cattle cart...
...and some thick blankets to hide wanted fugitives.
It's enough to let me fool myself that I'm safe.
But not for long.
RASCAL...

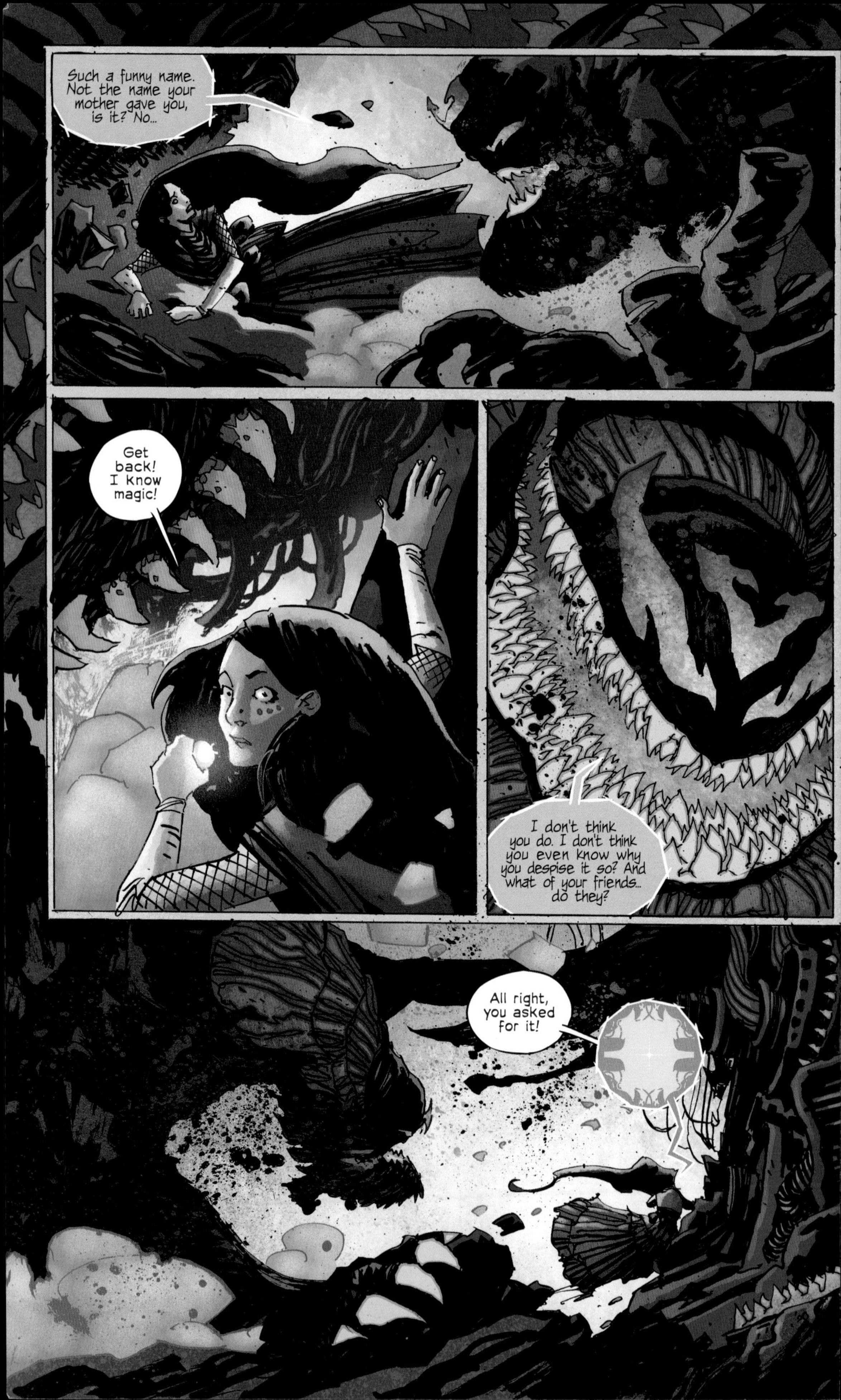
Such a funny name. Not the name your mother gave you, is it? No...
Get back! I know magic!
I don't think you do. I don't think you even know why you despise it so? And what of your friends... do they?
All right, you asked for it!

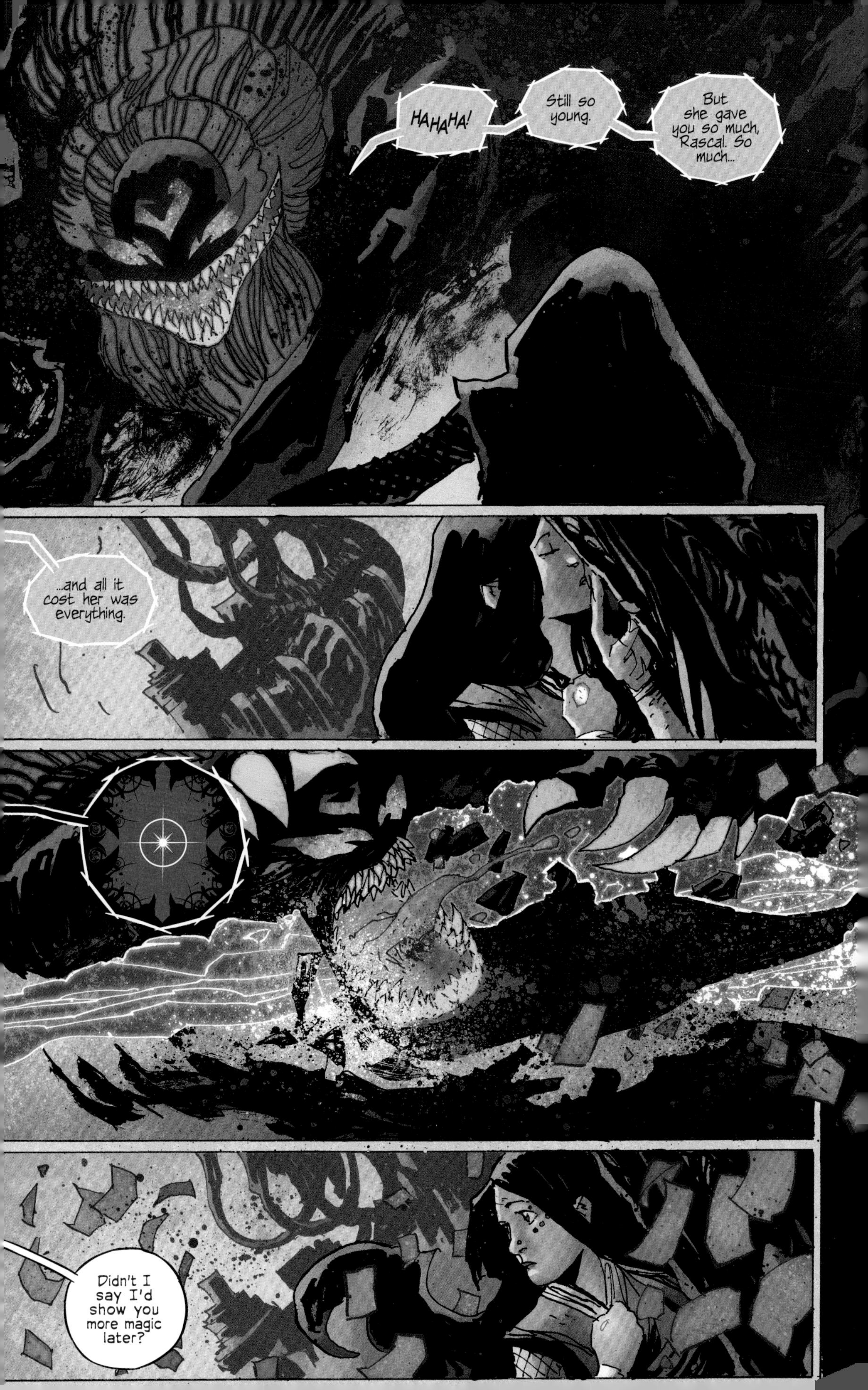
HAHAHA!
Still so young.
But she gave you so much, Rascal. So much...
...and all it cost her was everything.
Didn't I say I'd show you more magic later?

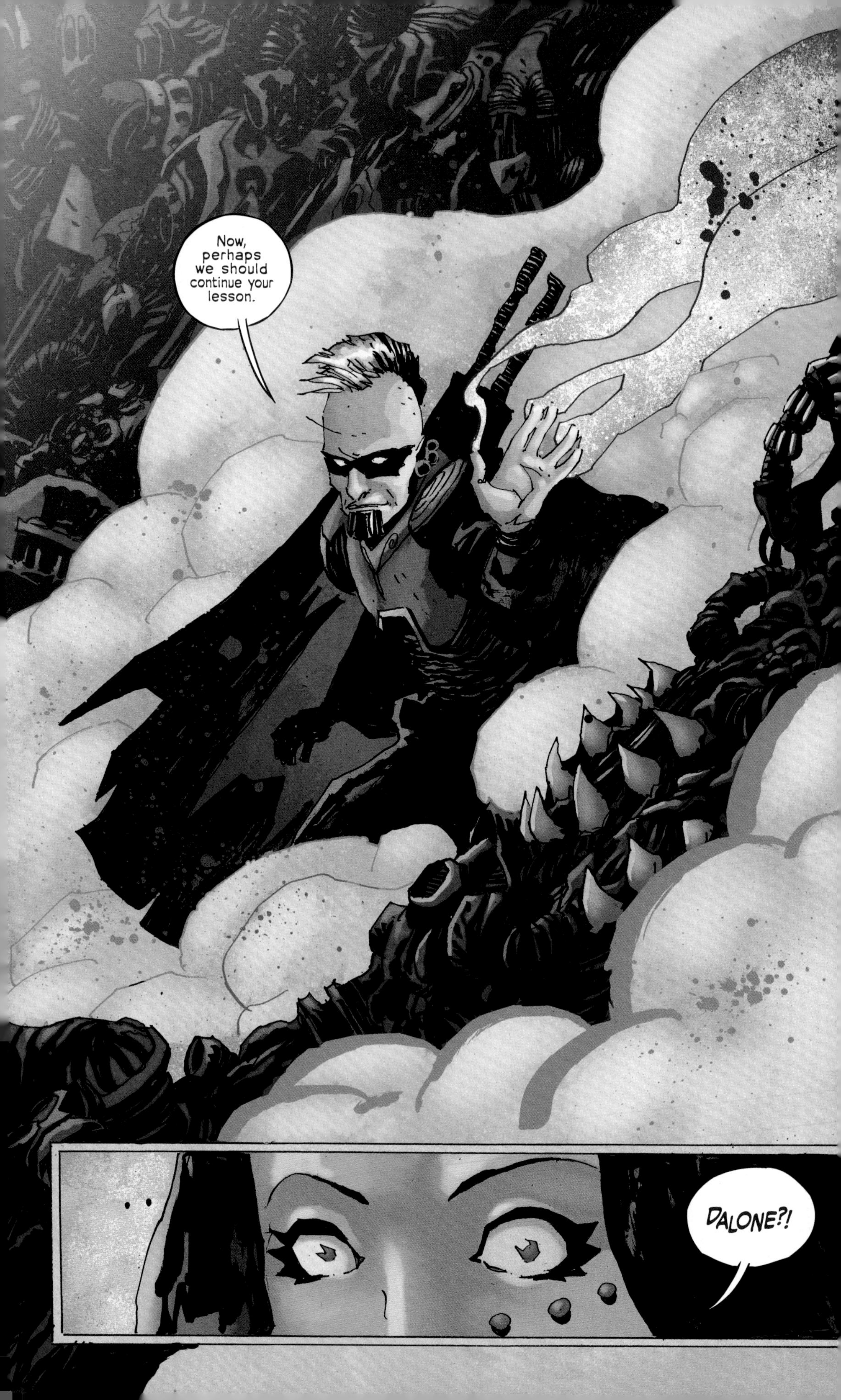
Now, perhaps we should continue your lesson.
DALONE?!

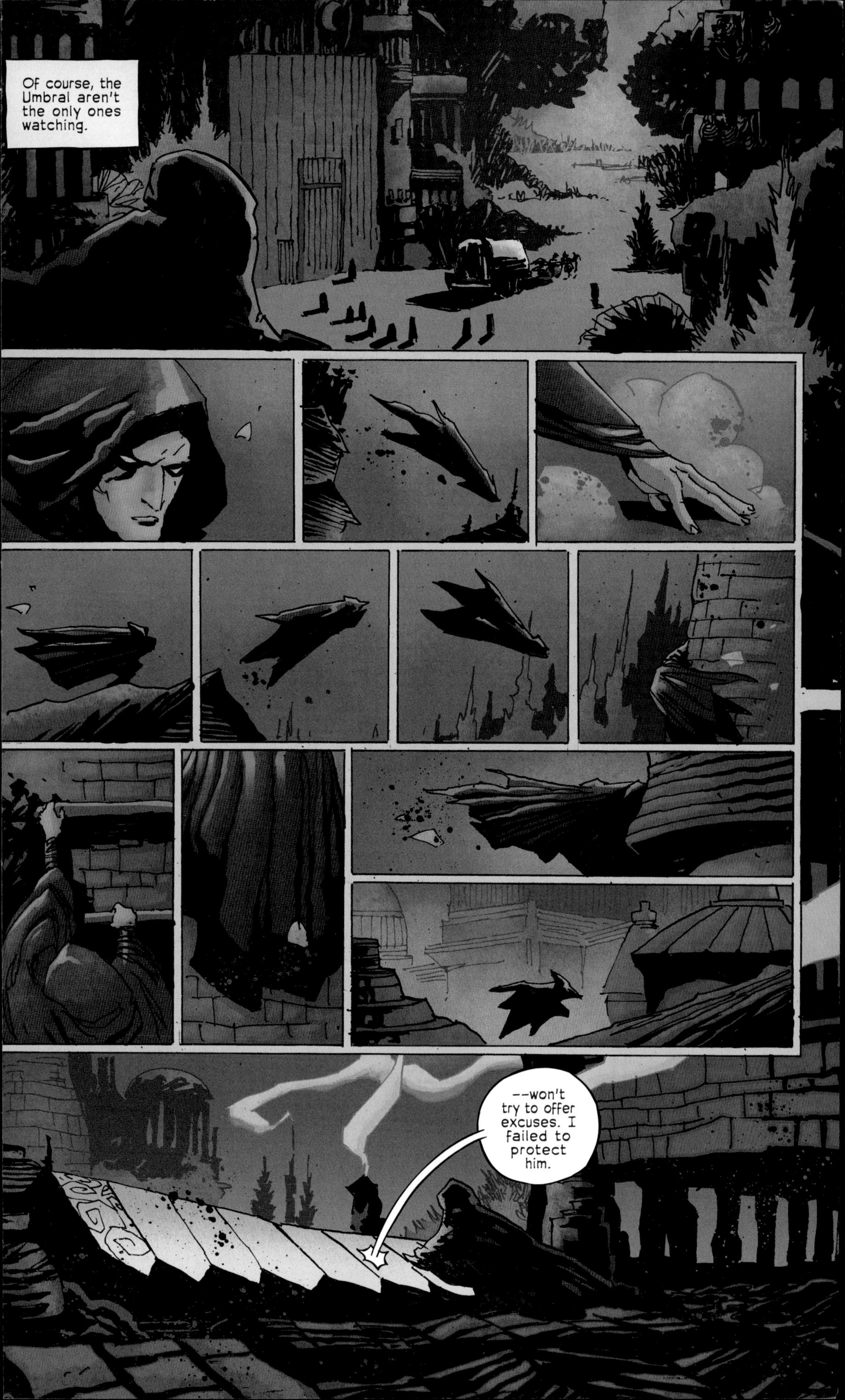
Of course, the Umbral aren't the only ones watching.
--won't try to offer excuses. I failed to protect him.

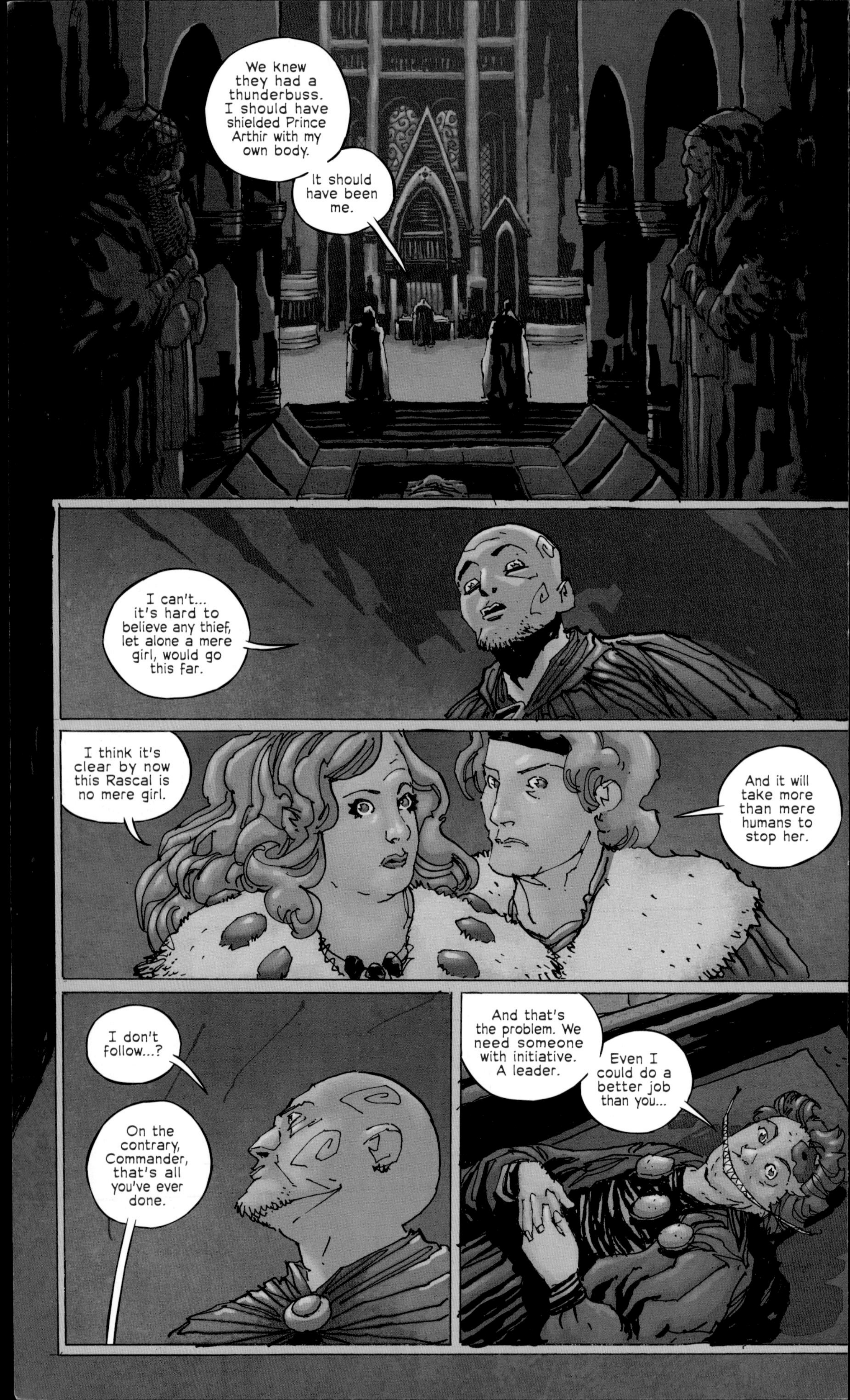
We knew they had a thunderbuss. I should have shielded Prince Arthir with my own body.
It should have been me.
I can't... it's hard to believe any thief, let alone a mere girl, would go this far.
I think it's clear by now this Rascal is no mere girl.
And it will take more than mere humans to stop her.
I don't follow...?
On the contrary, Commander, that's all you've ever done.
And that's the problem. We need someone with initiative. A leader.
Even I could do a better job than you...

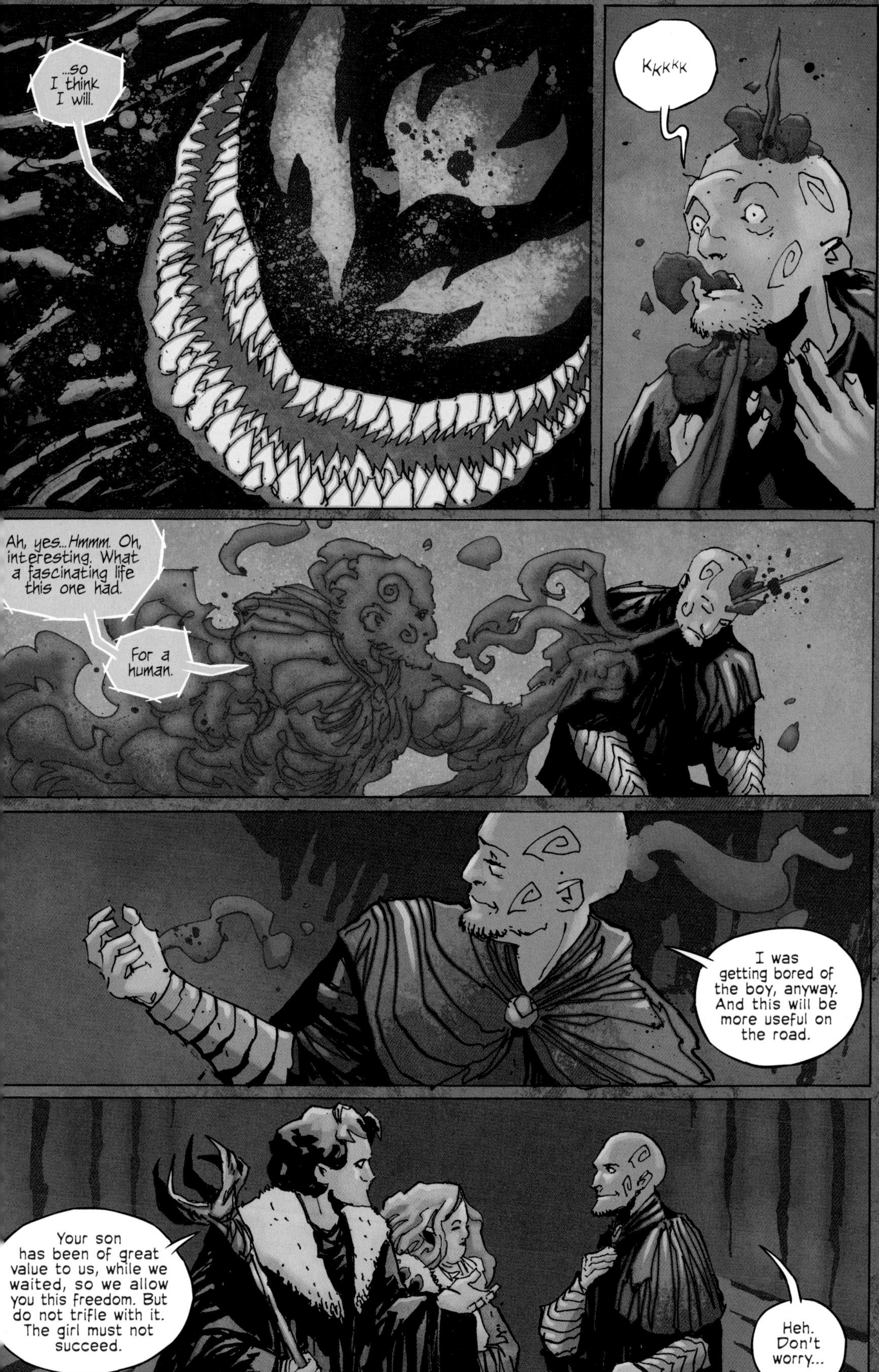

...so I think I will.
KKKKK
Ah, yes...Hmmm. Oh, interesting. What a fascinating life this one had.
For a human.
I was getting bored of the boy, anyway. And this will be more useful on the road.
Your son has been of great value to us, while we waited, so we allow you this freedom. But do not trifle with it. The girl must not succeed.
Heh. Don't worry...

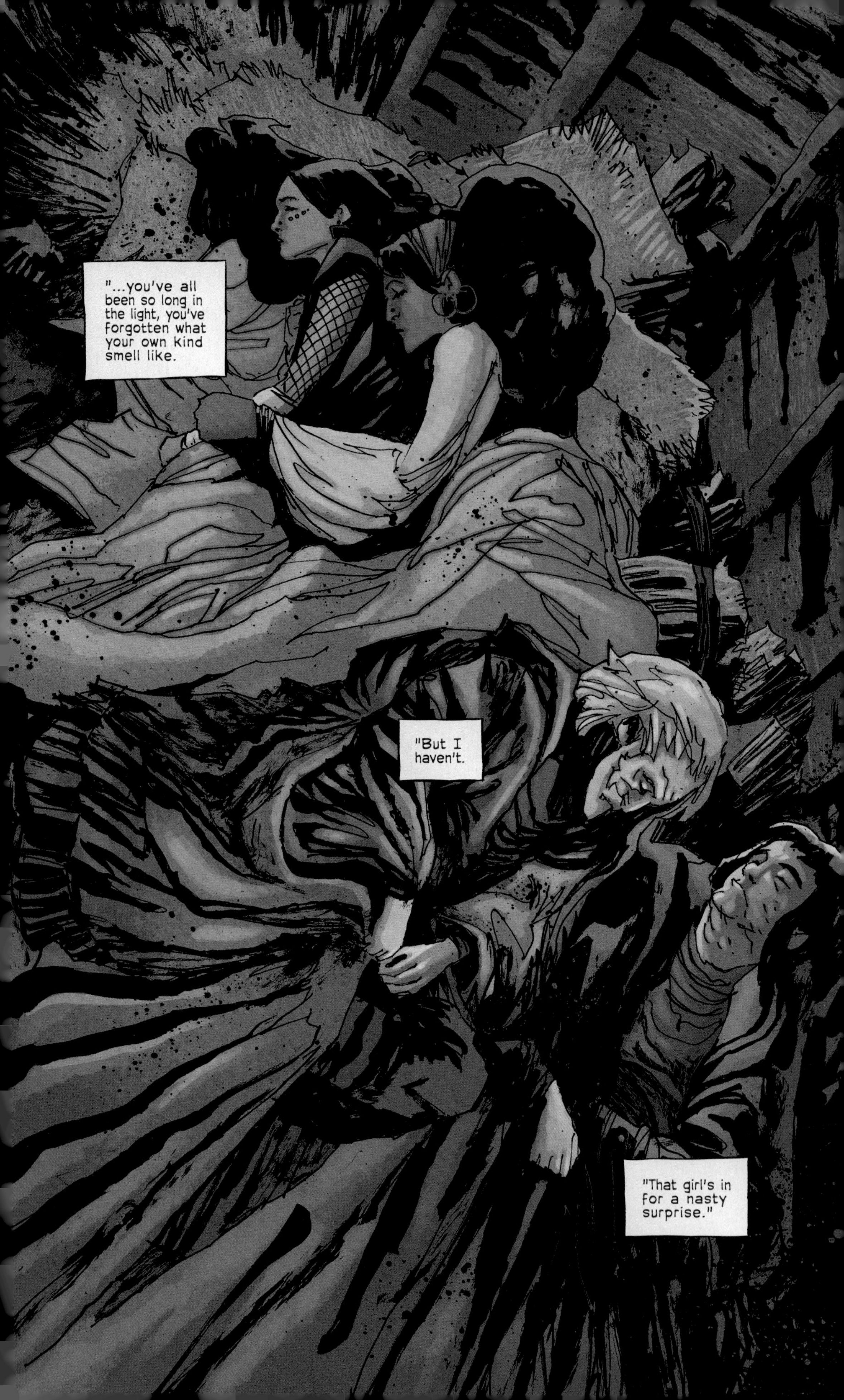
"...you've all been so long in the light, you've forgotten what your own kind smell like.
"But I haven't.
"That girl's in for a nasty surprise."

TO BE
CONTINUED

ANTONY JOHNSTON

Antony is an award-winning, *New York Times* bestselling author of comics, graphic novels, videogames, and books, with titles including *Wasteland*, *The Fuse*, *Shadow of Mordor*, *Dead Space*, *The Coldest City*, *ZombiU*, and more. He has adapted books by bestselling novelist Anthony Horowitz, collaborated with comics legend Alan Moore, and reinvented Marvel's flagship character *Wolverine* for manga. His titles have been translated throughout the world and optioned for film. He lives and works in England.

ANTONYJOHNSTON.COM

@ANTONYJOHNSTON

CHRISTOPHER MITTEN

Originally from the cow-dappled expanse of southern Wisconsin, Christopher now spends his time roaming the misty wilds of suburban Chicago, drawing little people in little boxes.

He has contributed work for Dark Horse, Oni Press, Image, DC Comics, Wildstorm, IDW, 44FLOOD, Dynamite, BOOM!, Black Mask, and Simon & Schuster.

CHRISTOPHERMITTEN.COM

@CHRIS_MITTEN

JOHN RAUCH

John is a comic book colorist whose credits include *Invincible, Teen Titans: Year One, Patsy Walker: Hellcat,* and other stuff not worth bragging about. He enjoys speaking about himself in the third person and pretending he's more talented than he really is to help fight off bouts of depression.

JOHN-ROCK.TUMBLR.COM

@JOHN_RAUCH

JORDAN BOYD

Despite nearly flunking kindergarten for his exclusive use of black crayons, Jordan has moved on to become an increasingly prolific comic book colorist. His recent credits include *Star Wars: Legacy* from Dark Horse, *King's Watch* from Dynamite, and *Knuckleheads* from Monkeybrain. He and his family reside in Norman, OK.

BOYDCOLORS.TUMBLR.COM

@JORDANTBOYD

THOMAS MAUER

Thomas has lettered and worked on a number of Harvey and Eisner Award nominated and winning titles, including the *Popgun* anthology series and the webcomic *The Guns of Shadow Valley.* Among his recent work are *Strange Attractors* for Archaia, Image Comics' *Bad Dog* and *Undertow,* and Monkeybrain's *Knuckleheads.*

THOMASMAUER.COM

@THOMASMAUER